BIGGER

and

BETTER

the book of

ENLARGING

BIGGER *and* BETTER

the book of ENLARGING

by DON D. NIBBELINK
FRPS, APSA
Technical Editor
Eastman Kodak Company

Drawings by
Sherman E. Nelson

Published by
John P. Smith Company, Inc.
for Garden City Books
Garden City, N. Y.

Printed in the United States of America

Table of Contents

Chapter 1

The Print's the Thing

THE TWO of us stood in the darkroom watching a fourteen-by-seventeen-inch print magically appear in the developer.

"Did you ever stop to think that a really top-grade print is never made from most negatives?" My photographer friend kept his eyes on the print being swished back and forth in the tray as he spoke.

"You don't have to be subtle with me. If you think that I'm making a mess of this print, just say so."

"No, no, I don't mean that! I mean all prints by all photographers. Take me, for instance. Usually, I'm so anxious to see what the picture looks like that I rush through the whole print-making procedure. That means that I'm careless about solution mixing, skip the test strips, give little or no thought about dodging, cut short the fixing time, and then decide I don't really care if it's washed an hour or not. It's pretty easy to get into a habit like that, and from some of the prints that I have seen at camera clubs, there are plenty of us who work just like that. The worst part about it is that many of us never realize what good pictures we take, because the first prints we make are such a sloppy job."

"You're perfectly right," I agreed, lifting the print by one corner to drain and putting it into the stop bath. "And what do we do with the few seconds we save by rushing the print through? Probably, spend it wishing we had done a better printing job! I find myself doing it every once in a while."

"Sometimes," he said, "I think that the difference between a good print and a poor one is just taking the time to do it right."

"That's pretty close to the truth," I answered. "I've seen some wonderful prints made from some pretty poor negatives . . . Prints

that proved the man who made them really knew how to use photography to get an idea across. But, there's a little more to it than that. I think any photographer who wants a really good print has to do a kind of exploring job. Every negative has some qualities we don't suspect. To find those qualities takes a little patience and a few tricks of the trade. Some people have the idea that these darkroom tricks are pretty difficult and mysterious. They'd be surprised if they knew how easy they really are." The print had been in the hypo long enough for a close inspection. "That corner should have been darkened a bit more," I admitted. The mistake was apparent with the room flooded with light.

"You know," my friend said, "someday you ought to write a book about print quality. Why don't you write one just about prints? Follow a print through the complete process, just as you did a few minutes ago. Take it all the way through until it is framed and hung on a living room wall, or accepted in a photographic salon, or bought by a customer, or whatever happens to it. Put each technique in a separate chapter. And don't just start with the operation of the enlarger! Start at the beginning, and talk about everything that goes into the final print—negatives, papers, solutions, toning, dodging—and you might even include a little bit about the darkroom. I think that there are lots of amateur and professional photographers who are like me. They just need to be coached a little on the right ways of working with those negatives. A book like that could do it, and for my money, you're the man to write it."

Who could resist a suggestion like that?

Chapter 2

Mixings and Fixings

PHOTOGRAPHY IS, of course, a chemical process. So, of necessity, a photographer has to use chemicals. But, since the *print* is your goal, let's take care of this discussion of chemicals and solutions in one brief, fell swoop. Then, let's make pictures.

First of all, the modern trend is toward packaged chemical preparations. These are either ready to use or need only to be diluted with water and, accordingly, offer many advantages to the photographer. While a published formula, to be practical, must be restricted to fewer than a half-dozen readily available ingredients, chemicals prepared by the manufacturer may contain many other beneficial components. For example, in addition to the usual developer ingredients consisting of buffers, restrainers, accelerators, developing agents, and preservatives, a packaged, ready-to-use developer may also contain agents which prolong solution shelf life, increase capacity, and keep the solution clear during use. These ingredients may be present in minute quantities—in fact, too small to be weighed accurately in a home darkroom—yet all are blended with professional skill and with uniformity from batch to batch. As a result, packaged chemicals are easier to use, longer in life, and more effective in doing the job for which they were designed.

When you go into a camera shop or photographic-supply store, the chemical counter may confront you with a baffling array of packaged chemicals. Which to choose? Perhaps you have noticed that, regardless of manufacturer, processing chemicals are packaged either as packets, as bottled solutions, or as canned or boxed powders. The packets—those handy, matchbook-size, metal-foil containers—are primarily for amateur use in making contact prints.

Their solution quantity is intentionally small enough to provide just about the right amount for one evening's fun of contact printing, when the "tired" solutions should then be discarded. Whereas the canned and boxed chemicals are primarily for professional use, the bottled ones are well worth considering from an advanced-amateur standpoint.

Bottled, concentrated liquids for developers, stop baths, and fixers are available in quantities to make more than enough for an evening of enlarging even with large-size papers, and they are easy to store. But, best of all, they need only to be diluted with water for *immediate* use.

"But," you ask, "which chemicals should I buy?" To help answer your question, a few of the most commonly used chemical preparations are grouped below according to purpose.

DEVELOPERS

KODAK VERSATOL: This all-purpose developer comes in concentrated liquid form, requiring only dilution with water. There is nothing to dissolve. It develops films, plates, and papers, but is especially suitable for cold-tone papers.

KODAK DEKTOL: For cold- and neutral-tone papers, this developer, of the Kodak D-72 Developer type, has long life in use and excellent keeping qualities. It shows little sludge or discoloration and gives the same high print quality as D-72 Developer. It is supplied in handy packets (for 16 ounces) as well as in larger quantities.

KODAK SELECTOL: This warm-tone paper developer, of the Kodak D-52 Developer type, has greatly improved capacity and longer life. It is compounded especially for Kodak Opal Paper, but also gives excellent quality with other warm-tone papers.

KODAK SELECTOL-SOFT: This developer, which is also suggested for warm-tone papers, is recommended for obtaining normal contrast prints from contrasty negatives or with regular Selectol Developer for producing intermediate contrast.

STOP BATHS

KODAK INDICATOR STOP BATH: There is no need to guess whether or not this stop bath is active. When exhausted, it turns purple.

One 16-ounce bottle of concentrated solution makes 8 gallons of working solution.

KODAK STOP BATH SB-1: This is not available in ready-to-use form but it is very simple to mix. The bath is comprised of 1½ ounces of 28 percent acetic acid to one quart of water. (To make 28 percent acetic acid from glacial acetic acid, dilute 3 parts of glacial acetic acid with 8 parts of water.)

There is one danger, however. How often have you seen a fellow photographer mix up a stop bath by filling a tray half full of water and then pouring in a few "glugs" of acetic acid directly from the bottle? Extra-strong stop baths may easily lead to trouble in the form of translucent water spots in the prints. These spots may disappear on drying but, in time and under unfavorable storage conditions, may accelerate fading or staining of the print. Also, water-spotted prints resulting from "spiked" stop baths may be the source of mottle if the prints are subsequently toned.

FIXING BATHS

KODAK ACID FIXER: A single-powder preparation containing fixer and hardener, this rapid, long-lasting, high-capacity fixer can be used for films, plates, and papers. It is packed in convenient darkroom sizes.

KODAFIX SOLUTION: This is a convenient, single-solution hardening fixer which needs only to be diluted 1 to 4 for film and 1 to 7 for paper. Incidentally, do *not* use the same fixing bath for both films and prints regardless of whichever fixer you prefer.

KODAK ANTI-FOG NO. 1 (BENZOTRIAZOLE)

This processing aid can be helpful in suppressing print fog in three situations. These are:

1. When papers tend to show fog from excessive age or unfavorable storage conditions.
2. When forced development is necessary, particularly with used developers.
3. When prints must be developed at higher-than-normal temperatures, such as during warm weather.

Kodak Anti-Fog No. 1 is supplied both in tablet and powder

form. For use, dissolve three tablets (crush them first) per quart in the developer working solution. If you have the chemical available as a powder, make a 0.2 percent stock solution by dissolving 30 grains of the powder in 1 quart of hot water, then add 2 ounces of this solution per quart of developer working solution.

NOTE: Under normal conditions, benzotriazole is *not* required. Also, it is a *helpful suppressor* of fog, not a cure-all. If used in greater quantities than recommended, it may produce a loss in emulsion speed and a change in print image tone.

MIXING SOLUTIONS

As handy as packaged chemicals are, however, they do not relieve the photographer of *all* mixing responsibility. With developers, for example, there is little difference in the speed of mixing at temperatures from 90 to 125 F. But, with some developers, the

"Now, it said pour, not dump; continuous stirring, not a lick and a promise."

manufacturer recommends that the water used be at 90 F so that the final mixed solution will be nearer to the recommended working temperature at 68 F. So, don't think all directions are alike.

If a developer is of the two-component type, the photographer *must* remember to see that all the developing agent—the first chemical added—is completely in solution before adding the rest of the chemicals. An undissolved crystal here and there can "seed" the whole batch and result in crystallization, particularly if the solution is stored at comparatively low room temperatures. Also, incorrectly mixed developers may contain complex crystals that are quite insoluble even at elevated temperatures.

Let's take a packaged fixer for another example. The directions may say, "Pour the contents of this package, with continuous stirring, into one gallon of water, not over 80 F (20 C)." Now, it said *pour,* not *dump*; *continuous* stirring, not *a lick and a promise*; and *80 F,* not *whatever temperature the tap water happens to be.*

Many photographers who are used to mixing prismatic hypo crystals at 125 F don't understand that the anhydrous (water-free) hypo and hardener in the modern fixer won't take such high temperatures. With prismatic hypo crystals, which in their apparently dry state contain water, a lot of water is absorbed in dissolution, but the temperature doesn't rise appreciably. With the anhydrous hypo, more water is absorbed faster, and the heat generated results in an unusable milky solution. It is therefore important to start at the recommended temperature of 80 F.

In cold weather, some stock solutions may crystallize because, as pointed out above, undissolved particles of chemicals can serve as "crystallization centers" and thus hasten the crystallization of the chemicals which are in "excess" at that temperature. Some chemicals are sold in concentrated-solution form. There's not much of a storage problem here because most of these solutions naturally have a low crystallization point and will withstand temperatures as low as 10 to 20 F without crystallization. Lower temperatures than this may cause a "needled" appearance in the solution, but on warming up, the crystals will go back into solution and without detriment to the solution.

An exception is glacial acetic acid which freezes at about 60 F.

On warming up, however, it liquefies readily and its subsequent use is not impaired in any way.

There seems to be a fairly widespread impression that glacial acetic acid expands as it freezes and can break its glass container. This is not true. Acetic acid, like so many other liquids (water is the exception), contracts as it freezes. The attendant danger is that the crystals hang in a rather heavy mass, often near the top of the glass bottle. Partial thawing allows this mass to drop and break the glass by impact.

Incidentally, bottles for developer stock solutions should be the right size; if you mix a quart of solution, it should be stored in a one-quart bottle—not a half-gallon or larger size. To further this end, a well-fitting screw cap or a rubber stopper is preferred. Remember, a poorly kept chemical solution may deteriorate: a partially deteriorated developer has a short life and may produce stained prints.

After preparing the developer—or any photographic solution for that matter—be sure to label the bottle. Unidentified solutions can cause many sorts of trouble in the darkroom. If you wish, you can coat a gummed paper label with melted paraffin or clear nail polish so that spilled solution won't blur the lettering.

TESTING SOLUTIONS

It's best that you know a little about testing solutions. Not that they are solutions you actually need. But it's a good thing to have them at least listed here for reference purposes since they can come in very handy, especially if you are a careful print maker and want to make permanent prints.

Obviously, an acid stop bath or a fixing bath should not be overworked. We all know that the use of an exhausted bath frequently leads to stains and streaks on the prints. When produced by a fixing bath, such stains may become evident only after a period of time.

Since the *appearance* of an acid stop bath or a fixing bath does not change appreciably during its useful life, the question is: How can you tell when it is unsafe for further use? One convenient way is to use the Kodak Testing Outfit. Here is how to use it:

Testing an acid stop bath. Fill the clean, empty vial, supplied with the outfit, about three-quarters full with the acid stop bath; then add 2 drops of the Kodak Testing Solution "A." The tester is yellow in an acid stop bath, but turns purple when the acid has been neutralized.

Under a Kodak Safelight Filter, Wratten Series 0A, the yellow color is not noticeable, but the purple color appears dark.

The Testing Solution "A" can also be added directly to the tray or tank containing the stop bath. Add the Testing Solution to the stop bath, while stirring, as recommended in the table.

SOLUTION	TRAY			TANK (*White card or tray on bottom*)	
Acid stop bath	1 quart or 1 liter	2 quarts or 2 liters	1 gallon or 4 liters	1 gallon	3½ gallons
Testing Solution "A"	40 drops or ¼ dram	½ dram or ¼ vial	1 dram or ½ vial	½ dram or ¼ vial	2 drams or 1 vial

In either of the above tests, when the liquid darkens (under safelight) or turns a light purple (in daylight), the bath is exhausted and should be replenished or discarded. Prints should not remain in the stop bath containing the Testing Solution much longer than 2 minutes; otherwise, slight yellow stains may result.

Testing a fixing solution for papers. Fixing Baths for Papers: To 5 drops of Kodak Testing Solution "B" in the vial provided with the outfit, add 5 drops of water and 10 drops of the fixing bath to be tested. If the bath is exhausted, a heavy yellow precipitate will form immediately. Any slight milkiness should be disregarded. Do not use or keep an exhausted fixing bath!

Testing for permanency. There is another simple way to test for an exhausted fixing bath or for insufficient time in the fixer—either of these malpractices constituting improper fixation.

Improper fixation is detected readily by using a sodium sulfide "drop test." The testing solution is made by dissolving 70 grains of sodium sulfide in 16 ounces of water (or 1 gram in 100 cc. of water). Place a drop of the sulfide solution on the emulsion side of the washed and dried print. If the print turns the sulfide solution yellow or brown, you may assume that the print contains silver compounds. And that's undesirable, to put it mildly, since in time these silver compounds can stain or yellow the print. The obvious remedy is to refix the print in a fresh fixing bath and then wash and dry as usual.

You should not have to test for improper print washing. Just follow the print washing recommendations in Chapter 6 (see page 78 in particular) and your prints should last a lifetime. If you ever do want to check this matter, testing for adequate washing is done with the Kodak Hypo Test Solution HT-2. This solution and its method of use are fully described in the Kodak Data Book, Processing and Formulas.

P.S. *A final thought before leaving this subject of solutions and chemicals . . . You may hear or read elsewhere that packaged developers can often be "improved" for a specific purpose by the addition of either a "pinch" of potassium bromide to decrease print contrast or a "dash" of sodium carbonate to increase print contrast. What's the real truth about this situation?*

In the first place, if the manufacturer had felt that his developers would be improved by altering the proportions of their components, then the developers would have been changed long ago. While the addition of the above chemicals has the described effect, the degree of control is exceedingly small and, from a practical standpoint, not worth the trouble. The contrast control is, in fact, usually less than that effected by changing the paper contrast by one grade or by switching, for example, from Kodak Selectol Developer to Kodak Selectol-Soft Developer. And these developers, when used in a two-tray technique, will yield any desired intermediate range of print contrast. Finally, if you should add some bromide to the developer to lower the contrast of the first print you made during an evening, what would happen to the contrast of prints made thereafter from different negatives and developed in the same print developer?

So, if some chap you know likes to "get his hands wet," and is fond of beakers, balances, and the rest, let him go ahead and add a pinch of bromide. But, in the meantime, you'll be making enlargements.

Chapter 3

About Darkrooms

THE MOST important thing about a darkroom is to have one! Probably you do already. And since you're primarily interested in enlargers and how to use them, this is going to be one of the shortest discussions on darkrooms you have ever seen.

If you don't have darkroom facilities available, and have been pleading "lack of space," take heart that excellent prints can be made with an enlarger set up in a kitchen, a bathroom, a corner of the basement, or even a large closet. A full-fledged photo-lab can be established in a space as compact as 6 by 8 feet—or less.

Although a "real" darkroom is not essential, it is convenient. Besides, it makes enlarging even more fun if you can work under ideal conditions. So, if you'd like an efficient, special place to make your superprints someday, here's a good basic darkroom plan.

PLANNING NOTES

The basic plan illustrated is 6 by 8 feet (each square is 12 inches) . . . This plan can be condensed easily to 5 by 7 feet; its shape can be varied . . . A dry basement is the best location (attics tend to be too warm in summer, too cold in winter) . . . Walls can be of thin wallboard on light wooden frames . . . Don't try to use curtains; they catch dust . . . Paint or asphalt-tile the floor . . . Use the largest flat-rim sink you can afford; put a frame of 1-inch slats in it as a base for tanks and trays . . . Buy trays at least one size larger than you think you will need. Linoleum, coved up at the rear, makes the best counter top . . . Provide on-edge storage below the sink for extra trays and ferrotype plates . . . Plan at least one electric outlet on each wall . . . Forced-air ventilation is not im-

HERE'S A BASIC DARKROOM PLAN

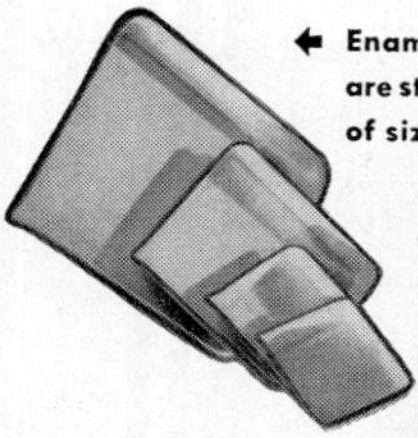

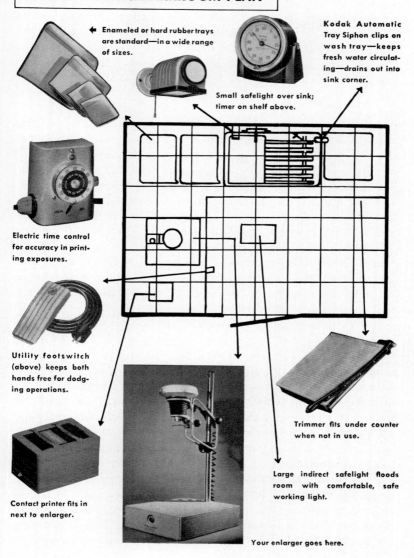

← Enameled or hard rubber trays are standard—in a wide range of sizes.

Small safelight over sink; timer on shelf above.

Kodak Automatic Tray Siphon clips on wash tray—keeps fresh water circulating—drains out into sink corner.

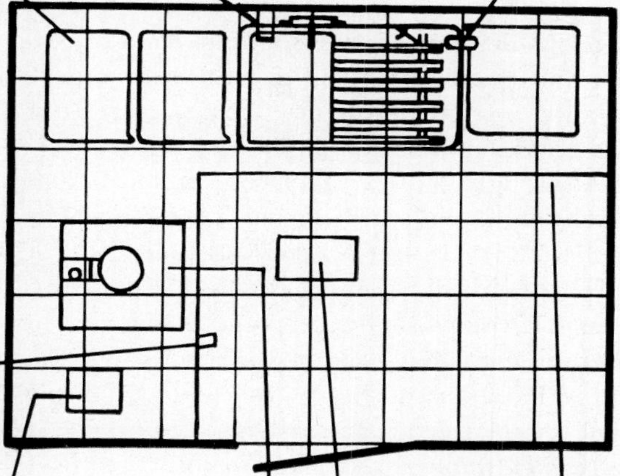

Electric time control for accuracy in printing exposures.

Utility footswitch (above) keeps both hands free for dodging operations.

Trimmer fits under counter when not in use.

Contact printer fits in next to enlarger.

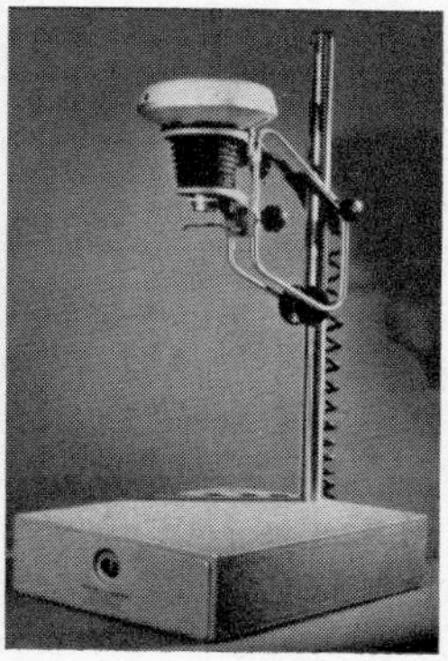

Large indirect safelight floods room with comfortable, safe working light.

Your enlarger goes here.

perative; just leave the door open when you step out for a rest or a smoke . . . If possible, provide a mixing faucet for hot and cold water—and keep the bib at least 15 inches above the sink bottom . . . Counters need be no wider than 24 inches . . . Underneath, provide cheesecloth stretchers for drying prints, or space for Kodak Photo Blotter Rolls . . . Remember that workability is more important than fancy finish.

THE SAFELIGHT

Although you're anxious to get on with the business of making good enlargements, the safelight is one feature of any darkroom that must be emphasized as having an important bearing on print quality. So, for *top* quality, it's a good idea first of all to learn the "do's and don'ts" of safelights.

A safelight is often taken for granted but, actually, how safe is a safelight—the one in *your* darkroom, for instance? It may come as a shock to you, but there is no such thing as an absolutely *safe* safelight. Ideally, a safelight should emit the maximum illumination of a color to which the eye is sensitive but to which the photographic paper you use is least sensitive. Since there is no sharp cutoff in paper sensitivity, the safeness of any darkroom illumination is a relative matter.

It is extremely important to follow the safelight recommendations of the manufacturer of the photographic paper you are using. It is not enough to assume that a certain safelight gives "better, safer illumination," as one advertisement put it, because a safelight which is ideal for papers of one kind or of one manufacturer may not be at all suitable for use with another. Be careful also not to exceed the suggested wattage for the safelight lamp, to use the safelight too close to the working area, or to leave photographic paper exposed too long to safelight illumination.

The obvious danger is, of course, fog. Fogged prints have grayish instead of white borders and are characterized by "veiled," degraded highlights. In extreme cases, print contrast is noticeably decreased, and the prints have an objectionable muddy appearance. The insidiousness of unsafe darkroom illumination however, lies in the fact that *print quality can suffer even though the borders of the print are visibly free from fog.* It happens in this way: Small amounts of safelight exposure, which in themselves are not sufficient to produce fog, may expose silver in the image portion of the print and cause it to develop to a higher density than if it had not been exposed to the safelight. Thus there is sort of a double exposure—first, the exposure caused by the safelight, and second, the exposure caused by projecting the negative image onto the paper. Almost without your realizing it, this combination can be enough to add up to a faint highlight veiling—just enough to detract from the clean, sparkling quality that distinguishes a fine print. And high-contrast papers used for line copy work may show marked degradation of quality without producing visible highlight fog.

Be sure your safelight filter isn't obsolete. Kodak Safelight Filters in the new Wratten Series bear the same designations as older filters—but are quite different. Except for Wratten Series No. 7 (infrared), the new filters are single sheets of glass, coated with dyed gelatin of correct spectrophotometric characteristics, and Tenite—dipped for surface protection against wetting and vapor. Incidentally, the Wratten Series 0A is recommended for use with most photographic papers; use a 10-watt bulb if the work is to be illuminated directly. To add to your operating convenience, a

The "ideal" darkroom would look something like this. Do you see any ideas you can use in your darkroom?

Is your safelight safe? This shows what can happen if it isn't. The light area received the negative exposure only but the darker panels received, respectively, the negative exposure plus 30 seconds, 1 minute, and 1½ minutes of safelight exposure.

large, *indirect* type of ceiling safelight lamp with a 25-watt bulb is suggested for general darkroom illumination.

As with almost everything else, time takes its toll with safelight filters. Check them periodically to make sure that they haven't become faded or cracked with age.

Checking safelight illumination. When it is suspected that safelights are causing trouble, a simple but sensitive test can be made as follows:

1. With the paper and the printing method you commonly use, make an exposure with your enlarger from a typical negative. Mask the borders of the paper so as to produce an unexposed area around the picture. *Do not have the darkroom safelight turned on for this portion of the test.*

2. Position the exposed paper about as far from the safelight as you generally work and expose it to the safelight illumination by covering successive areas of the paper for different, specific lengths of time. Keep one area covered all the time.

3. Process the exposed paper and notice in the print the amount of safelight exposure which can be given without any appreciable change in print quality.

Remember, some papers are more susceptible than others to safelight fog because they are more sensitive, either in speed or to a particular color of light. Accordingly, a separate test should be made for each distinct type of paper used. If you find that your prints are degraded quality-wise or actually show fog, the cure is simple. Use a *safe* light.

P.S. *By all means, keep everything in your darkroom* clean—*not only equipment but the walls, the workbench and your hands as well. Change the darkroom towels frequently. Occasionally dust the table tops, shelves, and cupboards with a damp cloth. Any chemical solutions accidentally spilled on the floor should be removed immediately with a damp cloth. Photography may be a fickle mistress but cleanliness is one of her necessary virtues.*

And now let's start using the enlarger!

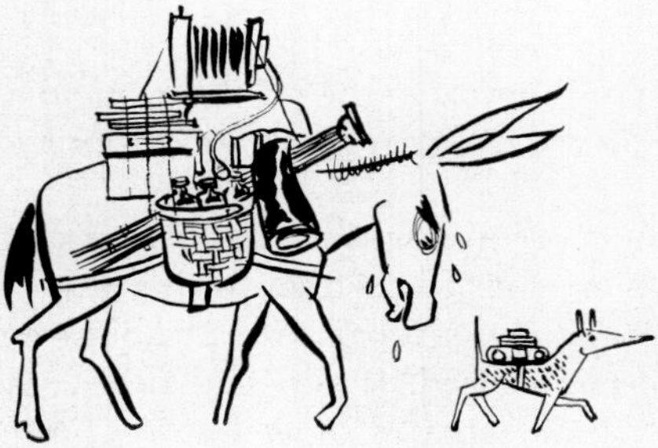

About Enlargers

A MULE LOAD of 20 by 24-inch glass plates for his camera was once carried to Mesa Verde by the pioneer photographer, William Henry Jackson. He wanted to be sure that his prints—which were to be made by contact—would be large enough to convince audiences of the significance of the ancient cliff dwellings which he had explored. Today, the same job could be accomplished more easily with a miniature camera taking pictures little, if any, larger than a postage stamp. And a major portion of the great difference between these two extremes is due to a single instrument, the photographic enlarger.

The contact print is, by no means, either dead or dying. It has a definite place in modern photography, such as in photofinishing, in commercial work, and particularly in the newer industrial field of documentary reproduction. However, for producing pictorial results conveniently, the enlargement reigns supreme. Studio portraits, photo-murals, and prints for most newspaper and magazine reproductions are made with an enlarger. Because details in small prints may become "lost" and therefore fail to assume a desired relative importance, all modern exhibition prints are also enlargements. Furthermore, from a perspective standpoint, enlargements usually appear more natural than contact prints. Commercially speaking, an enlarger is used to secure a print of a given size, whether enlarged or reduced.

Basically, an enlargement differs from a contact print in that it is made by projecting a larger image of the negative onto a piece of especially sensitive paper. To do this requires that a light source be placed behind the negative to illuminate it and a lens be mounted in front of the negative to project a large image of the negative onto a paper holder. An enlarger therefore consists of a light source, a means of illuminating the negative uniformly, a negative-carrier support, a lens and lens support with bellows to shield the light rays, and a paper support or easel.

If you are thinking of buying an enlarger, no one can tell you which one is "best," or which one to choose. There are enlargers to fit different purposes and different-size pocketbooks. However, there are basic features that every good enlarger should have—things you should check carefully before acquiring one. For example, the enlarger construction should be sturdy. The head should not have any tendency to vibrate unduly long if the enlarger is jarred accidentally. In fact, you can test this feature for yourself by giving the enlarger head a slight tap and seeing if it is as rigid as seems advisable.

Although it is difficult to ascertain, the plane of the lens board should be exactly parallel with the plane of the negative. Also, interior reflections should be at a minimum. It may help here to remove the lens or lens board, turn on the enlarger and peer critically up into the bellows-negative carrier area. No bright metal should be apparent since any good reflecting surfaces at this location will increase the flare in the optical system.

Let's consider a few more salient points.

LENS

The covering power of the enlarging lens should be adequate. This means that the lens should be able to project a fairly sharp image of the entire negative, including the corners as well as the center. To do this, the enlarger lens usually has to have a focal length equal to or greater than the diagonal of the negative.

Some photographers use their camera lenses also as enlarger lenses in order to save the expense of buying a separate lens for enlarging. If you have wondered about this matter, here is the answer: A camera lens may *not* necessarily perform equally well on an enlarger, particularly at low degrees of magnification. For the most part, this is because the camera lens was designed and corrected for normal camera-to-subject distances. This means from infinity down to three or four feet, depending how close the camera will focus. Enlarging lenses, on the other hand, are designed and corrected for working distances of from three or four feet down to about twice the focal length of the lens. So you see, the enlarger lens design sort of "takes over" for producing images of optimum quality where the camera lens design "leaves off." For example, it would be unreasonable to expect that a lens from an aerial camera designed to photograph objects a great distance from the lens would satisfactorily serve double duty as an enlarger lens also. In addition, "fast" camera lenses of high aperture suffer from curvature of field at magnifications below about 10-to-1 and thus are not suited for use on enlargers.

This is particularly true if lenses such as these are used at or near their maximum apertures. But stop them down from *f*/11 to *f*/22 and you will find that many of these lenses can be used for non-critical enlarging. However, many top-quality unit focusing lenses which are normally used for taking still photographs can also be used with a high degree of satisfaction in many instances for enlarging. Let's repeat: For best results with any camera lens on the enlarger, be sure to stop it down before making the actual print exposure. Don't overdo it if a lens happens to stop down more than *f*/22, since with a smaller lens opening than this, the image may become less sharp due to diffraction, the relatively large amount of "spread" light rays passing through a small lens aperture.

Optimum quality is, of course, obtained with flat-field enlarging lenses especially adjusted for short working distances. Enlarger lenses used for making color-separation negatives must also be well corrected for lateral color (the different magnification of colored images most noticeable at the edge of the image) to help insure against "color fringes."

Most enlarger lenses available today are coated with a thin, hard layer of magnesium fluoride to reduce intersurface reflections. As compared with the noncoated variety, coated lenses have, therefore, less tendency to project flare light onto the easel and tend to give improved highlight separation, especially from dense, high-contrast negatives.

ILLUMINATION SYSTEMS

There are two types of illumination systems: diffusion and condenser. Which is better? This question cannot be answered in a word, for each has its advantages, depending on the type of work it will be used for. Let's take a look at both of them:

Diffuse illumination. There are several methods used by enlarger manufacturers to produce diffuse illumination. Some 5 by 7-inch and 8 by 10-inch enlargers employ a parabolic-shaped reflector to direct the rays through the negative. A sheet of sand-blasted glass above the negative helps to provide even illumination. This kind of an enlarger has an illumination quality about halfway between the condenser type and the usual diffuse type. The customary components of diffuse-enlarger illumination are a frosted enlarging lamp and a sheet of ground or opal glass. And now, too, of course, there are the newer "cold-light" enlargers which provide diffuse illumination; these will be discussed on page 26.

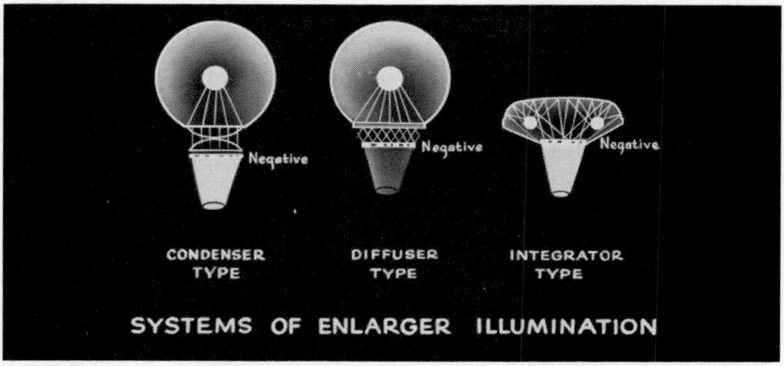

Diffuse means scattered. Since diffuse-enlarger illumination is scattered thoroughly, its rays strike the negative at all angles. The illumination is scattered additionally by the negative—particularly in the dense portions representing subject highlights. As a result of this "light from everywhere," the lens sees and projects an image of lower contrast than if a point source of illumination had been used.

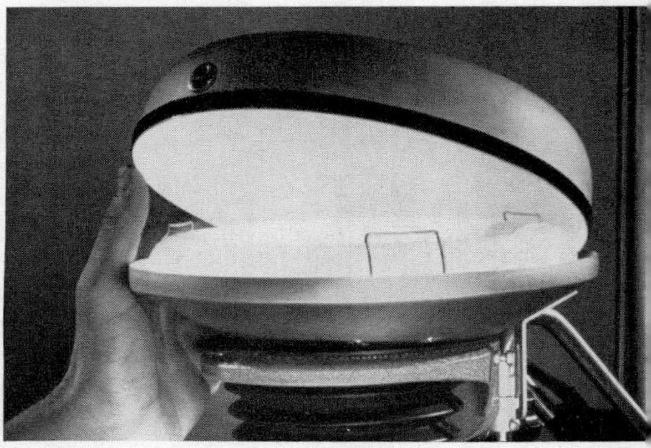

Kodak Flurolite Enlarger showing 8¼-inch Circline Lamp and white interior finish.

Cold-light enlargers. The newer fluorescent-tube enlargers employ a coiled or circular glass tubing. This contains a coating which fluoresces with a "cold" illumination. Argon enlarger illumination is also classified similarly. The word "cold" is fitting primarily because the operating temperature is much lower than that of tungsten lamps, and the negative is therefore in considerably less danger of overheating. This feature makes the cold-light enlarger useful in color-separation work, since the color transparency would not be exposed continuously in a warm enlarger lamphouse assembly which might affect the register of separation negatives made from it. Filters can, of course, be used with these enlargers to control the color of the illumination, if necessary for color-print-making purposes, but with different filter factors than required for tungsten illumination.

An important consideration is that all cold-light enlargers are of the diffuse type. Therefore, contrast differences between them and conventional diffuse-tungsten enlargers are quite minor. What minor differences in contrast exist may do so because of the differing color quality of the illumination. Many cold-light enlargers, such as the Kodak Flurolite Enlarger A—a reflecting diffuse type, make use of the 4500 white fluorescent tubes. The light from these tubes is between tungsten and daylight in color, that is, it is bluer than tungsten light. And how does this concern us? In general,

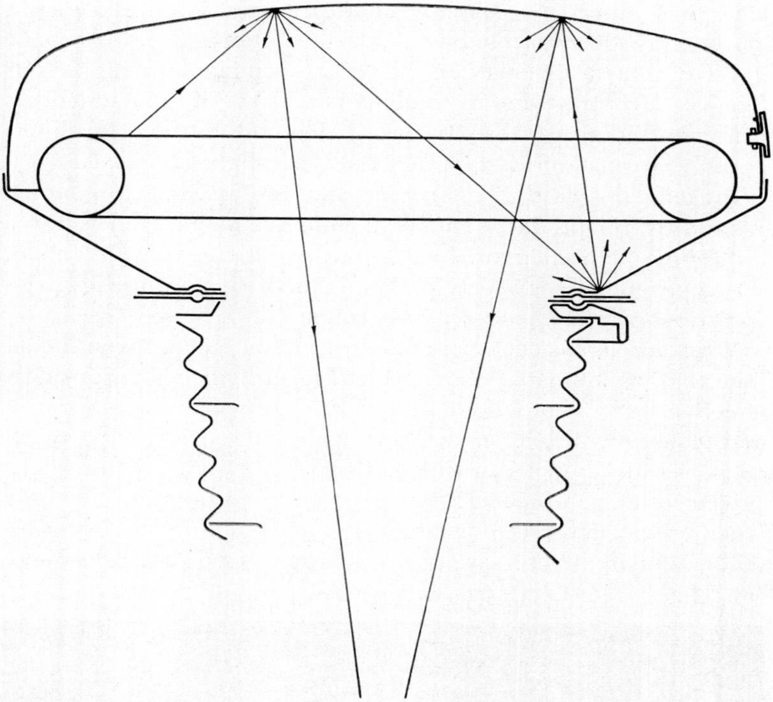

(Above) A cross section of the Flurolite Lamp House showing multiple reflections. (Below) Proportion of heat, light, and effectiveness of tungsten and fluorescent lamps.

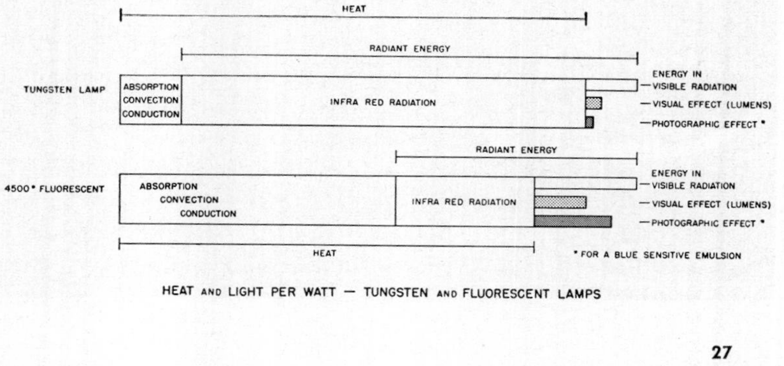

HEAT AND LIGHT PER WATT — TUNGSTEN AND FLUORESCENT LAMPS

enlarging papers give slightly contrasty results to yellow light and slightly soft results to blue light.

When comparing enlargers, however, keep in mind that the difference in contrast due to condensers versus diffusion systems is considerably greater than any effect due only to the color differences between a diffuse-tungsten and a cold-light source.

In general, *speed relationships* and the spacing of *contrast grades* are about the same for a fluorescent enlarger as for a diffuse-tungsten enlarger. In other words, there would be about the same "jump" between No. 2 and No. 3 paper contrast grades regardless of which enlarger was being used.

While discussing the color of fluorescent illuminants, you should note that, as intimated above, their bluish light is a surprisingly effective light. Photographic papers are primarily blue-sensitive and, consequently, a projected image on the easel may appear weak visually but it can expose the paper rapidly. Because the projected image may *seem* dim, extra care is required in focusing when using a fluorescent enlarger, and a magnifying glass or some other, similar direct-focusing accessory may be especially helpful. This is even more true when using argon-type enlargers.

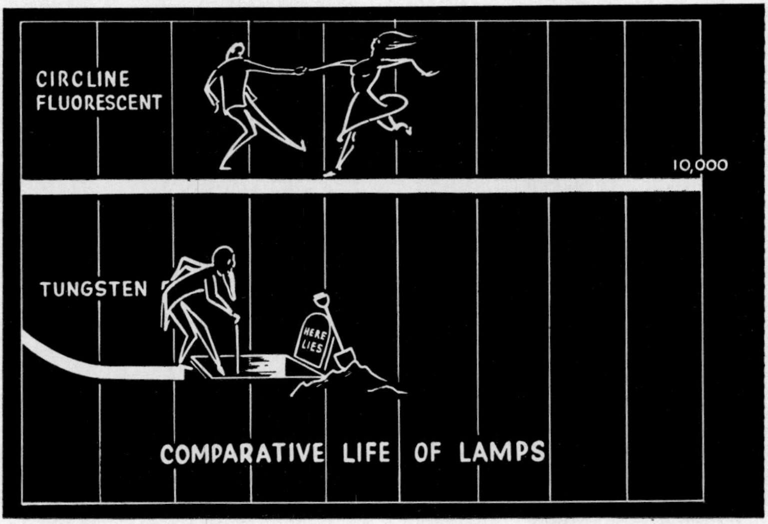

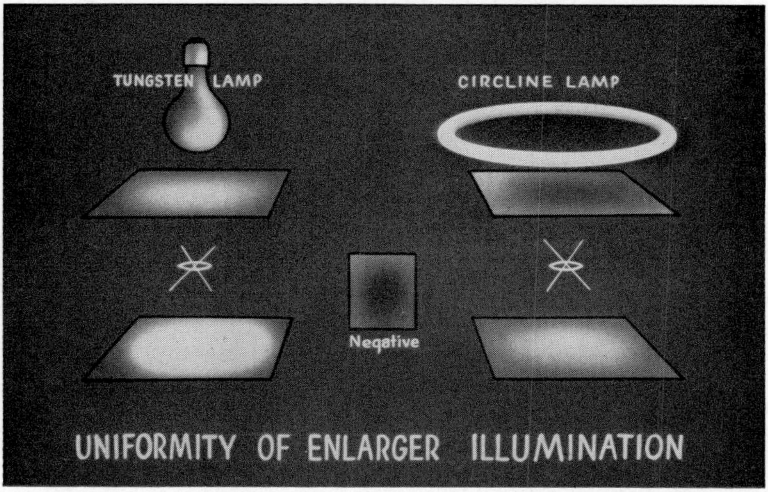

Condenser illumination. The experts tell you that a "pure" condenser enlarger would be one with a point light source, or at least a very small light source, such as would be provided practically by the filament of a projection lamp of the kind employed in amateur motion-picture projectors. And there is no such enlarger commercially available unless you except some types of fixed-enlargement printers used only in photofinishing plants. But the important thing is that a true condenser enlarger for ordinary enlarging purposes would not be desirable anyway. Prints from it would be excessively contrasty, and negative defects, such as scratches, would be accentuated and would limit its application. Today, the term "condenser enlarger" has come to mean an enlarger which uses both a light source covering a relatively large area, such as a white-glass G-E Photo Enlarger Lamp No. 212, and a pair of plano-convex condensers which are usually arranged in a "bucket," or collar, to support the two condensers. This type of arrangement is intermediate in characteristics between specular or "directed-ray" illumination and diffuse illumination—in fact, in about a 50 to 50 ratio. Using condenser illumination is especially advantageous where small negatives—up to 2¼ by 3¼

—are to be blown up to large size prints and without excessively long exposures. In other words, there is not the same optical need for condensers to print large size negatives. This is probably fortunate since large size condensing lenses are expensive.

The advantages of using condensers are threefold: They direct through the negative and lens most of the illumination they collect, with the result that a relatively short printing time is usually required for the enlargement. The two glass condensers act as fairly good heat-absorbers, and they, plus the short exposure times, therefore keep the negatives from becoming overheated during enlargement. Thirdly is the type of print quality afforded by this illumination.

This matter of print quality deserves special mention since it is this point around which the condenser versus diffusion controversy rages. Generally, a print made with a condenser enlarger is more contrasty than one made from the same negative with a diffusion-type enlarger. Depending on which two specific enlargers are being compared, this difference in contrast varies from about one-half to one grade of paper contrast. This means, for example, that a negative which prints well on No. 2 paper with a condenser enlarger would probably be printed on No. 3 paper with a diffusion enlarger. The added contrast of a condenser system gives the appearance of slightly sharper results. But, *there is no appreciable difference in sharpness between the two illumination systems.* In general, sharpness is controlled instead by the negative characteristics, the lens design and aperture used, the parallelism of the negative plane, the lens board, and the printing paper.

Let's assume that the contrast was adjusted by selecting appropriate paper grades for use with each enlarger—what about quality differences then? Well, it all depends on what you mean by "quality." *Insofar as contrast and tone reproduction are concerned, there is no difference in the prints from the same negative obtained with each of the different systems of negative illumination.*

Another aspect of print quality as influenced by the system of negative illumination is that minor negative defects, such as scratches, small abrasions, and even dust and coarse grain, are considerably less apparent in prints made with a diffusion enlarger. This is practically desirable since it minimizes defects and eliminates much of the need for spotting prints. Consider, for example, how this helps and saves time for the unfortunate photographer enlarging a scratched or grainy negative, or how it is appreciated by the professional portrait photographer who must print negatives containing minute retouching marks. Actually, a professional photographer usually strives for soft, often "misty," results in his portraiture. He is not so concerned with somewhat more contrasty results and optimum highlight separation as is the commercial photographer.

It may help to visualize the results obtained from diffuse versus condenser enlargers if we consider the illumination from the two types of enlargers analogous to the illumination obtained from floodlamps and spotlights, respectively. Each has its own characteristics. Which is better, you ask? One factor which argues against the tungsten-source diffusion enlarger is the sacrifice of light caused by the light-absorbing properties of ground or opal glass. Thus exposures must be, on the average, longer for this type of enlarger than for the condenser type. Longer exposures mean inconvenience in printing and dodging comparatively dense negatives, particularly at large magnifications; they also mean higher lamp-house temperatures with—in extremely long exposures—the possibility of overheating the negative.

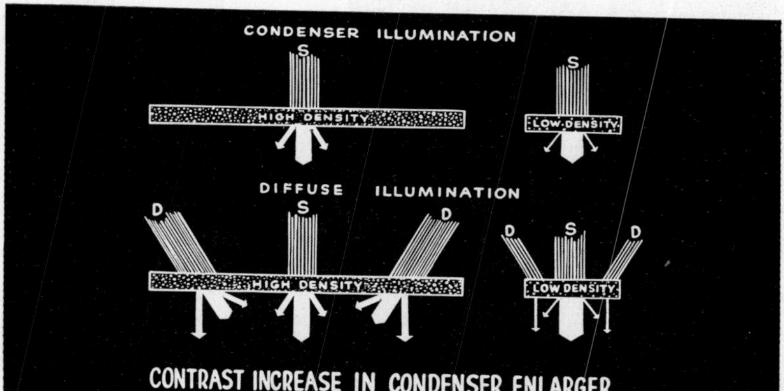

CONTRAST INCREASE IN CONDENSER ENLARGER

Because of the light-absorbency of diffusers, don't think it would be a simple matter for you to convert your condenser enlarger to give diffuse-illumination results by placing a sheet of matte acetate above the condensers. Yes, the print results will be what you expect, but you will be dismayed by the speed loss.

For *best* results—and, after all, that's what you're most interested in—you should make the negatives to "fit" the enlarger you have. Normally exposed and developed negatives will be fine for diffusion-type enlargers. But normal exposure and *somewhat less development* (about 20 percent less) will yield negatives which will give excellent results in condenser-type enlargers. The reason is that less-than-normal development means both smaller grain and lower negative contrast; these characteristics, teamed with the grain-emphasizing, specular illumination of the condenser enlarger, approximately cancel each other. So, you see, a graininess or quality comparison between two prints made from the same negative and enlarged in the two types of enlargers is not strictly a fair comparison. As far as scratches are concerned—well, anyone who exercises reasonable care in processing films and in filing negatives should not have appreciable trouble with either enlarger. After all, anyone interested in top-quality enlargements does not shuffle negatives together like a pack of playing cards!

No matter what kind of enlarger you own, it should be protected from dust when not in use. A little care here will save print spotting time later.

ACCESSORIES

The enlarger easel. If you own an enlarger, you probably also have an easel or paper holder to use with it. The easel is a very handy accessory for holding the paper flat in the plane of sharp focus, for providing white print margins of the desired width, and for masking the paper in the desired print format. Besides, it provides a convenient method of shifting the paper around on the enlarger baseboard to secure the desired composition.

Most easels accommodate paper sizes up to 11 by 14 inches; larger than that, the easels are fairly expensive. However, you can easily make salon prints or other large prints of 14 by 17 inches in size or larger even if you do not have a commercial-type easel; in fact, some photographers prefer not to use one since most easels

Some enlargers, such as the Kodak Flurolite Enlarger, can double as view cameras. With the appropriate accessories this particular one can be used to take both 35mm and 2¼ by 3¼ films.

"steal" a little bit from the picture area in the borders which usually have to be trimmed away when the print is mounted. Although keeping the paper flat is very important, this can be done easily by placing a sheet of clean glass on top of the paper before making the exposure. The glass should be slightly larger than the paper size being used.

Of course, plate glass has its objections of being unwieldy, susceptible to dust, scratches, and fingerprints. So if this last sentence has made you join the objectors' ranks, you can easily make a large easel from a large drawing board. Tack down along two adjacent edges strips of the metal molding material commonly used for edging linoleum on kitchen counter tops. This molding has a slot that will readily accept the paper and hold it flat. This takes care of two edges. To hold down the opposite corner of the paper, do this: On the corner of the drawing board opposite the molding install a spring clip, such as used on clip boards for taking field notes. This easel won't give white margins all around but it is a comparatively inexpensive method of holding flat large sheets of photographic paper.

You will want to check over the other accessories available for various enlargers since they may also influence you in selecting a particular model.

For example, some enlargers have accessory copying lights, exposure-meter brackets, filter holders, etc., which make them suitable for use as cameras. A few models incorporate an automatic focusing feature. This convenience is scarcely necessary for home use, and, as a matter of fact, is not always desired, but where the enlarger may be in constant use to produce a great volume of prints, usually professional, the automatic focusing arrangement is a timesaver. "Deluxe" enlargers may have the so-called "distortion controls" of a tilting negative carrier or a swinging lens board. These adjustments are helpful in straightening out converging lines caused by taking pictures while the camera back is tilted out of a vertical position. If you're interested in doing color printing, check to see that the lamp house-negative carrier assembly is reasonably lighttight.

How about the negative carrier? Will it take different-size nega-

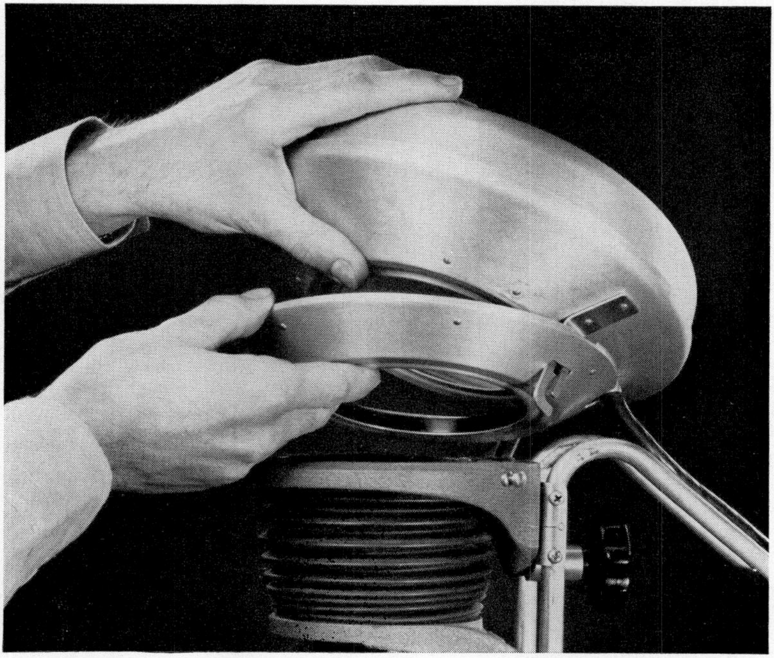

Accessories may determine your enlarger choice. This Flurolite Color Head Adapter A positions color filters for color printing, and can be used with Kodak Wratten Filters, 5-inch Gelatin Film Circles. Lamp House and Color Head are lighttight.

tives? Is it of the glass or glassless type? Many photographers using miniature negatives prefer the glassless-type carrier because it eliminates four glass surfaces on which dust can collect. Dust can be a problem when making large prints from small negatives.

Another disadvantage in using a glass-type negative carrier is that Newton's rings sometimes form between the back of the negative and the top glass of the carrier. Newton's rings are patterns of light interference which can be projected down with the negative image as practically "unretouchable" print defects. They are formed most frequently under atmospheric conditions of high humidity so if the printing can be postponed until a drier day, the trouble will probably disappear.

One of the best ways to combat the problem immediately is as follows: Make a thin "soup" of talc or magnesium carbonate and Kodak Film Cleaner or carbon tetrachloride. The particles will be held in suspension by the liquid. Place the negative to be printed on a flat clean surface with the emulsion side down. Dip a tuft of cotton in the suspension and rub it *lightly* over the back side of the negative. The liquid evaporates in a few seconds leaving a thin even coating of the talc particles. Use a camel's hair brush to even out any streaks or concentration of the particles. That's all there is to it; the particles provide just enough separation between the back of the negative and the glass of the negative carrier so that the objectionable Newton's rings will not form. The talc particles are small and will not be apparent in prints made with diffusion enlargers. Condenser enlargers customarily employ glassless or "dustless" negative carriers and therefore this treatment is not necessary for condenser enlargers.

EXTENDING THE MAGNIFICATION RANGE OF ENLARGERS

High magnification. Occasionally it may be desirable to "blow up" a negative beyond the maximum range of the lens-to-baseboard distance. For example, you may want to make a giant enlargement from an entire negative or to enlarge greatly a small area from a negative. Some enlargers have a lamp-house assembly which can be tipped to project horizontally. Others can rotate around the post so that, with the enlarger baseboard clamped or weighted securely in position, the image can be projected down onto the floor.

Using an accessory positive lens over the enlarger lens is still another method of obtaining increased magnification. Although somewhat of an emergency procedure, this is particularly helpful for relatively inexpensive enlargers which cannot be adapted in either of the other two ways provided the lens can be moved closer than usual to the negative. The accessory lenses recommended are the Kodak Portra Lenses which normally are used to give a close-up effect. They can be adapted to many enlarger lenses with the appropriate Kodak Adapter Ring, depending on the diameter of the enlarger lens mount.

Reductions. What about making unusually small enlargements—prints which may be used as miniatures, in lockets, or in billfolds? Many enlargers can project an image about as small as the actual size of the negative itself. It is usually necessary, however, to find some way of propping the easel so that it is nearer to the lens than ordinarily. A pile of magazines or a small wooden box can be used conveniently. An example of an application where this procedure is useful is given in Chapter 16 on slide making.

Reductions can be made by projection if the enlarger has a sufficient bellows extension to extend the lens *more* than twice its focal length from the negative. These extremely small projection prints are probably made most conveniently by using a lens with a shorter-than-normal focal length. However, an ordinary enlarger can often be used for making reductions by merely adding Kodak Portra Lenses. The action of the Portra Lens is to shorten the effective focal length of the enlarger lens so that the projected image will normally give approximately a 1-to-1 magnification; the Portra Lens will act as a reducing attachment so that the image will be smaller than the negative. For reductions smaller than a 1 to 1 ratio, turn the front of the lens *toward* the negative. This will help to produce a sharper image.

The heads of some enlargers will not approach the paper board closely enough for this application; in such a case, as mentioned above, the easel should be raised. Incidentally, this must always be done with an auto-focusing enlarger.

Note that when the enlarger is operating near a 1-to-1 magnification, focusing is complicated by the fact that moving the lens alone changes both the object and the image distance at about the same relative rate. The result is that it is impossible to focus by moving the enlarger lens alone. Therefore, the proper focusing technique is to set the lens distance at an approximate position and then move the whole enlarger head, or if necessary, to raise or lower the easel. Should the image thus focused be incorrect in size, a further adjustment must be made in the lens-to-negative distance and the focusing done again by moving the whole enlarger head.

At the comparatively small apertures generally used in enlarging, Portra Lenses do not appear to have any objectionable effect on definition at low magnification even when the strongest Portra Lens, the 3+, is used. In some cases, it is even possible to combine the Portra Lenses 2+ and 3+, if a small aperture is used.

Do you have a magnifying glass handy? One of those large-diameter ones with a handle—the kind often used for retouching? Since the retouching glass is a positive lens—much stronger than Portra Lenses—it *may* be satisfactory for making reductions if it is centered as well as possible over the enlarger lens and *if a small aperture is used in the enlarger lens.* Try it and see.

The following table indicates approximately the extension of lowest magnification possible with various enlarger lenses by the addition of Portra Lenses. Only those figures of less than 1.00 represent a reduced image. For example, suppose you were printing a 4 by 5-inch negative with a 6⅜-inch enlarger lens and the enlarger would normally focus down only to a 1 to 1 ratio. The addition of a 2+ and 3+ Portra Lens makes a 1½ by 2-inch print.

EXTENSION OF LOWEST MAGNIFICATION (Approximate)

Kodak Portra Lens	*Minimum magnification* 1			1.5			2			3		
	1+	3+	2+ and 3+	1+	3+	2+ and 3+	1+	3+	2+ and 3+	1+	3+	2+ and 3+
Enlarger Lens												
50mm (2 in.)	0.9	0.75	0.65	1.35	1.1	0.9	1.75	1.4	1.15	2.5	1.9	1.5
75mm (3 in.)	.85	.7	.55	1.25	0.95	.75	1.65	1.2	0.95	2.3	1.6	1.2
100mm (4 in.)	.85	.65	.50	1.2	.85	.65	1.55	1.05	.8	2.15	1.35	1.0
128mm (5 in.)	.8	.55	.45	1.15	.75	.6	1.45	0.95	.7	2.0	1.2	0.85
135mm (5⅜ in.)	.8	.55	.45	1.1	.75	.55	1.4	.9	.65	1.95	1.15	.8
161mm (6⅜ in.)	.75	.5	.4	1.05	.7	.5	1.35	.8	.6	1.8	1.0	.7
190mm (7½ in.)	.7	.45	.35	1.0	.6	.45	1.25	.75	.5	1.7	0.9	.6

USING THE ENLARGER AS A COPYING CAMERA

There are on the market several versatile enlargers, such as the Kodak Flurolite Enlarger A, for which complete accessories are available, including ground-glass focusing backs, camera-back adapters, and copying-light stands, which permit their use as efficient copying cameras. However, few photographers realize that many ordinary enlargers can be used successfully as copying cameras with no conversion or special equipment needed—that is, if you don't call two inexpensive copying lights in reflectors "special equipment." Actually, nearly any type of light source can be used for this purpose, such as two reflector-type photographic flood lamps, gooseneck desk lamps fitted with No. 1 photoflood bulbs, etc.

It is important to be able to position the lamps so that their illumination is directed downward toward the enlarger baseboard, one from each side of the enlarger, at about a 45-degree angle. The illumination on the baseboard need not be intense, but it should be distributed as evenly as possible. The evenness of the illumination can be checked with an exposure meter, if one is available.

Either film or paper can be used, depending on the requirements of the copy job at hand. Suppose that you wish to make a reduction copy of a document. Here's the simple procedure:

1. Using the enlarging easel as a paper holder, position the center of the document to be copied directly under the enlarger lens. Drop a plumb line from the lens to the easel to locate this point.

2. Place a sharp test negative in the enlarger negative carrier and project an image of it onto the document. Adjust the height of the enlarger so that the area of the projected image coincides with the borders of the document to be copied. This will assure you that all of the document will be included in the copy.

3. With the enlarger lens at its maximum aperture, focus the test negative sharply on the document.

4. Remove the test negative and insert a sheet of enlarging paper, emulsion side down, in the enlarger negative carrier.

5. Stop down the enlarger lens to about *f*/11 and make a test exposure, using the two copying lights and controlling the dura-

tion of the exposure by means of the light switches.

6. After correct exposure has been determined by trial and error, expose a sheet of paper.

This procedure will, of course, result in a reversed paper-negative copy; i.e., if the original has black printing on white paper, the reduced size copies will have white printing on a black background. Furthermore, any printing is wrong-reading. It is a simple matter to perform the next step. This is done by placing the paper-negative copy on the easel in place of the original and repeating the process. Tones of the copy from the paper negative will again be reversed to the positive form of black printing on a white ground. If this second step is undertaken, it probably would be advisable to lower the enlarger head so that the enlargement ratio is in the neighborhood of 1 to 1 (that is, so that the paper negative on the easel is the same size as the sheet of photographic paper in the enlarger).

Film copies. Suppose on the other hand, that instead of a single small copy of a document, you want to make several enlargements of it. The procedure in this instance is the same as outlined previously except that you will now use a sheet of film—a slow-speed, orthochromatic film is suggested instead of a sheet of paper in the enlarger negative carrier. Since even this film is considerably more light-sensitive than paper, the following precautions will have to be taken:

1. Illumination on the easel "copy board" will have to be considerably reduced in order to control the exposure accurately with the quite crude light-switch method.

2. After the enlarger negative carrier with the film has been inserted into position in the enlarger, it may be necessary to tape up any cracks or chinks around the negative carrier which might leak light (from the copy lights) and possibly fog the film.

3. The film copy, like any other film negative, should be processed in complete darkness.

After this copy negative has been made, processed, and dried, it can, of course, be enlarged in the normal manner and for the desired number of positive prints.

Chapter 5

Getting Ready to Print

IF YOU WANTED to build a new house, would you order a load of miscellaneous building materials to be delivered to your lot *before* you had decided what kind of house you wanted or before you had a completed set of plans? Obviously not. But so many photographers do just that sort of thing when it comes to making an enlargement; they throw the negative into the enlarger and proceed with abandon to use up a package of paper to get just the "right effect." And even then, they are not sure if it's printed the way it ought to be.

Come, now—let's be sensible and avoid this waste of time and materials! Photography is a wonderful way to express one's artistic thoughts. And when you make a print, it represents everything that you have put into the entire conception and execution of the picture. Prints, therefore, should not be mere piles of paper to be ground out like hamburger; if they are worth making, they are worth making well. The answer is very simple: Make a proof print; study it carefully; then make the final enlargements.

Just for fun, let's assume that you have a negative from which you want to make an excellent enlargement—it can be a pictorial landscape with salon possibilities, a portrait of your best girl, a commercial shot taken for a customer, or what have you. Let's make a proof print from this negative and see what we can learn from analyzing it carefully.

The actual method of proofing naturally varies with your preference. Some people can get along with a contact print of a 35mm negative—and a magnifying glass; others use an 8 by 10-inch enlargement; a few top-flight salon exhibitors have a more elaborate procedure. They make a 14 by 17-inch print, mount it and hang it some place in their home where it can be seen every day. Then, only after a week or so of careful observation and planning, do they make the final prints.

Ideally, the size of the proof print should be the same size as the final enlargement you plan to make. It will then be of most help in deciding about contrast, distribution of tones, compositional emphasis, and the like. However, regardless of which size you prefer, the important point is not to exclude this step from your plan of attack.

The first step is, then, to take the negative you have selected and make a "straight" enlargement of normal contrast. The term "straight" is used to designate a print that has not been dodged, diffused, or altered in any manner. The entire negative area should be included.

The paper to be used in making the proof print is relatively unimportant so long as it is not glossy. If glossy paper is all you have on hand at the moment, be sure not to ferrotype it because you will want to mark it up with pencil lines or smudges and with chalk. A suggestion at this point is to use, if possible, Kodabromide Paper N or Kodak Medalist J. These particular surfaces are perhaps unexcelled for their ability to accept all types of retouching media and are physically hard enough to withstand erasures or alterations of pencil markings.

After the proof print has been completely processed according to the manufacturer's recommendations for the paper in use, you are ready for the next step in the production of your masterpiece —the analysis. There are five questions you should now answer after studying this proof print. These are:

1. How should the picture be cropped?

2. Should the image be reversed?

3. Should any local areas be lighter or darker than they now are?

4. How large should the final print be?

5. Which paper should be used for the final print?

HOW SHOULD THE PICTURE BE CROPPED?

"Painting is dead from today on!" Paul Delaroche cried out when he saw his first "sun picture" more than a hundred years ago. But artists took hope again when they discovered that the trouble with the camera was that it saw too much. True, the composition of a picture is largely determined at the moment the film is exposed. But many times, in making the final print, a picture can be improved by using only the most interesting portion of the negative. Thus, by eliminating, through careful selection, an extra bit of foreground, for instance, or other areas or features surrounding the center of interest, it is possible to discover a "picture within a picture." This elimination of unwanted parts of the total negative area is known as "cropping."

Probably the best way to determine if and how a picture can be cropped to advantage is to cut two L-shaped masks from lightweight cardboard or a discarded print. The size of the pieces should be adequate to mask the longest dimension of the proof print: If the proof measures 8 by 10 inches, the sides of each L should be about 10 inches long. An inch or two in width will be sufficient. Place the two masks on the print so that they conform to the square or rectangular outside dimensions of the proof. Print making is, of course, both an art and a science. The science part of it is largely taken care of by the manufacturer. But now here is your chance to begin to add your contribution or artistic judgement. Fortunately, there is something of the artist in everyone, so let's be at it!

First, ask yourself whether the picture should be horizontal or vertical. Could the composition be improved if a portion were eliminated from any of the four sides? Is there too much foreground? Does a towering expanse of sky overbalance the picture? Does the center of interest need to be moved to the right or left, and does it assume its proper size with relation to the entire picture area?

As you consider each of these factors in turn, slide the masks about on the print and see if the composition can be improved. *Try every reasonable possibility.* Then try the unreasonable possibilities! For instance, the sides of the masks don't always have to be kept parallel with the proof borders. Rotate the masks together, first one way and then the other, until you find the most artistic position possible. Of course, a strong horizon line cannot be tilted out of its exact horizontal plane, or trees and buildings cannot lean over and still appear normal, but often a head-and-shoulders portrait can be improved by tipping the subject forward or backward.

The purpose of this procedure is to determine the shape and size of the area of the negative to be used in making the final print. When this is accomplished, hold the masks firmly in place and outline the selected area with a soft-lead pencil. Do not trim the print; you may change your mind tomorrow or next week with regard to which area makes the best composition. Also, it is a good idea to retain this print in your files, for you may wish to print that particular negative in the future, and it will greatly facilitate matters if the proof is available as a guide to the cropping.

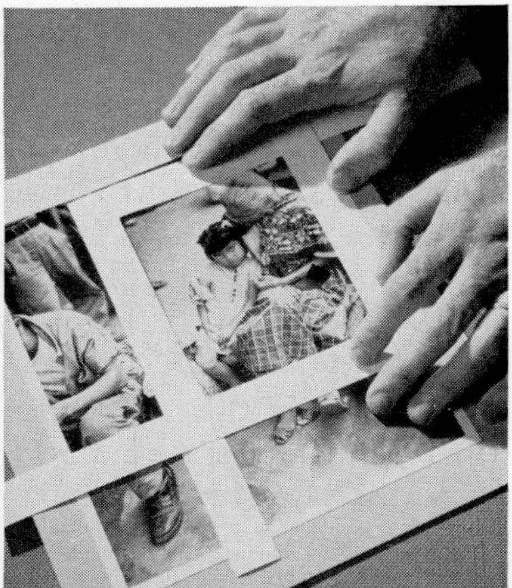

(Left) A snapshot taken in a crowded Manila street. The center of interest is surrounded by too much area and distracting details. The picture looks promising, so—

(Right)—the question is, how much to crop off? The answer is readily provided by a pair of L-shaped croppers which can be easily cut from a sheet of cardboard.

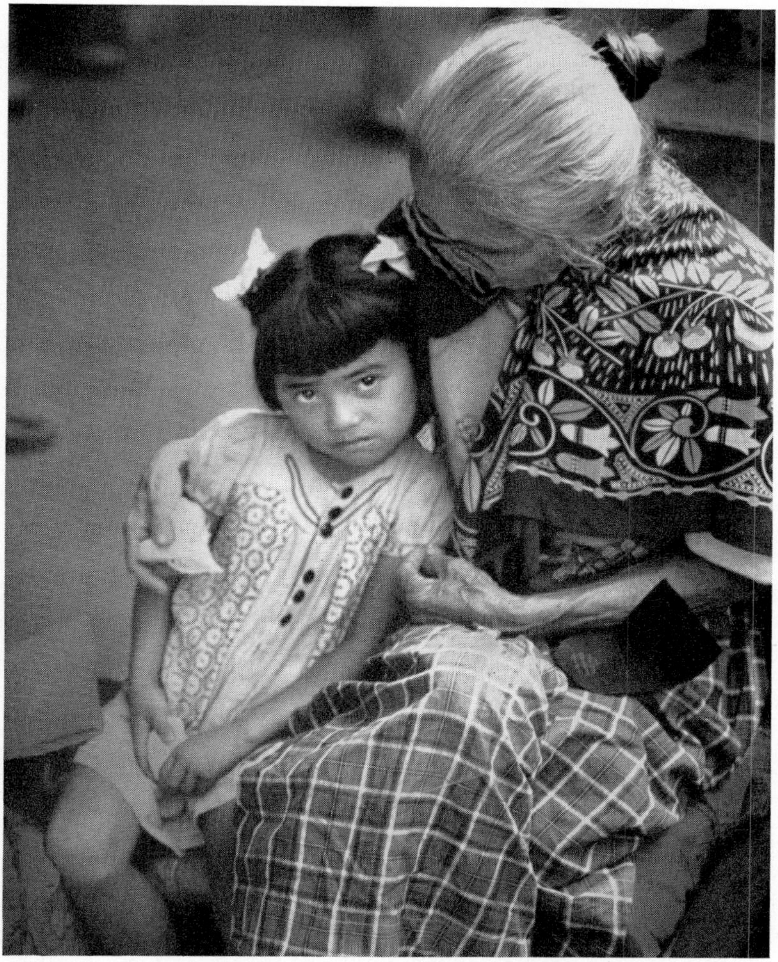

And here is the finished picture, now more than a mere snapshot, cropped to include only that part of the entire scene which best tells the story of the shy little girl. To complete the presentation, the corners and excessively light areas were darkened by printing in. Compare both the cropping and the dodging with the "before" version on page 44. Both improvements were planned with the help of a contact proof print. It is changes such as these—the decisions of how much to crop and which areas to alter in value—that give enlarging its appeal.

SHOULD THE IMAGE BE REVERSED?

When the proof print was made, the emulsion side of the negative was toward the enlarging paper. This means that everything in the print is orientated in the same manner as it was in the original scene. The snow-covered mountain peak that you saw at the left side of your direct camera view finder is still on the left side of the print; the little group of pine trees in the lower right-hand portion of the foreground is also found in the same relative position in the print. But would the composition be improved if their positions were reversed so that the trees were at the *left* and the mountain at the *right*? That is another matter to be determined. In this, of course, truth of representation is discarded.

To do this, hold the proof print with the image side toward a strong light source—an ordinary electric light bulb will serve—and examine it from the back. The image will thus be seen in reverse. Is the arrangement of the subject matter now more pleasing than before? If so, print it that way later. This procedure is rarely, if ever, applied in portraiture. The subject may object to having his hair parted on the "wrong" side or seeing his right ear where his left ought to be. Your picture of the downtown business district also should not be reversed. To say the least, it would be odd.

Are the illustrations on these two pages made from the same negative or not? Which is better?

SHOULD THE PRINT BE DODGED?

Dodging the print, as the term indicates, is a method of *locally* lightening or darkening the tones in a picture. At this point in the analysis, ask yourself if any local area of the picture would be improved if it were slightly darker than it is in the proof. Suppose a cloud is nothing more than a white blob on the proof print, with no suggestion of contours or fleeciness. But you suspect that if just the cloud were allowed to print a little longer, while the rest of the picture remains as it is, the defect would be eliminated. To help you decide on this aesthetic effect, place the proof print on a flat surface and lightly shade in the cloud with a soft-lead pencil. Smear the graphite with your finger or a small tuft of cotton so that the deposit will be more even. Does that help? Try it a bit darker. If you put on too much graphite, remove some with an art-gum eraser, and reblend the pencil lead for just the right effect.

Try the same technique on that three-quarter-length portrait you took the other evening—the one in which the hands compete with the face for interest. Pencil in those hands a bit darker and see if that doesn't subdue them to their proper degree.

Many prints are improved if the borders are darkened slightly. Maybe yours will be too. With a razor blade, scrape off enough lead

Reversing the image and dodging made possible these two interpretations from one negative.

from the end of the pencil to make a little pile of graphite dust. Pick up a small quantity on a tuft of cotton and gradually work it around with a circular motion on the corners and edges of the print. Is the unity of the composition improved? Does the eye have less tendency to wander out of the picture? Remember all these things when making the final print and try to give each portion of the paper the right amount of exposure to approximate the effects seen in the proof.

It is slightly more difficult to ascertain beforehand if some shadow areas should be printed lighter and, if so, how much. Some workers find that white chalk, used in a manner similar to that used with the graphite, is helpful. Others, however, simply make a mental note of those areas to be printed lighter and "hold back" some of the exposing light when making the final prints. Both techniques of dodging—"printing in" and "holding back"—will be fully explained in Chapter 8.

Are you ready for the salons? It may help if your prints have a high visual impact.

HOW LARGE SHOULD THE PRINT BE?

If you are making this print for a friend, for a Christmas greeting card, or for your living room wall, you doubtless have the size requirements well in mind. If you are concerned with salon exhibitions, the matter may be a little more involved.

Salon print sizes. Salon print sizes are following a typical American trend—they are getting bigger as well as better. Time was when 4 by 5-inch and 5 by 7-inch prints were accepted frequently by salons. But now even an 11 by 14-inch print is considered small for this purpose. This excepts foreign entries which may be governed by material shortages and mailing restrictions. In most salons the accepted prints are about equally divided between the 14 by 17-inch and the 16 by 20-inch sizes.

Before going on, let's explain one point: In the language of the salon exhibitor, any print larger than 14 by 17 inches, even though it measures somewhat less than an actual 16 by 20 inches in size, is called a 16 by 20 print. This is because the print was probably made on 16 by 20-inch paper. In the finishing process the print borders or easel marks and any frilled edges may have been trimmed off. Or perhaps the print was cropped somewhat on the trimmer so that the shape of the print would better fit a particular composition. Actually, you will find very few full 16 by 20-inch prints that are mounted flush with the edges of the mount board. In their travels about the country from one salon to another, full-size 16 by 20-inch prints are liable to collect more than their share of bent corners through careless handling as compared with slightly smaller prints where the mount board alone takes the bruises. Since the large prints cannot be conveniently remounted, this also helps to shorten their exhibition life.

Suppose you were trying to decide what size to make your exhibition prints. Here are some additional points you should consider:

1. The paper cost.
2. Salon prints are often accepted or rejected by the jury after only a few moments' consideration. Accordingly, the visual *impact* is an important factor. And, in general, the larger the print size, the greater the impact.

3. Of all the prints submitted to a salon, a greater percentage of the 16 by 20s are accepted than of any other print size.

4. An analysis of accepted print sizes compared with the photographers' names shows that the more experienced and consistently successful exhibitors generally make their prints on 16 by 20-inch paper. In other words, it is the newcomer to exhibition work who makes his prints on 11 by 14-inch or smaller paper. As soon as he learns the ropes, he graduates to the giant sizes.

Prolific salon exhibiting isn't easy on the pocketbook and this trend toward larger prints doesn't help in that respect. But most dyed-in-the-wool exhibitors feel that they would, if necessary, rather make fewer 16 by 20-inch prints with that extra edge of acceptability than more smaller prints which might not fare so well. You have probably heard these photographers say that enlarging is the acid test for a negative; that enlarging makes a good picture better and a poor picture worse. And, with 16 by 20 inches as a top limit, they may have a point at that!

Size and perspective. There is another matter which may help you determine what size to make the finished print. This matter is concerned with perspective which, the dictionary says, is the science of representing, on a flat surface, natural objects as they appear to the eye. So for a moment, let's think of a photograph as a *perspective view;* furthermore, let's call the camera lens the *center of perspective.* Now follow this reasoning:

(a) If a photograph is to look most natural, its perspective must be correct.

(b) The perspective is correct only if you look at the print the same way the camera lens viewed the original scene.

(c) Thus a print should be viewed at the center of perspective. *This is a distance from the print equal to the focal length of the camera lens times the degree of enlargement.* For example, for an 8 by 10 enlargement made from a 4 by 5-inch negative (a 2× enlargement) taken with a camera that had a 5-inch lens, the best viewing distance would be 10 inches. The most natural perspective would be obtained by viewing a contact print from this same negative at a distance of five inches. However, since the normal eye

Try this test: Cover up one eye and look at these two pictures from a distance of about eight inches. The left-hand picture represents a contact print. However, the right-hand enlargement should appear more natural because your eye is closer to the center of perspective. The accompanying paragraphs of the text give more information on the relation of realism to image magnification and viewing distance.

does not focus clearly at five inches, the small print is held further away at a more comfortable viewing distance. Here, then, is the reason why enlargements are generally more natural or realistic than contact prints: It is easier to view enlargements than contact prints from their center of perspective.

How does this work from a practical standpoint in determining print size? Well, you have already seen from the preceding paragraph why it would be better to show somebody an 8 by 10 print than a contact print if you knew that the print was going to be held at a normal reading distance of about ten inches to one foot. Suppose you knew that a group of salon judges were going to sit six feet away from your print entry. Or that prospective portrait customers were going to look at a print display case from a distance of about six feet. How large should the prints be for the most natural impression? If the camera lens had a focal length of six inches, then a 12 times enlargement would place the center of perspective at 72 inches (six feet) where it should be. Of course, many other factors, such as available space to hang the picture or the intended print purpose, will also determine the actual print dimensions. However, this matter of viewing the print from the center of perspective is often overlooked when making the best possible print from any particular negative.

Just a minute: You're not convinced that the scene will look much more natural when viewed from the center of perspective as compared from any old place, are you? Then make this test: Look at a contact print first with both eyes at a comfortable viewing distance. Then look at the same print with a reading glass and notice how much more realistic the scene becomes—it almost seems to take on a third-dimensional quality. The reason is, of course, that the reading lens places your eye closer to the center of perspective and probably forces you to look at the print with only one eye, as the camera did.

The above statement probably causes you to wonder if pictures will appear more realistic if you view them with only one eye. The answer is, definitely yes! But since no one is going to do this anyway, we won't discuss the subject further. Let's take a look at the characteristics of paper.

SELECTING THE PAPER

Whatever the intended purpose of the final print, the paper used plays an important part in producing a picture of quality, beauty, and character. In your selection of a paper, you give the picture another creative touch and help to express your own artistic interpretation of the subject.

Many considerations enter into the selection of the printing paper. The intended use of the print will determine its size, the character of the negative will influence the printing grade of the paper used, and personal preference will govern the tint of the paper stock and the texture and gloss of the paper surface. Let's look briefly at these characteristics.

PAPER CHARACTERISTICS

Achieving *consistently* good print quality does not result from a will-o'-the-wisp chase from one paper to another—either from surface to surface or from manufacturer to manufacturer—but more from learning thoroughly the characteristics of one or, at most, a few papers. This advice may have whiskers on it, but it's nonetheless true.

The total characteristics of a paper include its speed, contrast, image color, exposure latitude, development latitude, how it reacts to various toning baths, how much the surface "dries down," and certain other factors which may be less obvious but also have an important bearing on print quality. As an example of the less obvious characteristics, when an exposed sheet of paper is placed in the developer, its image may "come up" fast and then "level out," gradually building up density until the normal development time is completed, or its image density may build up in a more gradual fashion.

Here's another item: Some papers increase contrast with increased development, while some other paper may keep practically the same degree of contrast regardless of whether the development is short, normal, or long. Does a particular paper you have selected increase contrast with increased development? You *should* know. This might be quite desirable if you have only a No. 3 paper grade on hand and wish to print a negative requiring a No. 2 paper grade. The procedure would then, of course, be to give a slightly more-than-normal exposure and compensate for this by developing for somewhat less than the recommended normal development time. On the other hand, the contrast of a print made on Kodabromide Paper does not change with development time. This characteristic meets the requirement of those photographers who have on hand a selection of papers of various printing grades and who wish uniform contrast regardless of the development time selected.

Incidentally, some photographers personally prefer a particular grade of paper over another grade; it gives "better tones," they say. True, a particular grade may fit most of their negatives better than some other grade. But such photographers are doubtless prejudiced since, *with appropriate negatives which fit the paper grade being used,* there is no difference in quality between prints made on No. 2 grade paper, No. 3, or even the high-contrast No. 4 paper. Of course, it's best to aim your negative contrast so that you usually print on a No. 2 or No. 3 paper grade so that you will have some contrast latitude on either side of normal.

Because it's worth-while advice, it's repeated: Choose one kind of paper and then stick with it until you are completely familiar with it—until it's as "comfortable as an old shoe."

A warm image tone plus a fine-grained paper surface would be ideal for this scene.

Stock tint. Generally speaking, papers are furnished in three stock tints: white, cream white, and old ivory or "buff." The choice of tint will depend upon both the subject itself and the color quality of the lighting of the subject.

White is recommended for high-key subjects; for cold-tone subjects, such as portraits, landscapes, and interiors taken with artificial light.

Cream White is suited for general use for both sunlighted and artificially lighted scenes.

Old Ivory is ideal for prints which require extreme warmth, such as sunlit interiors, firelight scenes, and sunsets, and for many character studies of elderly people.

Keep in mind that high-key prints tend to emphasize the tint of the paper; low-key prints, to subdue it.

Speed. The speed of photographic papers is normally less than that of negative materials. It is determined primarily on the basis of the amount of exposure required to produce satisfactory shadow details. Enlarging papers are relatively higher in speed than contact printing papers, but some moderately fast papers, such as Kodak Opal, can be used for both purposes.

American Standard Paper speeds of some of the commonly used Kodak enlarging papers are given in the following table:

Kodak Paper	American Standard Paper Speed
Opal G	160
Illustrators' Special	160
Portrait Proof R	320
Ektalure	350
Platino F-2	500
Medalist F-2	1000
Mural R-2	1000
Kodabromide F-2	1000
Resisto Rapid N-2	1000

These values are of particular interest in determining exposures when different papers are used interchangeably. For example, if the exposure for a given set of conditions for Opal Paper G is 72 seconds, Kodabromide Paper F-2 would require 4.5 seconds.

Texture. Although each paper manufacturer's designations differ somewhat, surface textures can be grouped into the following classifications:

Smooth paper has no discernible surface to interfere with the reproduction of fine detail. Consequently, it is well suited for small prints.

Fine-grained paper has a slightly pebbled surface which adds distinctiveness with no appreciable loss in definition. It is useful for close-ups of young people and for architectural subjects; it is also a popular surface for exhibition prints.

Rough paper has a definite surface texture which has a slight tendency to subdue fine detail and thus focus attention on the larger planes of the picture. It is for this reason that rough-textured papers are used widely for making portrait proof prints (where the negative has yet to be retouched) and for photomurals (to help conceal any tendency toward graininess).

Tweed paper has a coarser surface texture than "rough," and therefore gives a further opportunity to emphasize the masses in landscapes and character studies.

Tapestry paper offers an extremely rough surface for the maximum subordination of detail. Its most effective use is in large prints.

Silk paper has a shiny, clothlike surface which adds sparkle and distinction to high-key portraits, snow-covered landscapes, and water scenes.

Suede paper resembles in texture the leather of that name. Its deep blacks are particularly suited to low-key pictures. The surface is extremely matte and is useful where annoying, light reflections from the print surface should be eliminated.

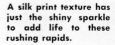

A silk print texture has just the shiny sparkle to add life to these rushing rapids.

Image tone. The color of the silver image in the finished print is referred to as the "image tone." Enlarging papers vary in manufacturers' designations but can be arbitrarily grouped into classifications such as those given for the following Kodak papers:

Neutral black	Brown black
Kodabromide	Opal
Resisto Rapid N	Ektalure
	Illustrators' Special
Warm black	Portrait Proof R
Platino	Translite Enlarging
Medalist	
Mural	

The warmth of tone of the warm-black and the brown-black papers can be varied somewhat by using cold-tone developers (such as Kodak Dektol Developer or Kodak Developer D-72) or warm-tone developers (such as Kodak Selectol Developer or Kodak Developer D-52).

Weight. Paper stock varies in thickness, the two common types being designated as Single Weight (SW) and Double Weight (DW). For the most part, double-weight papers are preferred for enlargements.

Contrast capacity. Many papers, such as Kodak Platino or Kodabromide, are supplied in several printing grades to fit negatives which vary in density scale due to differences in subject lighting, exposure, or degree of development. Other papers, such as Kodak Opal, are intended for use with negatives of uniform quality made under carefully controlled conditions; for this reason they are supplied in only one printing grade. Choosing the right grade for a particular negative is somewhat of a trial-and-error procedure, although the selection is usually not difficult. If you are in doubt, start by making a print on paper grade No. 2 which is intended to yield a print of normal contrast from a normal negative. If you have a "soot-and-whitewash" effect, with few middle tones, try grade No. 1. If the result is "flat" or "muddy," try grade No. 3.

Surface gloss. Surface gloss or sheen is a very important factor in your selection of a paper, and for this reason it is worthy of a little extra consideration. Generally, surfaces are classified as glossy, lustre, and matte.

Glossy paper is favored for prints which are to be reproduced and for small prints in which fine detail is important. To increase the degree of gloss, this paper is usually dried on ferrotype plates.

Lustre paper has a subdued gloss and is the all-purpose choice for general-exhibition and portrait work.

Matte paper has a fairly dull surface and is frequently the choice for high-key pictures and atmospheric shots.

There are two effects produced by the degree of paper gloss. First, there is the control of the range of tones in the prints. The higher the gloss, the higher the density a particular paper can produce. Zero density—that of white paper—is practically the same for all papers, and the range of tones from light to dark is therefore dependent on the maximum density or, to put it simply, on the "blackest black." A long range of available tones is highly desirable for printing most scenes because most negatives, being transparencies, have a greater range of tones than can be reproduced in a paper print which is viewed by reflected light. The more accurately a paper can reproduce the range or density scale of the negative, the more realistic the result will be.

From a practical standpoint, it is therefore most desirable to use glossy or high-lustre papers for subjects which have a long tonal range. These subjects are typified by low-key portraits, night scenes, or any scenes in which fairly dark shadow details contain relatively important subject details. On the other hand, many high-key subjects or fog scenes have most of their important details encompassed by a relatively short tonal scale which can be satisfactorily reproduced by a short-scale, matte paper.

The remaining consideration is that, when removed from the wash water, matte papers tend to dry down and lose more of their apparent wet tonal range than do glossy papers. However, a matte-texture paper can be selected as best suited to a particular subject, and then a high gloss imparted subsequently by means of Kodak Print Lustre or by lacquering.

Chapter 6

Enlarging from Eight to Late

LET'S FACE IT: Good enlargements are the result of carefully following simple, straightforward directions, plus a liberal pinch of photographic horse sense. So here is a chapter dealing with elementary enlarging and including "beginner's" instructions. Yet, it should not be passed by as "elementary stuff." Perhaps you have already made good enlargements. Then why not consider this chapter as a helpful review? Even the concert pianist has his scales and exercises to play, and the professor occasionally has to review the fundamentals of his field to retain full command of his subject. And that's the way it is with photography.

CLEANING THE NEGATIVE

Before any print is made, the negative should be CLEAN. This means freedom from dust, dirt, greasy fingerprints, etc., since, if present, these deposits will print as though they were part of the negative image and will show up as objectionable white spots on the print. The smaller the negative, the greater the degree of magnification, and the more important it is to work with dust-free negatives. Also, as mentioned on page 30, condenser-type enlargers show negative defects more readily than do diffusion enlargers.

If your negatives have been treated with care ever since they were made, for example, if they have been stored in a suitable negative file, it may be sufficient merely to dust them off with a soft brush. Other "less fortunate" negatives may have surface streaks or dirt which is seemingly embedded in the emulsion. It is quite important to remove these particles, if present, since they may do further damage to the emulsion by scratching it if the neg-

Make it a firm habit! Dust off each negative before printing it to save a lot of spotting time later.

ative is used in a "glass-sandwich" type of negative carrier. In this instance, it may be best to rewash the negative for about 15 minutes and then carefully swab the surfaces with a piece of wet cotton. Before drying the negative, immersing it in Kodak Photo-Flo Solution will help prevent the formation of water spots during drying; otherwise, water spots may show in the print.

Fingerprints and other surface deposits are best removed with a grease solvent, such as Kodak Film Cleaner or carbon tetrachloride. Film cleaners are usually volatile solvents which produce harmful vapors and should be used with adequate ventilation. Avoid breathing the vapor and prolonged or repeated contact with the skin. Don't use too much cleaner, avoid "scrubbing" the film, and use the cleaner quickly so that pools of liquid do not form or stand on the film surface.

One more suggestion: The use of carbon-tetrachloride-type cleaners often creates enough static electricity to attract dust particles to the film. This is not serious, particularly if you use a lintless applicator, but it does warrant a final check of the negative for dust particles just before placing it in the enlarger.

Scratches in the negative are serious, however. Although there is no remedy which is completely satisfactory, you can fill the scratch with a light application of Vaseline or glycerin or one of the commercial scratch repair preparations available in camera stores and which are helpful in lessening the "printing effectiveness" of the scratch.

MASKING THE NEGATIVE

With the negative cleaned free of grease marks (such as fingerprints) and brushed free of dust particles, place it with its emulsion side (the dull side) down in the enlarger negative carrier. This next step is important and should not be omitted: Cut a mask from a piece of opaque paper—some photographers use a sheet of Kodapak Sheet, Ruby, for this purpose—so that only that part of the negative will be projected which you intend to include in the print. Some enlargers have built-in, adjustable masks, but if yours does not, keep the individual mask you make and it won't be long until you have a collection which will accommodate most new masking requirements.

The purpose of this mask is to prevent any "stray" light from being projected down to the easel-baseboard area where it could degrade the quality of the print by bouncing around and being reflected by various glossy or white surfaces in the darkroom onto the sensitive paper. Reflecting surfaces might include light-tone darkroom walls, the metallic post of the enlarger, a large, white focusing surface on the easel, or even your white shirt! "Never bothered with making a mask, and my prints aren't degraded," a well-meaning friend may tell you. Well, perhaps you can get away with it. But perhaps you cannot. The case where a mask is most needed is where the negative is smaller than the maximum size the enlarger was designed for, say, printing a 2¼ by 3¼-inch negative in a 4 by 5-inch enlarger. The white light that escapes past the edges of the negative can really bounce around them and cause trouble by creating a "flare"-light condition in the enlarger lens. Also, in passing the edges of the negative, some of the light is bent or refracted directly onto the printing area. You can test this yourself by cutting a sheet of black paper the size of your negative, placing it in the "over-size" carrier, and turning on the enlarger light. It can easily be seen that the printing area is receiving some of this unwanted "bent-and-splashed" fogging light.

It is also important to mask down the negative to the desired area if (a) the negative is abnormally dense or (b) if the exposure time is abnormally long, due to a combination of a slow-speed enlarging paper and a relatively large degree of magnification. Thus, under print-exposure times of a minute or more, the scattered-light exposure has a cumulative effect which, added to the normal print exposure, can have a degrading influence, particularly on the print highlights.

Are you convinced that masking is worth while?

Remember, just before placing the negative carrier in the enlarger, give it a final check to see that no dust particles have settled on either the negative or the glass of the carrier.

COMPOSING ON THE EASEL

After adjusting the easel to the desired print size, insert a blank piece of white paper—the reverse side of an old print will do—on which the projected negative image can be focused and composed. Switch from normal room light to safelight illumination, and turn on the enlarger. Next, raise or lower the enlarger lamp house so as to make the image area on the easel correspond exactly with your cropping of the proof print. Tighten the vertical lamp-house adjustment if necessary, make sure the lens diaphragm is set at its widest opening, and bring the image into focus.

This is a very critical time in the making of your picture; let's think for a moment about composing the image within the size format you have selected. Now is the time to review the thoughts you had in cropping the proof print. Or, if you skipped the proof-print step entirely, it is even more important to know how you want your print to look before you proceed further.

Contrary to popular opinion, the composition or arrangement of objects within a photograph is not completely and irrevocably fixed when the film is exposed in the camera. Far from it; many things can change a picture's "face" in the darkroom. Probably most important is the elimination of distracting, irrelevant, or unnecessary details, or in other words, using only the best "story-telling" portion of the negative to make the print. In addition, perhaps the easel should be rotated clockwise or counterclockwise for improved subject emphasis. Maybe the final print would make a better horizontal composition than the vertical picture you had planned originally. All these things and many more discussed in the following chapters can alter the composition of the picture. Of course, a photographer isn't expected, as is the artist, to be able to move trees about at will; nevertheless, *you should seriously consider each one of these "fielder's-choice" possibilities before each different print is made.*

It may help in composing on the easel to ask yourself questions such as these: Just how much prominence should be given to a figure in a landscape? How large should it be in relation to the size of the print? Where should it be placed in relation to the print borders? Where should the horizon line be positioned? If these problems trouble you, you may find this helpful:

On the back of the discarded print which you are using to view the projected image, draw in the rectangular outline of the print area. (See page 100 for determining rectangular print shapes of pleasing proportions.) The easiest way to do this is to run a pencil around the inside edge of the easel masking arms. Next, using a ruler, draw in diagonal lines across the rectangle from each of the opposite corners.

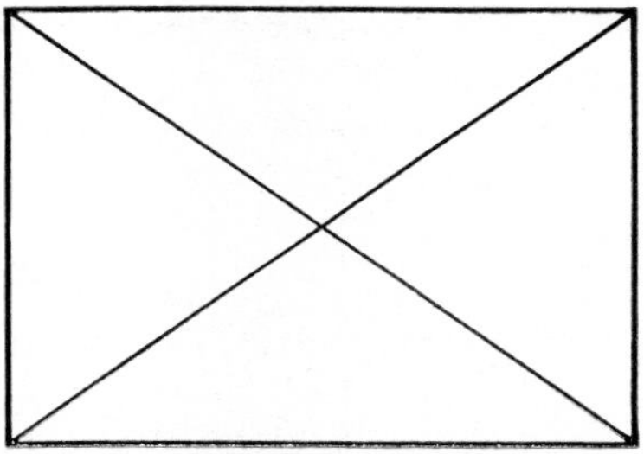

Step 1

Using these diagonals as base lines, construct a perpendicular line to each of the opposite corners.

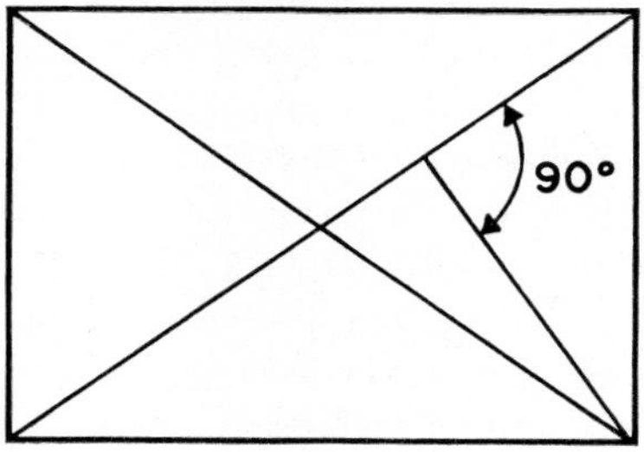

Step 2

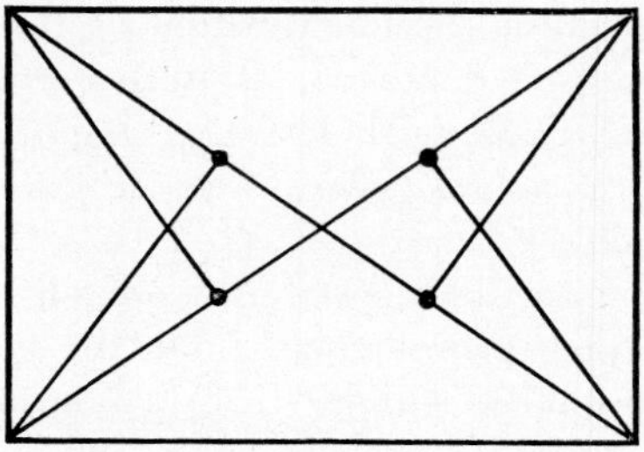

Step 3

At the intersections of the diagonals and the perpendicular lines, you have now located focus points in the picture area which may be used as "interest points," that is, places where centers of interest may be located. Since these interest points are important, darken them heavily or circle them.

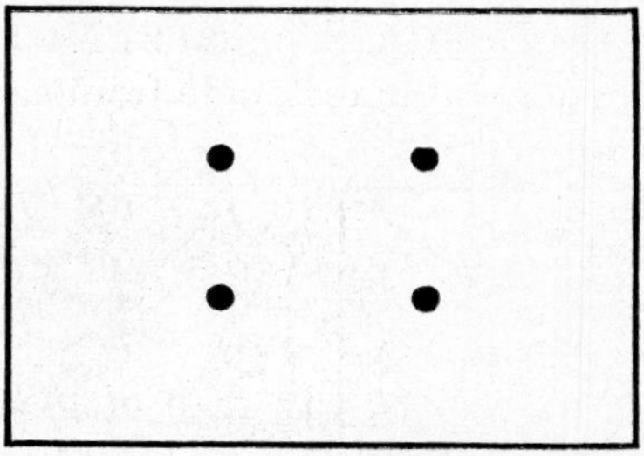

Step 4

To complete the compositional guide, draw parallel lines from opposite borders through the four points. Each line will be about one-third of the distance to the nearest edge of the rectangle and will serve as "horizon location lines."

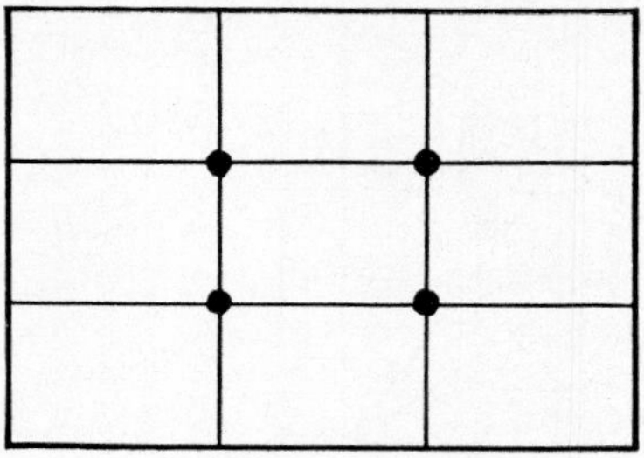

Step 5

Now let's put this guide to work. Replace it in the easel and turn on the enlarger. The general rules to follow are these: Move the easel about on the baseboard, and raise or lower the enlarger until:

1. The primary and secondary centers of interest are located as near as possible to any of the nearest appropriate "interest center points."

2. No print detail of *major* importance to the composition is positioned outside of an imaginary boundary line formed by the four interest points.

3. The horizon is located at or near one of the lines drawn through the interest points. This obviously gives you two choices in placing the sky line in either a vertical or a horizontal picture.

4. Strong vertical or horizontal lines of importance to the composition are located at or near one of the four "horizon" lines.

These guide lines suggest horizon line placement as well as positions for interest points. Keep in mind that this guide only suggests, not demands, that it may not fit all subjects.

The system works equally well with portraits, landscapes, or other subjects. For example, if your print-to-be is a three-quarters portrait in a vertical format, you will probably want to position the face at one of the top interest points. A subordinate center of interest, such as the hands, will then be as near as possible to either of the two lower points. In a landscape, a lone tree on the horizon may be located at one of the vertical "horizon placement lines" while a figure in the foreground will probably be aesthetically located at one of the lower points. Horizon lines are generally in a pleasing position if located by this guide system.

No one, however, wants to walk always with a crutch. A guide such as this should be used at first to avoid stumbling awkwardly from a compositional standpoint. A feeling for tasteful arrangement is something which can be cultured and developed. So, don't limit your picture making to the narrow confines of rules. Break them now and then; dare to make a different picture—dare to be yourself.

TILTING THE EASEL

Did you ever take a picture of a building in which the building appeared to be leaning over backwards? This so-called distortion, most commonly seen in architectural pictures, is caused by a convergence of lines which are parallel in the original subject. Such results are inevitable when the film in the camera is not parallel with the front surface of the building. To counteract this, professional view cameras are equipped with rising-and-falling fronts and swinging-and-tilting backs by which the necessary parallelism may be secured. But pictures taken with less flexible folding or reflex cameras must, therefore, be remedied by tilting the easel when the enlargement is being made. Thus, if you aimed your camera upwards a few degrees from horizontal to include, for instance, the spire on the steeple of a picturesque New England church, the easel must be tilted a like amount in the opposite direction to compensate for the convergence in your negative.

Actually, it is incorrect to say that distortion was induced by tilting the camera or that the distortion is eliminated by tilting the easel. More properly, these are matters of altering perspective.

Furthermore, tilting the easel introduces an actual form of distortion by elongating the image. However, the elongation is usually the lesser of the two "evils" and the results generally warrant the slight "stretching" of the subject.

This "stretching" of the print subject has an interesting practical application that is often overlooked by many photographers. For example, in portraiture, it is easily possible to widen a too-narrow face by tilting the easel up from one side. Similarly, a round face may be narrowed by tilting the easel from the top or bottom. True, in many cases the portrait subject himself may object to having his features distorted. The answer here is, of course, that a *little* distortion may be flattering and may not be noticed by the subject. Certainly, few short people would object to appearing slightly taller; or stout people, slightly thinner.

For an even more practical example, suppose that you are printing a three-quarters portrait from a negative in which the hands in the subject's lap were made unduly prominent because they were located somewhat closer to the camera than was his face. Furthermore, the prominence of the hands was emphasized by a comparatively short-focal-length lens on the camera. In printing this negative, tilt the easel so that the bottom part of the picture is brought closer to the enlarger lens. Because the hands at the bottom part of the picture are now *nearer* the lens than the subject's head and shoulders, the hands will be made somewhat *smaller* in proportion to the rest of the subject. Thus, your problem may be solved.

When the easel is tilted from its normal horizontal position, refocusing is naturally necessary. Some enlargers have a built-in control, such as a tilting negative carrier or tilting lens board, which greatly facilitates this focusing problem of trying to cover a comparatively great depth of field. For enlargers without this convenience, it is best to focus on a spot in the projected image approximately one-third the distance from the top edge of the easel, as shown in the accompanying diagram. Focus the image with the enlarger lens wide open, and then stop it down until all parts of the image are critically sharp. Usually this means that the lens will have to be stopped down about as far as possible.

There are, of course, practical limits to tilting the easel. They must be determined by the particular picture and your good judgement. Do not expect this technique to perform the miracle of changing Mrs. Five-by-Five into a glamorous pin-up model. Rather, it's a technique for inducing subtle improvements, and *the possibility of using it should be considered before each print is made.*

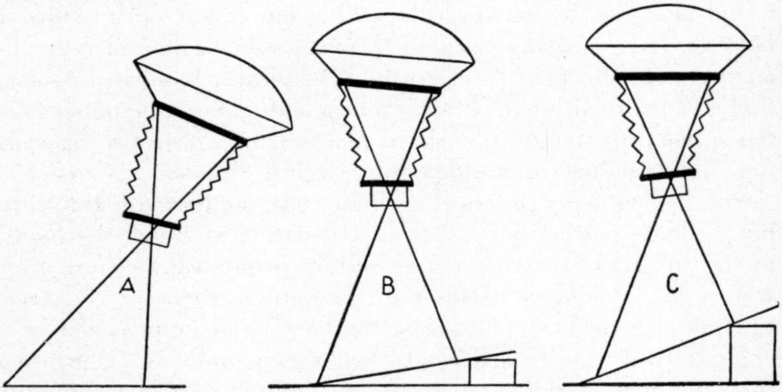

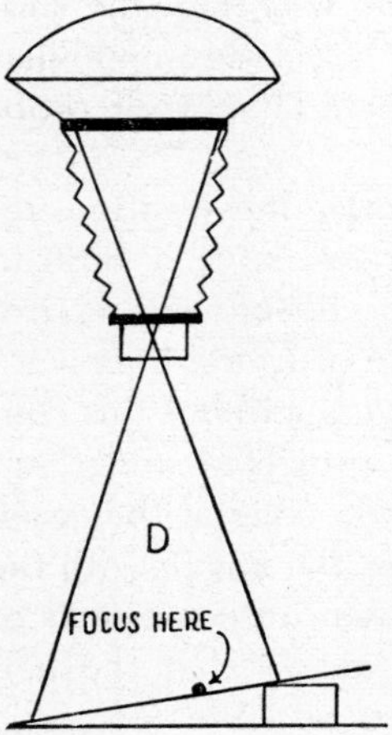

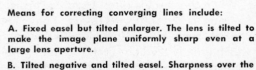

Means for correcting converging lines include:

A. Fixed easel but tilted enlarger. The lens is tilted to make the image plane uniformly sharp even at a large lens aperture.

B. Tilted negative and tilted easel. Sharpness over the image area is provided by tilting the negative in the indicated direction.

C. Fixed negative but tilted lens and easel. Notice that this condition is similar to A except that the enlarger is upright.

D. Fixed negative and lens but tilted easel. In this case the depth of field is quite shallow and lens must be well stopped down.

FOCUSING THE IMAGE

As a final precaution before exposing the print, check to be sure that the projected image is as sharp as it possibly can be. For best visibility, focus with the lens at its maximum aperture, and then stop it down from about *f*/8 to *f*/16 for a normal enlarging time. When using a cold-light enlarger, the bluish light is visually weak and you may have some difficulty in focusing fairly dense negatives at a relatively large degree of magnification. In this case, you have two alternatives: The first, and most convenient, is to use one of the optical focusing accessories of the type incorporating a magnifier. These are usually available at camera stores and are a useful accessory for a cold-light enlarger. The second method might well be called "focusing by substitution." With the enlarger lamp house firmly in place, remove the (dense) negative and replace it with a discarded negative into the emulsion of which you have intentionally drawn some deep scratches. It will be an easy matter to focus on these marks and then replace the negative.

Is there any difference in image sharpness in using the enlarger lens wide open or stopped down? To answer the question directly, sharper enlargements generally result with the lens stopped down. Of course, it depends on the lens in question. Some, such as the Kodak Ektar Enlarging Lenses, have a flat field and are sharp even at their maximum aperture. Other enlarging lenses are the curved-field type; this includes camera lenses which may be used temporarily as enlarger lenses. If it is absolutely necessary—to avoid unusually long exposures when working with dense negatives and slow papers—to use the enlarger lens at its widest aperture, as a general recommendation try to focus on a point about one-fourth of the distance away from the center of the projected image toward the corners. This will make for better over-all image sharpness than by focusing either in the exact center of the image (in which the corners may be slightly out of focus) or at the corners of the easel (in which the center of the picture may be slightly out of focus). But to eliminate as much of the lens aberration as possible, regardless of the lens used, remember the advice to stop the lens down if circumstances permit.

EXPOSING THE PRINT

Determining print exposure is of particular consequence in influencing the technical quality of the print. The exposure must be quite accurate since, if the paper is appreciably overexposed or underexposed, it will have to be discarded, with the only recourse being to make a new print. Test strips represent an easy and economical method of determining the exposure time. A first guess at the exposure when printing a new negative is almost never exactly correct, even for experienced workers. So try to avoid that understandable impulse to put a full-size sheet of paper in the easel the first time. Like impulses in general, this can soon be an expensive habit!

So, with scissors or a trimmer, cut a full sheet of paper into about four equal pieces. Replace three of them in the paper box and put the remaining one, emulsion side up, on the easel where an important area of the image will be projected. If the picture is a portrait, this will be the face; if it is a landscape, try to include a portion of both the sky and the foreground. Now cover up four-fifths of this strip with an opaque black paper and switch on the enlarger light. Keep a close check on the time with the second

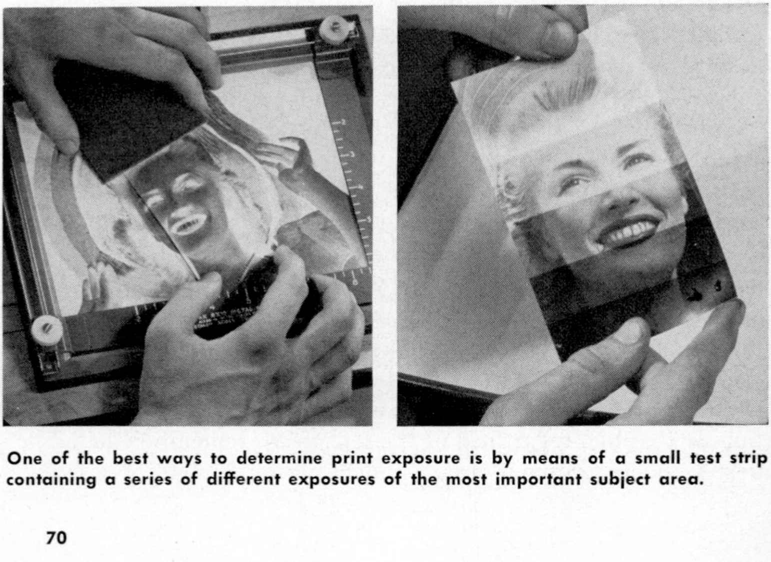

One of the best ways to determine print exposure is by means of a small test strip containing a series of different exposures of the most important subject area.

hand of a watch, clock, or any audible timer. After 32 seconds, quickly move the black paper so that it covers three-fifths of the test strip. Be careful not to change the position of the strip. In this position, expose the test strip for the next 16 seconds. Now cover all but two-fifths for an 8-second exposure, and the next-to-last portion for a 4-second exposure. Remove the black covering paper entirely and give the whole strip another 4-second exposure. Switch off the enlarger light.

Now take a breath and see what you have. You gave the small test print a staggered series of five exposures in the ratio of 32, 16, 8, 4, and 4. In reverse order, these five sections received 4, 8, 16, 32, and 64 seconds of exposure; in other words, one received twice as much light as did the one exposed immediately before it. Develop this test strip exactly according to the instructions packaged with the paper. You now have—if the negative was anywhere near normal—a suitable range of print densities from which to choose the correct exposure for a full-size sheet of paper. Which of the five sections seems neither too dark nor too light? If you think that the one which received 8 seconds' exposure is normal, the next obvious step is to try exposing a full-size sheet of paper for 8 seconds. If the exact exposure seems to be between 8 and 16 seconds, for example, try exposing a full sheet for 12 seconds; there is no real need for a second test strip with a 12-second exposure since there is considerable development latitude which you can use to adjust print density in cases of small exposure errors. It is often helpful in selecting the print-exposure time to compare the processed test strip with one or two full-size prints even if they were made from different negatives.

In addition to determining exposure, the test strip should also give you a clue as to the correctness of print contrast. Here again, comparing the test strip with finished prints of normal contrast and density will be helpful.

A streamline method of making a test strip to determine the correct exposure time for any enlargement is by using a Kodak Projection Print Scale. The procedure is quick and simple:

1. Place a negative in the enlarger and focus sharply.
2. Turn off the printing light.

3. Place a small piece of enlarging paper on the easel.

4. Lay the scale (shiny side up) on the paper and locate it over the place where the center of interest will be projected.

5. Expose the paper for 60 seconds and develop it as recommended by the manufacturer.

6. Inspect the image and select the best-appearing sector. The correct printing time *in seconds* will be found on the rim of that sector.

7. Without disturbing the enlarger, expose a full-size sheet of the same kind of paper for the indicated time and develop it in the same manner as the test print.

Measuring negative densities with a densitometer, a spot photometer, or a Density Kodaguide can serve as an accurate guide to predicting the print exposure or the necessary paper contrast.

One of the best methods combines the use of both the Kodak Color Densitometer, Model 1, and the Kodak Print Exposure Computer. The information on the Print Exposure Computer can be made into a chart and correlated with the magnification scale of the enlarger, if desired. When working with negatives which include different subjects and were taken under a variety of lighting conditions, it is best to base the system on shadow-density readings (as suggested in the Color Densitometer instruction book). This system of negative-density measurement has its most practical application in large portrait studios where the photographer turns out negatives of consistently high quality and is willing to exercise close control over his equipment and processing. When working with portrait negatives exclusively, however, diffuse-highlight readings are used. With this, as with all other density-measurement systems, it is necessary to make a new control test for each type of paper used and, preferably, for each different emulsion number of a particular kind of paper.

But here's an important consideration: *The best way of "predicting" the proper exposure and contrast grade is to make a number of prints, varying the exposure and, if necessary, the contrast grade, and then to select the best print by careful comparison.* Be sure to view the prints in sufficiently bright illumination when making your selection.

For enlargements, the ideal exposure time should fall between about 8 and 25 seconds. Exposures shorter than 8 seconds make dodging difficult and reproducing the exposure time accurately for subsequent duplicate prints almost impossible. Exposures longer than about 25 seconds make exposing a tedious chore, particularly if considerable dodging is required. To keep the average exposures at a convenient working level, you may find that the aperture of the enlarger lens will have to be increased or decreased, depending on the negative density, the speed of the printing paper, and the wattage of the enlarger lamp. However, if your print exposure time tends to be appreciably higher, use a fast enlarging paper to increase your prints-per-evening output.

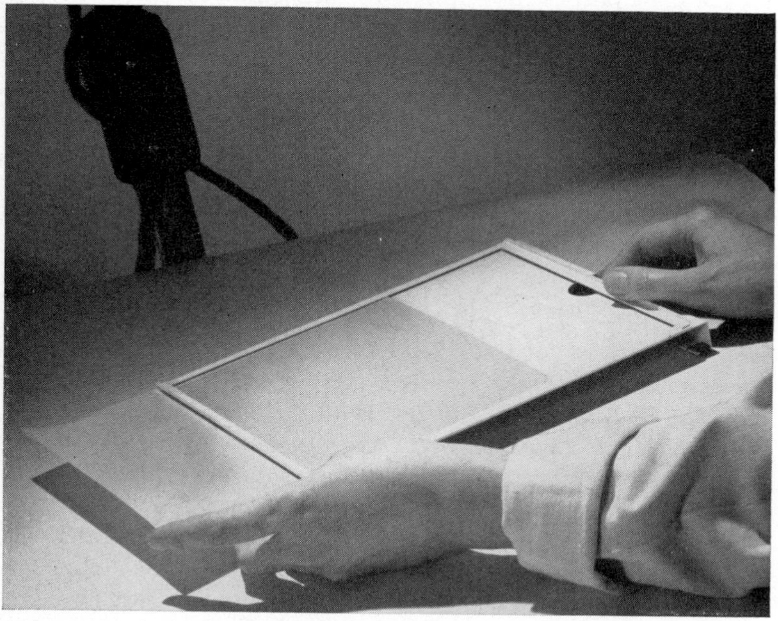

A print difficulty which may plague any photographer, and especially beginners, is fingerprints which appear unaccountably in the picture area. This may be largely prevented by handling the paper only by the very edges as shown here and by carefully drying the hands before handling the sensitive paper. This easel, by the way, is one with non-adjustable margins, but is inexpensive and convenient to use.

PROCESSING THE PRINT

The trays are customarily arranged in the order, left to right: 1—developer, 2—stop bath, 3—fixing baths, and 4—wash. Space them a short distance apart so that one solution will not be splashed into another. The trays for the developer and the stop bath should be slightly larger than the largest print to be made; because the trays for fixing and washing will probably contain several prints at a time, they should be about twice as large as the other trays. Be sure to use sufficient solution in each tray to cover the prints by at least ½ inch. Incidentally, when you have finished printing, do not leave the trays scattered about. Clean them well inside and out and stand them up on edge to dry. Always use the same tray for the same purpose to help prevent the solutions from becoming contaminated.

Handling the test strips may have left traces of the processing solutions on your fingers, so be sure that your hands are rinsed thoroughly and dried on a clean, dry towel. Incidentally (to help prevent fingerprints from being incorporated into the picture area), this precaution should be taken before handling each new sheet of photographic paper. If your fingers are naturally oily, the use of print tongs will solve the fingerprint problem. You'll need two: one for the developer, and the other for the stop bath and the hypo. Do not mix up these tongs—use each only in the proper solutions.

Developing. Hold the exposed paper by an edge (with dry fingers!) and *emulsion side up*. With a glance at the timer or clock, slide the paper smoothly and quickly into the developer. Be sure the print remains completely submerged, particularly during the first few seconds of development. Paper which has been stored in a dry place may have a tendency to curl. Watch out for this because if a part of the paper protrudes unnoticed above the surface of the solution and consequently receives less development, a line of demarcation may show in the finished print.

Incidentally, do you know why the above emphasis was placed on inserting the paper into the developer *emulsion side up*? It's this: a rough-textured paper may have a tendency to trap small air bells on its surface as the paper is being immersed in the developer. By inserting the paper emulsion side up and then agitating it quite vigorously during the first few seconds of development, any air bubbles present will be freed and will rise uninhibited to the surface. But if it were immersed emulsion side down, these bubbles would really be trapped and would prevent the print from being developed wherever they might be. Then too, another reason for developing the print emulsion side up is that the emulsion —which rapidly becomes soft and susceptible to abrasion while wet—will not chance being pushed down and scratched against a rough tray bottom.

For the remainder of the developing time, the print should be kept under the solution as much as possible and agitated constantly by gently tipping the tray backwards and forwards to help promote uniform development. Try to control a rather universal urge to pick up the print every few seconds to examine its progress. Otherwise you will only increase the possibility of fogging it by holding it nearer than recommended to the safelight and of staining it if the developer is not fresh.

Obviously, the longer the print is left in the developer, the darker it becomes. But do not infer from this that the time of development should determine the proper density. Print density should be almost entirely controlled by print exposure. The duration of development varies with different paper-developer combinations, but this information is always found on the instruction sheet packed with the paper. Note that there is a recommended development time in minutes, and that this is in the center of a useful range of development times.

The sacrifice in print quality begins when either limit of this range is exceeded. There is a natural tendency to "pull" a print out of the developer if it is sufficiently dark even before the lower limit of the range of recommended times has been reached. However, an underdeveloped print is usually flat and "muddy" with blocked-up shadows. The image tone may be warmer than normal but, worst of all, the print may be grainy or even mottled. On the other hand, "forced" development (development beyond the maximum time recommended) may cause fog or yellow stains,

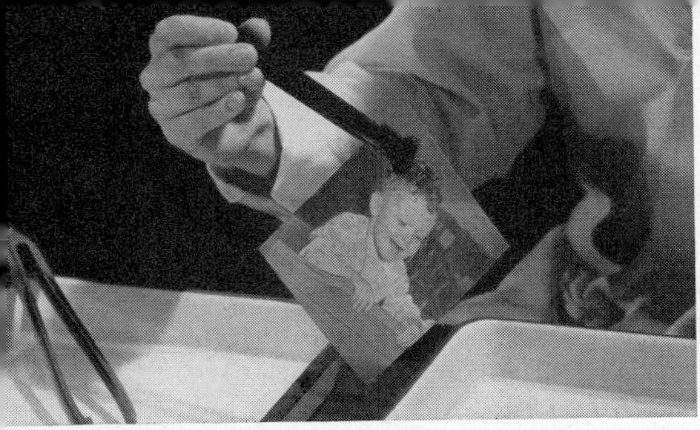

If you are troubled by finger marks in your prints, keep your hands out of the solutions by means of print tongs. Use one tong for the developing tray, another for the stop bath and hypo trays.

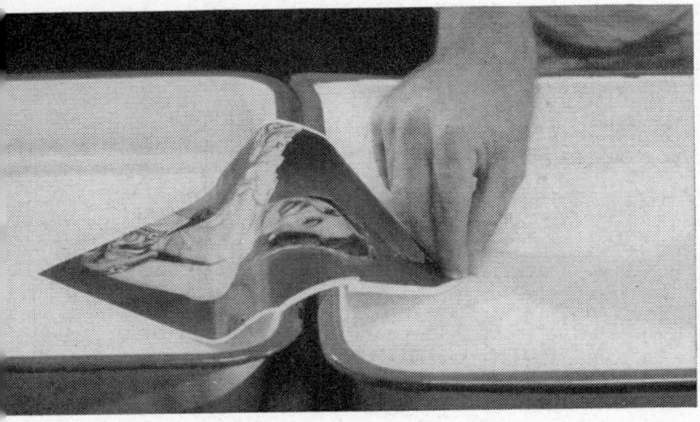

But don't ever do it this way! This means that a lot of developer will be carried off without being allowed to drain back into the developer tray, plus rapid exhaustion of the stop bath as well.

both of which will be most noticeable in the highlight portions of the print. The maximum development time that can be used decreases with old or partially exhausted developers and at higher-than-normal temperatures.

If you have no alternative to working at high temperatures, you may want to keep in mind that, for most developers, this safe maximum development time decreases about thirty seconds for each five-degree rise in temperature above 68 F. However, this is only a general rule.

With the majority of papers, the developing tray is not the place to control print contrast. The paper contrast is largely inherent in the emulsion and the type of surface; in some papers, such as Kodak Opal Paper, it can be controlled only within very narrow limits by varying the time of development. However, with Kodak Medalist Paper somewhat greater control is possible. The principle is that overexposure and underdevelopment reduce contrast, while underexposure and overdevelopment increase contrast. Remember that, in general, the degree of control is very small—smaller, actually, than that effected by changing the paper contrast by one grade.

Rinsing. Immediately after development, rinse the prints in fresh Kodak Stop Bath SB-1 or Kodak Indicator Stop Bath for at least 15 seconds at 65 to 70 F (18 to 21 C). If the prints are drained for 1 or 2 seconds before they are put into the bath, the equivalent of approximately twenty 8 by 10-inch prints per quart can be processed. This bath checks development instantly, provided the acid has not been neutralized. It also tends to prevent spots and streaks in the prints when they are immersed in the fixing solution. This is a simple step in the processing of a print—just move and separate the prints in the stop bath to insure thorough access of the solution to all parts of every print.

Fixing. After rinsing the prints carefully, fix them for 10 minutes at 65 to 70 F (18 to 21 C) in a solution prepared from Kodak Acid Fixer or Kodafix Solution or in Kodak Fixing Bath F-5 or F-6. *Agitate the prints frequently while they are in the fixing bath.* These fixing baths will fix about one hundred 8 by 10-inch prints or their equivalent per gallon if a stop bath is used between development and fixing.

Avoid "overfixing" prints—that is, by not leaving them appreciably longer than recommended in the fixing bath. This is particularly true with warm-tone "portrait" papers. "Warm-tone" is another way of saying "fine-grained," and fine silver grains are more readily dissolved than are coarse grains. Thus, overfixation can lead to loss of image warmth and, if continued even further, to severely bleached and ruined prints. Be especially careful of overfixation during warm summer months. At 68 F, a very noticeable loss in density and change in image tone may occur in a fixing time of about 20 minutes; only about 10 minutes in the fixing bath is required to raise the same havoc at 80 to 85 F. This effect is, of course, most pronounced with fresh fixing baths and decreases gradually as the bath becomes exhausted.

For complete fixation, it is desirable to use two fixing baths, the second one being freshly made. This is particularly true when permanence is necessary or when the prints are to be sepia-toned in a polysulfide-type toner. Fix the prints for five minutes in each bath with a five-second drain between baths.

You may find the reason for using two baths quite interesting: used fixing baths are "loaded" with silver salts from previously fixed prints. Thus, it is difficult to remove all the unused silver salts from any print subsequently fixed in this old bath. These silver salts cannot be removed completely from the emulsion even by extending washing times up to two hours or more. Eventually, the silver salts are gradually converted during the life of the print to brownish silver sulfides and show up in the form of highlight stain. Residual silver salts show immediately if the print is brown-toned because the toner does not distinguish between the metallic silver image and the unwanted silver salts. However, immersion in a second relatively silver-free hypo bath removes most of the silver salts and thus lessens the highlight stain when prints are toned in the brown toner.

Kodalk treatment. The use of Kodalk Balanced Alkali after fixing will improve the final image stability, reduce washing time, and lessen the staining tendency of toners. In fact, the procedure is so worth while—it cuts print-washing time in half—that every photographer should adopt it as a part of his standard processing procedure between fixing and washing.

After the prints have been fixed, rinse them in water; then place them in a 2 percent solution of Kodalk Balanced Alkali and agitate them for about 2 minutes. Separate the prints frequently to insure complete soaking of both paper base and emulsion. A gallon of solution will treat a hundred and fifty 8 by 10-inch prints or their equivalent.

Washing. Prints given the Kodalk treatment should be washed for at least 30 minutes in running water which flows fast enough to provide active agitation. The rate of water flow should be sufficient to change the water every 5 minutes. The prints should be separated or turned over frequently. Prints not given the Kodalk treatment should be washed in the same way for 1 hour. Be careful not to contaminate prints which have nearly finished washing by adding other prints directly from the fixing bath. Otherwise, *all* of the prints must be washed for the time required by new prints.

During the winter months, if the water temperature cannot be brought up to the recommended minimum of 65 F, the washing time must be approximately doubled. In addition to the troubles arising from inadequate washing, cold wash water can cause over-hardening of the emulsion with consequent curl and ferrotyping problems.

Drying matte prints. When washing is completed, remove from the prints as much excess water as possible. They can then be placed on cheesecloth stretchers; on stretched plastic screening; between clean, white photo blotters; or on a belt dryer.

Did you ever hear the word "plum" applied to photographic prints? Some papers have a tendency to change image color when dried at excessively hot temperatures, shifting slightly toward a purplish "plumlike" hue. This trouble occurs mostly with electrically heated drum driers, and is really nothing to be concerned about if the drying temperature does not exceed about 180 F.

Forced drying has still another effect on most matte papers. In general, the hotter and faster a print is dried, the higher its surface sheen becomes. This difference in sheen between cold-dried prints and hot-dried prints is not great, but nevertheless it is readily apparent. The only real precaution in this respect is to avoid using excessively high drying temperatures since some papers may evidence high-sheen spots.

Drying glossy prints. If your print has been made on glossy paper, it should be dried on ferrotype tins or drums. Matte-surfaced prints, with the exception of Medalist J Paper, cannot be treated in this manner. The principle of ferrotyping is the compression of surface gelatin when a wet print is dried in close contact with a very smooth surface. This compression causes an increase in the reflectivity of the print. Usually, a ferrotype "tin" consists of sheet iron coated with black, baked enamel or a plating of chromium, or a sheet of stainless steel. Never allow the surface of ferrotype tins to become scratched by placing the tins in contact with each other. Preferably, when not in use, they should be stored in an upright position in a grooved cabinet.

Stainless steel or chromium tins do not require waxing but before using enameled ferrotype tins, they should be thoroughly washed with soap and water, dried, and then polished with either commercial ferrotype plate polish or the following solution:

	Avoirdupois	*Metric*
Paraffin	10 grains	0.7 gram
Carbon tetrachloride.	1 ounce	32 cc

Be sure the paraffin is dissolved completely before use. Apply this solution sparingly to the plate with a tuft of cotton and then polish it *well* with a soft cloth such as canton flannel. The plate should show no visible trace of the polishing solution, since an excess of paraffin will impart a waxy appearance to the prints. For best results, black-enameled ferrotype plates should be repolished after they have been used five or six times.

Each time before use, ferrotype tins, whether made of stainless steel or sheet iron, should be rinsed in clean, warm water to remove dust and lint. The wet, glossy print is put emulsion side down on the plate and squeegeed firmly in place with a hand print roller or print wringer. No air bubbles should remain under the print because perfect contact is necessary to produce a uniform glossy surface.

Any excess water on the back of the print should be carefully blotted or wiped away, and the plate put aside to dry in a current of warm air. Do not use excessively high temperatures to hasten the drying. This may cause drying marks, often called "oyster-shell markings," particularly on double-weight papers.

When completely dry, the prints should fall off the ferrotype plates of their own accord; if this does not happen, slide an old piece of film under the edge of the print and gently pry it loose.

One of the most frequent problems encountered by photographers making glossy enlargements is the sticking of the paper to the ferrotype tin. Usually, the sticking is due either to insufficient hardening of the paper in the fixing bath or to a film of dirt on the ferrotype tin. Although black or "japanned" ferrotyping tins should *not* be subjected to the following treatment, stainless-steel or chromium-plated tins or drums can be cleaned of all dirt by the use of a Carborundum product known as Aloxite Grade A No. 1 Fine Buffing Powder. Here are the steps:

1. Make a thin watery paste of the Aloxite Powder.

2. Apply this paste to the drum or tin with a soft cloth and over a small portion at a time. Continue to rub until there is no break in the water film. *This must be done at room temperature, not while the tin is heated.*

3. Allow the powder to dry and then wipe it off.

4. Polish the drum with Bon Ami until a broken film of water is obtained, indicating a high degree of water repellency over the entire surface. This is very important; otherwise, the prints will stick to the surface and be impossible to remove.

5. Allow the Bon Ami to dry and wipe the powder off with a clean cloth.

This procedure is recommended only when signs of sticking are actually encountered—not necessarily as a regular routine.

P.S. *Well, it took a lot of words to tell you how to make a good enlargement. But, if this is your first enlargement, the foregoing suggestions should help you get started on the right track. If necessary, use the information as would a cook in following a new cake recipe.*

If you are an old-timer at making enlargements, perhaps you realize better than before that there are no short cuts, no "royal road" to beautiful print quality.

Chapter 7

New Prints for Old

So AT LAST your print is finished. Or is it? Let's consider for a moment. First of all, is it too light or too dark? How dark or how light should you make a particular print, anyway? Why, of average, realistic lightness, of course! But although this answer seems simple enough, its attainment may be beset with pitfalls. For instance, you make a print that looks just right to you in the fairly bright "white-light" illumination of your darkroom. You find out subsequently, however, that the friend to whom you gave the print has hung it in a windowless hallway, and to everyone viewing it there, it looks too dark. Well, it *is* too dark for that level of illumination in the hallway!

This is but one of the pitfalls in trying to make a print of exactly the right density. Let's imagine you're back again in the darkroom —when the print is in the hypo bath to be exact—and where this problem is first evidenced. In the first place, a safelight, however bright it may be, is not a satisfactory light by which to judge print contrast, image tone, or density. A safelight has neither the proper intensity nor color quality to be used for this purpose. Yet, many photographers, wishing to make several identical prints from a negative, will examine the first test print by the darkroom safelight and, thinking the print exposure correct, will make the remaining prints on the basis of this often erroneous judgement.

The particular danger in this instance is when working with fairly warmed-tone and buff-stock papers. The yellowish safelight may be reflected quite strongly from the warm image tone; but the finished print may be viewed under subdued daylight or by bluish fluorescent tubes, causing the impression that the exposure should have been decreased by 10 or 15 percent for optimum quality.

Another danger to watch for is the "drying down" of normal-to-low-key prints made on a fairly dull-surfaced matte paper. While wet with the hypo bath or the wash water, the surface of matte papers acquires a temporary sheen due to water providing a more uniform reflecting surface than the irregular texture of the paper surface itself. While wet, the shadows of the picture appear more luminous, and darkish details can be seen more easily than when the same print is dry. Since low-key pictures generally depend more on shadow details than normal or high-key pictures, "drying down" is particularly evident with these subjects. Accordingly, if you want to appraise print density accurately, the print should be thoroughly dry; just blotting or wiping off surface water will not necessarily suffice since even subsurface moisture can give the emulsion an unnatural sheen. And, as mentioned previously, for best appraisal conditions, the thoroughly dry print should be viewed in about the same quality and brightness of illumination as that in which it will be eventually used or displayed.

Appraisal of the print under "use conditions" can be logically carried out even further. Keep in mind that a print placed in the center of a large expanse of white wall space will look darker than the same print placed in the center of a dark wall. Similarly, a print hung on a wall near a window must be printed somewhat lighter than normal for proper viewing. The window, in the same range of vision as the picture, causes one's eyes to "stop down," leaving a reduced eye sensitivity to view a print that was probably intended for more normal viewing conditions. This example of a print hung near a window may be somewhat unfair, since it is generally contrary to tasteful interior decoration. Nevertheless, the principles governing eye adaptability to viewing conditions in this instance are the same as those which cause successful salon exhibitors to judge proper print density in an illuminated viewing box similar to that which salon juries generally use to decide whether or not prints have sufficient quality to be acceptable for hanging in the salon.

As a final thought about print viewing conditions, remember that it is the relative brightness of the illumination on the print as compared with its surroundings which is important. At low levels of illumination, the difference in the better rendition of shadow details of a glossy print compared with a matte print from the same negative will not be so apparent. In other words, the brighter the viewing light, the easier it is to see the quality in a high-quality print!

Now let's take a good look at your print. Stand at arm's distance and study it carefully. Is it sharp? Or is it a bit *too* sharp and can you see every grain of the negative imaged faithfully in the print? Usually you cannot make a print that is too sharp. Usually, that is.

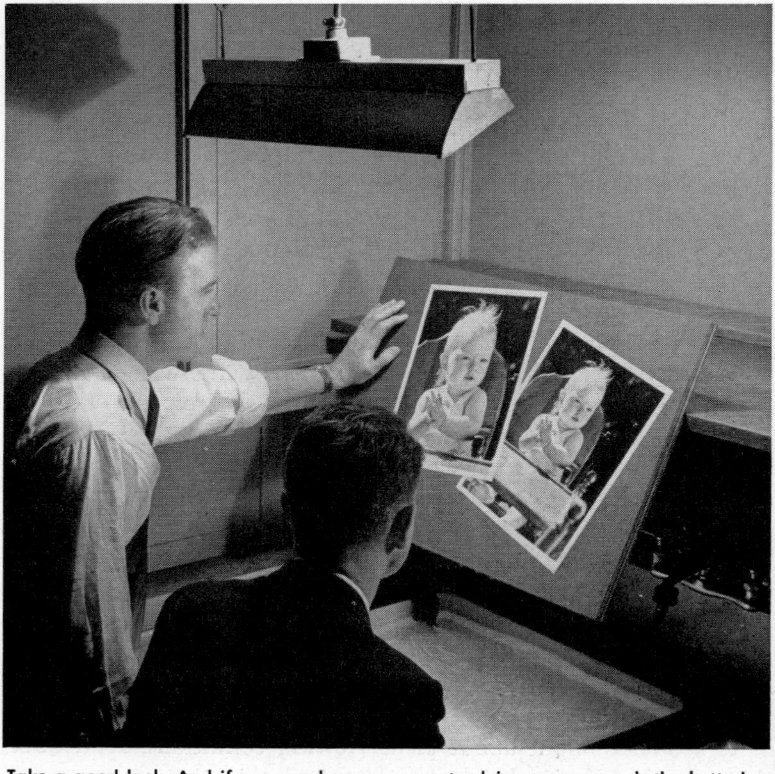

Take a good look. And if you can have an expert advise you, so much the better!

ASK YOURSELF THESE QUESTIONS

Is the contrast of the print satisfactory? Or would it look better printed on a harder or softer grade of paper?

See any spots, streaks, stains, or fingerprints which shouldn't be there?

Grain? Don't worry about it! And with that bit of advice, the problem of excessive grain size in prints should be taken care of. But you know how photographers are—they still will wonder if there isn't some magical means of reducing or eliminating the grainy appearance of large prints made from small negatives. In a word, there isn't. There are many published schemes for reducing the grain size in grainy negatives such as bleaching and redeveloping with fine-grain developers or with dye-coupling developers but in general, they are not satisfactory. If any reduction of grain size is obtained, it is usually done with a sacrifice of contrast or, and more serious, of image sharpness.

If you're a miniature negative enthusiast, use first of all a fine grain developer such as Kodak DK-20 or Microdol. Further than that, if less sharpness will solve your grain problems, print your negatives on rough or textured papers, or diffuse the projected image slightly. Constant worrying about grain size in normal enlarging procedure might well be taken as a danger signal; it may mean that you are spending too much thought on the technique of photography and *not enough on trying to say something with your pictures.*

Are you *really* satisfied with your print? Step back about fifteen feet from it. Do the details "carry"? If they don't, is it because the print is too low in contrast? Check the cropping and the composition in general. Now turn the print *upside down* and again check the composition for a balanced design.

The ideal frame of mind in which to be in asking yourself these questions is to imagine that the print had been made by someone else. *Now* what do you think of it? In brief, the general idea is to ask yourself frankly if you can think of any way that the print could be improved. If you are *completely* satisfied, then look again because nothing has ever been made that cannot be improved.

ASK AN EXPERT

The secret of making better prints lies in knowing how to improve those you have made in the past. If you honestly cannot find anything wrong with the print, perhaps you have not asked yourself the right questions. Perhaps some friends can help. Sometimes it requires an artist's trained eye to see errors in composition, a technician to indicate how the print quality could be improved, or a printing expert to show you the best way to dodge a problem negative. Well-meaning but incompetent praise can only be misleading.

Often it will be helpful to take the print to a camera club for the members' constructive criticism. Incidentally, if you can't take a bit of "needling," better stay at home, because this is often the "test by fire." You'll probably hear all types of suggestions, from a technical discourse on print reduction to "better crop about 20 inches off the top of that print!" Sift the wheat from the chaff and, after you come home, take a good look at your print and see where and if you agree with all the second guessers. Remember the salonists who put a picture in their homes where it can be seen every day for a week or so? Try it yourself. As you walk by the print with a sidewards glance, it won't be long before someone standing nearby will probably hear you mutter, "Let's see: the left side should be cropped off a bit more, this cloud lightened—wonder how that corner would look a little darker—" and before you realize it, you'll be heading down to the darkroom.

There are two kinds of faults which either will be self-evident or which the camera club members will be glad to point out to you. These are the "mechanical" print faults, such as spots, stains, streaks, fingerprints, etc., and the "artistic" print faults, such as insufficient contrast, lack of printing in where needed, etc.

First let's itemize some of the most common mechanical faults. You don't have to read this section—just remember that it's here, and that the faults are listed in alphabetical order for ready reference should you ever need to look one up. So now turn over to the section dealing with artistic print faults; these paragraphs ARE important and should be read.

MECHANICAL PRINT FAULTS

ABRASION MARKS

Cause:

Rough handling of prints.
High processing temperatures.
Excessive sodium carbonate in the developer.
Developing print face down in dirty trays.
Use of a non-hardening fixing bath.
Prolonged washing.
Washing too many prints together.

Prevention:

Always handle paper with utmost care.
Do not cut paper placed emulsion side down on trimmer.
At high processing temperatures, it may be advisable to add the photographically inert, swelling suppressor, sodium sulfate, to the developer. For processing at 80 F and above, add approximately one ounce of desiccated sodium sulfate per quart of stock solution.

Remedy:

If the abrasion is not severe, it may be treated satisfactorily by spotting the print.

BLACK SPOTS (a) Small, well-defined black spots.

Cause:

Undissolved chemicals in print developer.
Metol and/or hydroquinone particles on paper emulsion.
Dirt in any of the processing solutions.

Prevention:

Photographic chemicals should be mixed in a room other than that used for loading film or making prints.
Chemicals spilled on the floor should be mopped up, not swept away.
Processing solutions should be filtered.

Remedy:

Spots may be etched out of print surface.

BLACK SPOTS (b) Medium-size black spots.

Cause:

Failure to use an acid stop bath.
Not agitating the prints when first placed in the fixing bath.

Prevention:

Prints should not only be agitated when first immersed in the hypo, but periodically to insure even, complete fixation.

Remedy:

Make a new print.

BLISTERS AND FRILLING

Cause:

High processing temperatures.

Large temperature difference between solutions.

Excessively strong acetic acid stop bath.

Prolonged washing.

Allowing stream of wash water to strike print emulsion directly.

Prevention:

Prints should always be processed according to the manufacturer's recommendations.

Compound solutions as accurately as possible.

Remedy:

Make a new print.

BLURRED PRINTS (a) Local blurred spots.

Cause:

Negative buckled in enlarger negative carrier.

Paper not flat on easel.

Prevention:

Obvious.

Remedy:

Make a new print.

BLURRED PRINTS (b) Print generally blurred.

Cause:

Enlarger out of focus.

Movement of easel or enlarger during print exposure.

Excessive intentional diffusion during print exposure.

In contact prints, negative may be reversed.

Prevention:

If necessary, use a magnifying glass to focus the enlarged image sharply.

Remedy:

Make a new print.

BROWN SPOTS (a) Small well-defined spots.

Cause:

Rust in wash water.

Rust from trays with chipped enamel. Chips in the enamel expose the sheet iron underneath.

Prevention:

Water filter on faucet.

Chipped spots on enamel trays may be coated with clear liquid nail polish which is photographically inert and will prevent further rusting.

Remedy:

Print surface may be etched with knife.

BROWN SPOTS (b) Mottled areas.

Cause:
Contamination of the developer with hypo.
Oxidized developer.
Excessive heat when drying.

Prevention:
Hands should be thoroughly washed and dried on a clean towel after being in hypo bath.
Do not process too many prints in one tray of developer.
Developer stock solution should be stored in tightly stoppered bottles.

Remedy:
Make a new print.

CONTRASTY PRINTS

Cause:
Paper contrast not suited to negative contrast.

Prevention:
Use softer paper.
Use softer-working print developer.
Increase print exposure and decrease development.
Use of the Emmermann process.

Remedy:
If print contrast is not excessively great, it may be reduced in a super-proportional print reducer.

CRACKED PRINT EMULSIONS

Cause:
Rough handling of prints.

Prevention:
Use of a print-softening solution.

Remedy:
Make a new print.

CURLED PRINTS

Cause:
Drying prints too rapidly.
Drying temperature excessively high.
Surface water on prints during drying.

Prevention:
Obvious. Use a print-softening solution.

Remedy:
Same as prevention. Redampen prints on the reverse side with a cloth and dry underneath pressure between flat surfaces.

Dark prints

Cause:
Overexposure.
Overdevelopment.
Greater paper contrast than required.
Insufficient potassium bromide in developer.
Excessive sodium carbonate in developer.
Enlarger lamp too strong.

Prevention:
Careful evaluation of test strips.
Accurately compounded solutions.
Stop down enlarger-lens diaphragm.

Remedy:
Prints may be chemically reduced by a cutting, proportional, or super-proportional reducer as needed.

Dull spots on glossy prints

Cause:
Rapid drying.
Non-use of print-softening solution.
Improperly cleaned ferrotype tin.
Print not in perfect contact with ferrotype tin.
Premature removal of prints from ferrotype tin.

Prevention:
Obvious.

Remedy:
Resoak print for 5 to 10 minutes in a softening solution and referrotype.

Faded prints

Cause:
Overfixation.
Insufficient washing.
Non-use of a hypo eliminator.
Prints stored at high temperature and humidity.
Exposure of the print to harmful gases, such as hydrogen sulfide (present in illuminating gas).

Prevention:
Careful adherence to print-processing recommendations.

Remedy:
Reprint original negative if possible. Photograph print and print copy negative.

FINGERPRINTS (a) Light or white fingerprints.

Cause:
Handling sensitized paper with greasy fingers or when fingers are contaminated with hypo.

Prevention:
Each time after your hands have been in any of the processing solutions, they should be thoroughly washed and then dried on a clean towel.
Change towels in the darkroom frequently, as towels rapidly become hypo-laden and are often a source of fingerprints.

Remedy:
Spot the print.

FINGERPRINTS (b) Dark or black fingerprints.

Cause:
Handling paper with fingers contaminated with developer.

Prevention:
Same as for light fingerprints.

Remedy:
Etch print.

FLAT OR SOFT PRINTS

Cause:
Paper not suited to negative contrast.
Print underdeveloped.
Improperly mixed developer.
Dirty enlarger lens.
Moisture condensation on enlarger lens.
Negative not properly masked.
Use of old or improperly stored paper.

Prevention:
Wipe off enlarger lens each time before beginning work.
Use a harder paper.
Check test strip carefully against correct comparison print.

Remedy:
If print is both flat and dark, it may be reduced chemically with a cutting reducer.
If print is both flat and light, it may be intensified chemically.
Otherwise, a new print should be made.

FOGGED PRINTS—GRAY PRINT BORDERS AND HIGHLIGHTS

Cause:
Safelight illumination too strong.
Improper safelight filter.
Negative not properly masked.
Use of old paper.
Paper not kept in a lighttight container when not in use.
Developer too concentrated.
Insufficient potassium bromide in developer.
Exhausted fixing bath.
White light on too soon after print has been placed in the hypo.
Darkroom not lighttight.
Light leaks from the enlarger lamp house.

Prevention:
Test safelight illumination.
Compound solutions correctly.
Use fresh solutions.
Other preventive measures obvious.

Remedy:
Mild cases of general fog may often be treated successfully with a subtractive chemical reducer.

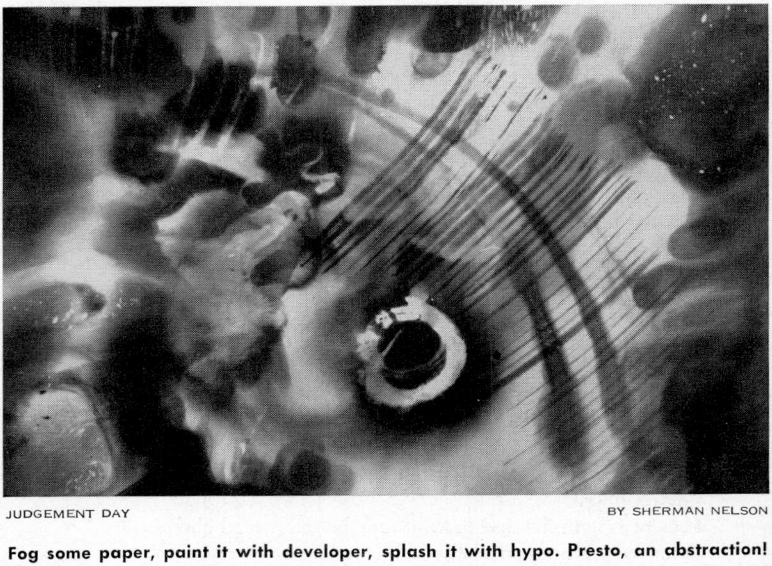

JUDGEMENT DAY — BY SHERMAN NELSON

Fog some paper, paint it with developer, splash it with hypo. Presto, an abstraction!

FREAK MARKS

Cause:

Uneven development.

Use of spoiled or outdated paper.

Developer too warm.

Old developer.

Developer too dilute.

Prevention:

Use sufficient developing solution—tray should be about half full.

Immerse the exposed paper in the developer evenly and quickly with a sliding motion.

Remedy:

Make a new print.

GREENISH-BROWN TONES

Cause:

Insufficient development.

Developer too cold.

Developer contaminated with acid or hypo.

Excessive potassium bromide in developer.

Prevention:

Maintain processing temperatures as close to 68 F as possible.

Process prints according to manufacturer's recommendations.

Compound solutions accurately.

Remedy:

Tone print.

Intensify print slightly.

GREEN STAINS

Cause:

Use of potassium chromium alum instead of potassium alum in stop or hypo bath.

Prevention:

Obvious.

Remedy:

Make a new print.

LIGHT PRINTS

Cause:

Underexposure.

Underdevelopment.

Overfixation.

Prevention:

Check test strip carefully with correct comparison print, compensating exposure and development accordingly.

Remedy:

Intensify print chemically.

MEALY, MOTTLED PRINTS

Cause:

Overexposure and underdevelopment.

Old paper.

Weak or worn-out paper developer.

Improper storage conditions for opened packages of paper.

Prevention:

Developing time should not be less than 45 seconds at 68 F.

Use fresh solutions; it does not pay to "squeeze" through extra prints in oxidized developer.

Remedy:

Make a new print.

NEWTON'S RINGS

(Small, dark, irregular, concentric circles of rings on the print).

Cause:

Humidity in darkroom is 50 percent or higher.

Prevention:

If humidity cannot be reduced, an electric fan directed on the enlarger lamp house helps to keep moisture from condensing on the negative and the glass in the enlarger negative carrier.

Remedy:

In mild cases, rings can be etched and spotted.

In serious cases, there is no remedy.

PURPLE DISCOLORATION

Cause:

Fixing bath is exhausted.

Prints are not sufficiently fixed.

Prevention:

Rinse prints thoroughly in acid stop bath.

Use fresh hypo.

Agitate prints in fixing bath, particularly when first immersed.

Remedy:

Make a new print.

STREAKS

Cause:

Lack of agitation of the print either in the developer, the hypo bath, or both.

Printing paper is edge-fogged, resulting in developable streaks on print borders.

Prevention:

Obvious.

Remedy:

Make another print.

White deposit on print surface

Cause:

Sulfur in the fixing bath has precipitated from excessive heat, excessive acetic acid, or insufficient sodium sulfite.

Prevention:

If the fixing bath appears at all milky, it should be discarded and a fresh solution prepared.

Remedy:

Refix print in a fresh hypo bath as a precautionary measure, rewash, wipe off the print surface with a damp cloth or sponge, and then dry.

White spots (a) Small, well-defined, white spots.

Cause:

Dirt or dust on the negative or on the paper surface when making the print exposure. Hypo particles on the paper surface.

Prevention:

Clean negative before printing.
Remove all spilled chemicals immediately with a damp cloth.

Remedy:

Spot the print with brush and spotting medium.

White spots (b) Large, irregularly shaped, light spots.

Cause:

Lack of print agitation in the developing solution.

Prevention:

Obvious.

Remedy:

Make a new print.

Yellow stains

Cause:

Excessively long developing times.
Exhausted developer.
Developer too warm.
Lifting print out of developer to inspect it frequently.
Insufficient potassium bromide in the developer.
Overfixation.
Sulfurized fixing bath.
Insufficient washing.
Storage of the print at high temperatures and humidity.
Exposure of the print to sulfurous gases, such as those present in coal (illuminating) gases.

Prevention:

Process prints according to recommendations. Use a hypo eliminator.

Remedy:

Make a new print.

ARTISTIC PRINT FAULTS

Print faults of the second, more intangible type are artistic in nature. Many of these are concerned with composition, which means simply the combining of the parts of a picture to form a harmonious whole.

A creative fault is somewhat more illusive than a mechanical error. A group of photographers will agree that a fingerprint will mar the appearance of a print; they will be in general accord over the best method of remedying the fault; they will all say it should be spotted down until it is no longer perceptible. But it is seldom that even two people agree on the seriousness of an artistic fault and the appropriate treatment. They may, for example, agree that a corner of your print should have been printed darker. However, the exact amount of density to add to produce an "optimum aesthetic quality" is likely to remain a matter of personal opinion. In other words, here are your instructions: Heed the majority's vote to darken the corner, but try to decide for yourself *how much.* After all, it is your picture and it is here that print making can give a wide interpretive range to your artistic ability. Photography has its rules, as does all art. But it is the individuality of brush stroke that helps to make the master painter's work unique. Likewise, you should desire, pursue, and strive to attain photographic individuality. Could your prints be identified without your signature?

Remember that photography has grown up. Modern photography is leaning more and more toward creating an impression or an effect. For example, photographers have largely outgrown the idea that full highlight and shadow detail—even "compressed" detail—must be preserved. Therefore, they have learned to omit details, particularly shadow details, which do not contribute to the main effect and may distract or even actually lessen the total effectiveness.

Here is why this is important to you: More often than not, a straight print does not utilize the full range or density scale of the paper. You think those shadows are *black* in the print you have just made? No, they're not; not usually. Some extra local exposure in the shadows will probably be required in order to achieve an actual *maximum* black for the paper you are using. Of course, a maximum black is very desirable from a print-quality standpoint, yet printing in shadows means that some shadow details will be darkened and lost. In other words, you have two choices with regard to shadow details: (a) to preserve them if they are important in contributing to the total print effect or (b) to print them down locally to a maximum black if they do not add to the print's effectiveness. Which to choose? This is a problem you'll have to decide for yourself and *for every new enlargement you make.*

Probably the most important aspect of making excellent enlargements lies in realizing that the composition of a photograph is largely determined at the moment of exposure *but not completely.* This is because both the method and the manner of print making also influence its composition. Therefore, if you think your print could be improved, check the individual elements of composition over which you still have some measure of control. For example, should the print be horizontal or vertical?

Since few scenes lend themselves to a square treatment, you should determine whether your print should be horizontal or vertical. Which shape tells the picture story better? Try both with a pair of croppers on a proof print of the entire picture area. Would you crop this picture of the ducks horizontally?

Or do you like this scene as a vertical picture with more "storm" showing?

To answer this, remember that a good recipe for picture making is economy of subject material coupled with satisfactory spacing. In turn, the spacing is partially determined by the physical proportions of your print size and shape. One of the great masterpieces, Raphael's (16th Century) "Madonna of the Chair" is a circular picture. The composition was originally planned on a barrel-top, for want of other material, and the figures fill the space admirably. It is difficult to imagine this particular painting in any format other than circular without losing some of its effectiveness. Yet this picture is exceptional; by far the largest majority of paintings and photographs are rectangular—not oval, square, triangular, or other various shapes. From the ancients to the moderns, artists have found the rectangle most suitable for presenting their ideas. Photographers also take the rectangle for granted. The matter is largely left to the manufacturers of photographic materials; consequently, most print compositions are squeezed into conventional paper sizes of 8 by 10, 11 by 14, 14 by 17, and 16 by 20 inches. Some of these popular rectangles are exactly proportional, the only difference being in size.

No one is likely to object, compositionally speaking, if you use these rectangles for practically all of your print making. Yet, you should not let convention dull your receptiveness to new ideas in picture shapes. Occasionally, an oval format is considerably more pleasing than the usual rectangle; sometimes a picture shape is square—any attempt to trim one side or another would introduce unwarranted restrictions or connotations on the subject. Rectangles themselves may be "stretched out" or heightened.

How does one know, you ask, when to alter a conventional rectangular shape, or exactly how much should it be changed? The "when" is answered by the mood or atmosphere of the picture. The "how much" is answered by the type of subject and your individual treatment of that subject. If you are looking for something different than the tired old 8 by 10-inch format, elementary geometry can be used to find a pleasing picture shape. You may be interested to know that the ancient Greeks found a rectangle so pleasing in proportion that it's named the "Golden Section." This rectangle has the mathematical proportions of .617 to .383, or,

A tall, narrow picture space suggests:
1. Tension
2. Aspiration
3. Limited distance
4. Vertical movement

Generally, a long panel-type rectangle suggests:
1. Restfulness
2. Stability
3. Expanse
4. Horizontal movement

another way to put it, proportions between the square root of two and the square root of three.

This is all a part of dynamic symmetry which you have probably heard about. Dynamic symmetry is, briefly, a sort of system of pleasing proportions and interesting balances in design. It's based on a series of rectangles known as root rectangles since they are all derived from a square which is a root one ($\sqrt{1}$) rectangle. A root two ($\sqrt{2}$) rectangle is made simply by using the diagonal of a square as the side of a new rectangle whose end is equal to one of the sides of the original square. You've probably guessed by now that a root three ($\sqrt{3}$) rectangle is made by using the diagonal of the root two rectangle to form the side of a new and slightly longer rectangle.

But school's out—it's really quite simple to construct these shapes by following the accompanying diagram. And after you're through, why not try to use one of these formats for an interesting new print size? Obviously, they will have both horizontal and vertical applications.

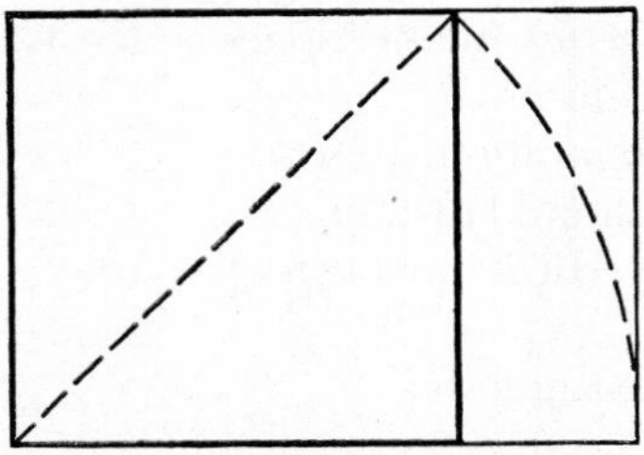

A root two rectangle.

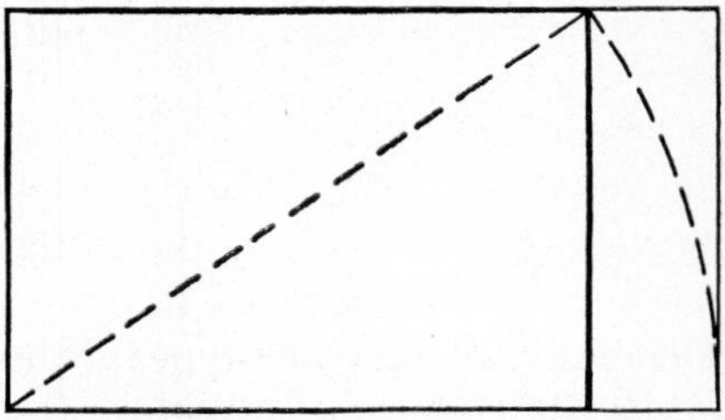

A root three rectangle.

Now look *inside* the picture frame. Can you alter to advantage print emphasis, unity, or balance? For example, is the principal subject—such as a sailboat in a marine picture—*emphasized* properly? Note the sailboat's location in the print, its size, how it contrasts with the water or with other boats. You might improve the relative position of the sailboat by cropping one side of the print; its size may be altered by changing the degree of image magnification by raising or lowering the enlarger; and the boat's contrast with the surrounding objects may be increased or decreased by dodging, flashing, printing in, or changing the print contrast—whatever you think is best. This particular photograph may achieve better *balance* if the foreground is darkened slightly. Or perhaps it will be more *unified* if that distant motorboat—the one at the left edge of the print which vies for attention with the principal subject—were eliminated either by cropping or by one of the control techniques described in a following chapter.

All photographs can be analyzed in a similar manner. Fortunately, no two prints are exactly alike; apply your artistic judgment to each new picture, and try to better each succeeding print.

If it will help, ask yourself candidly, "Does this print express what I saw when I exposed the negative?" Try to make a mental transition from the print to the original scene. See what may be missing, and then reprint accordingly. This may not be easy. Bernice Abbot says, "Prints which are made with lukewarm interest or a 'let the print take care of itself' mood are never good prints. In most cases, you have to sweat to get a good print. The error comes from the attitude that print making is purely mechanical. Alas, too many prints look just that way: They look too photographic!"

How to "reprint accordingly" is difficult for a book to tell you. However, a knowledge of printing techniques may well provide the answer. For this reason the following chapters are devoted to a selection of these essential print-making techniques: print flashing, combination printing, print reduction, and others. After you have read these chapters, think over all the possible ways of changing the appearance of your print. Which of these will help you make *the best possible picture?* Reprint accordingly!

P.S. *Print defects can be introduced intentionally to create unusual effects, such as "different" photograms or other abstractions. However, using print defects in this manner is exceptional; it is far better for these difficulties to be subservient to your wishes,* not *you to theirs. To paraphrase a saying, a cc of prevention is worth more than a wastebasket of faulty prints.*

Chapter 8

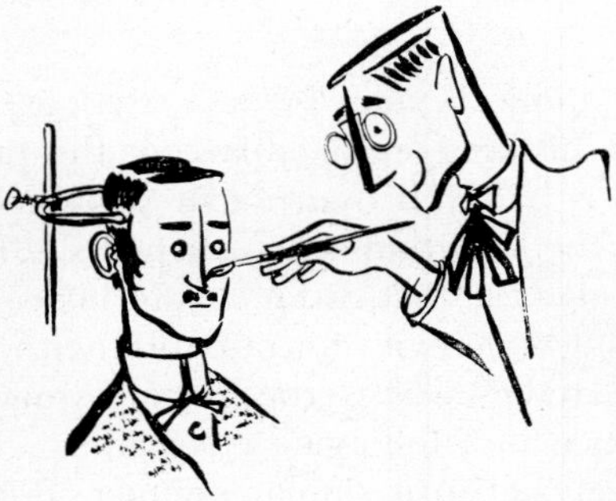

Painting with Light

"ANY PHOTOGRAPHER worth his salt has a set of cotton 'plumpers' to fill out sunken cheeks and some sealing wax to stick back prominent ears." So said Abraham Bogardus, one of the early photographers who made daguerreotypes, ambrotypes, and tintypes. For, with these processes, there was no negative and it was necessary to do any retouching on the subject.

This rather droll advice points out the fact that the subject—whether a portrait or a landscape—is not always perfect, and it is up to the photographer to do something about it. There are available to the modern photographer several worth-while control techniques. Some of these are concerned with the print, others with the projected image, but the beginning of control possibilities lies with the negative itself. Since working on the negative is definitely related to the making of good enlargements, let's begin by discussing three of the most useful techniques which involve the negative. These are pencil retouching, dye retouching—or "dye dodging," as it is sometimes called—and ground-glass printing. Each has a separate purpose, but often all three can be used to advantage in combination. And, "any photographer worth his salt" should need but a minimum of practice to use them proficiently. So let's paint with light!

PENCIL RETOUCHING

Pencil retouching on a negative can be an invaluable method—one which often cannot be supplanted—of improving final print results. For example, it is the best way of removing small facial blemishes from a portrait negative, a way which controlled dodging or after-work on the print could not easily duplicate. However, despite the popularity of retouching in the professional studio, the joint limitations of reduced negative size and requisite skill make the technique difficult for use with most amateur film sizes. You can often save time and trouble, in fact, by taking an occasional negative to a professional retoucher. Therefore, this section is not intended to be a complete treatise on the subject, but rather to point out that there are instances when a few adroitly placed pencil marks on a negative can help immeasurably to enhance print quality.

The smallest negative size which can be conveniently retouched is, customarily, 3¼ by 4¼ inches or, at the least, 2¼ by 3¼ inches, depending on the actual image size, although wonders can be accomplished with miniature negatives if necessary. Enlarged negatives can be made from all or part of the original miniature to facilitate retouching. This means, of course, printing the negative onto a sheet of film to make a film positive and then enlarging this positive onto another film to make the enlarged negative.

One successful portrait photographer retouches directly on the miniature negative by using a magnifying glass more powerful than the eventual degree of enlargement. For instance, if he is going to make an 8 by 10-inch print from a 35mm negative (approximately an eight-times linear enlargement), he uses a ten-power magnifying glass as a guide for the extremely fine retouching required. Then he feels safe in assuming that, if the retouching appears satisfactory under a ten-power glass, it should also be satisfactory in only an eight-diameter enlargement! But for most of us it is really more satisfactory to make an enlarged negative and use the normal procedure of retouching. In any event, a magnifying glass is a handy accessory when retouching.

Of the few materials necessary, the retouching stand is most important. While very good stands can be purchased inexpensively, or any negative viewer can be pressed into temporary service, it is also easy to construct a stand with a few pieces of board and a square of opal glass only slightly larger than the negative.

The important feature of the retouching stand or desk is the brightness of the illumination. Actually, it makes little difference if the source is a frosted lamp or reflected daylight, but too bright a light may cause eyestrain and obscure fine details.

For the retouching tools, H and 4H pencils will meet most of your needs. Be sure to sharpen them with No. 00 sandpaper to at least an inch-long point and keep them at needle sharpness for work on all negatives. Obviously, the finer the pencil point, the less noticeable the retouching will be on the print.

For a small amount of retouching such as required by most panchromatic portrait negatives of babies and children, no application of retouching fluid (a "dope" which provides an added tooth to the negative emulsion) will be found necessary. For orthochromatic portrait negatives or for other negatives requiring a relatively heavy graphite deposit, however, the use of retouching fluid will be helpful. In applying the medium, be sure the negative is placed with its emulsion up on a smooth, flat surface. Use a minimum amount of the fluid—one or two drops should suffice for small-to-average-size negatives—and rub it immediately and briskly with a tightly wrapped cotton pad in a circular motion in order to blend the retouching fluid out to the edges of the negative and leave no line of demarcation which might show in the print. Cut a hole slightly larger than the size of the area to be retouched in a black paper mask and place it over the negative on the inclined section of the stand. You are now ready to begin.

It is best to start first with a discarded practice negative and to work with an unretouched print from that negative as a guide. Then, as the work progresses, you can, if you wish, make occasional proof prints for reference until the retouching is completed. Just what to retouch and how much to retouch is up to your judgement, since it will vary from one negative to another and also with personal preference. Of course, you will want to soften, at least, or perhaps completely obliterate blemishes of miscellaneous types in a person's face. Go easy on lines or markings which give the face

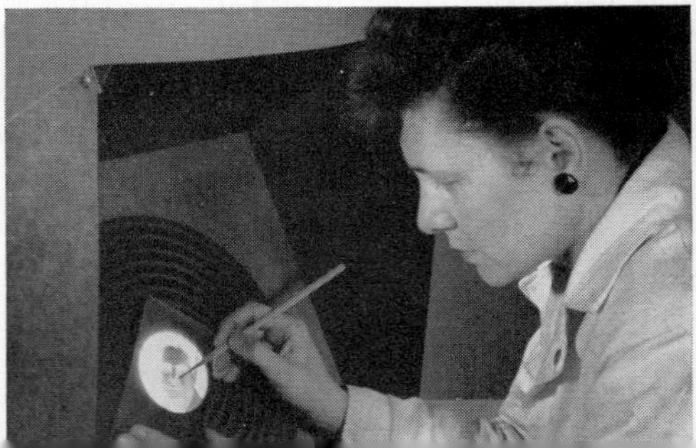

See that long, sharp point on the pencil? It helps to produce a light, fine retouching stroke.

its character and individuality of expression, since their removal would destroy the likeness or naturalness in a portrait. After all, your subject may feel like the old man who said, in commenting on his portrait in which he scarcely recognized himself, "Why, it took me eighty years to get those lines in my face, and then some retoucher took them out in ten minutes!"

If your picture is a landscape, check carefully to see if the result could be improved by retouching (i.e., softening) unsightly wires, tree or shrub branches, sticks, stones, and the like. Removing these objects completely is not in the usual scope of pencil retouching. It often helps if the highlights of clouds, reflections on wet pavements, and muddy roads are accentuated—particularly in backlighted scenes.

Throughout your retouching, remember that a light, extremely fine pencil stroke is necessary. The "stroke" is usually a series of minutely penciled lines resembling figure eights, sixes, nines, zeros, etc. Consequently, no two people have exactly the same stroke, just as no two people write the same. Straight lines should be avoided. The retouching should be built up gradually; if the 4H pencil does not deposit sufficient graphite, try the softer H pencil. If this still isn't enough, apply retouching dope to the reverse side of the negative and pencil there to add more density. Never bear down with the pencil, as excessive pressure may cut the emulsion, particularly if a hard pencil is used. Keep these three general rules in mind:

1. Match the density of the defect to the surrounding area.
2. Avoid the tendency to over-retouch a negative.
3. Create no abnormal retouching which will appear non-photographic in the print.

Finally, if the retouching is not to your satisfaction when the job is completed, all the pencil marks can be removed easily with another application of retouching dope, and you have a chance to correct your previous mistakes.

In one sense, a photographer may be compared to a magician—the fuller his bag of tricks, the more accomplished the performer. Fortunately, straight retouching is not difficult to learn and at the proper time is a good trick to have up a photographic sleeve.

DYE RETOUCHING

Changing a brunette to a blonde, adding needed detail to an underexposed tree trunk, adding clouds to a sky where before there were none—this list of near-miracles could go on and on—are all in the realm of a water-soluble, red dye called "Kodak Crocein Scarlet." Dye dodging steps in where pencil retouching leaves off. While it isn't suited to fine detail work, it is excellent for the local dodging of fairly small areas in the negative. The dye is easy to control because it is readily absorbed into the gelatin, and practically any degree of density may be added to the negative. If you wish to lighten the shadow side of a building in a strongly sunlighted outdoor scene, for example, an over-all, medium application of a weak dye solution will do the job much better than dodging the enlarger light manually when the print exposure is given. Or, if you wish to vignette a high-key portrait so that the image will fade out gradually at the edge of the print into clear white paper, repeated applications of a fairly strong concentration of the dye can be made at the edge of the negative until the dye acts like opaque in effectively blocking out all the light. Then, no matter how many prints are made from this negative, the vignette will be exactly the same in each print—practically an impossibility if accomplished by ordinary dodging.

Another outstanding advantage of this dye is its absolute freedom from grain or texture of any kind.

Kodak Crocein Scarlet is available in a 1-ounce bottle, but this quantity is deceiving because a little will last a long time. A suggested procedure is to mix 10 grains (about ½ a level teaspoon) in 1 ounce of water to make a strong stock solution which can be used to make up dilute solutions. For general work, a mixture of about 20 drops of this stock solution to 1 ounce of water will be satisfactory, but the actual circumstance will control the specific strength. Nevertheless, this mixture will serve as a guide, and you can alter it later as you see fit. Naturally, the working solution should be more concentrated if you intend to use the dye to build up heavy density appreciably more than if you only want to lighten slightly the shadow side of a baby's face in a delicate high-

A straight print. Note how the archway tends to merge with its surroundings. The problem is caused by the arch being too dark and the foliage too light.

The archway has now been lightened by means of dye retouching. Better, isn't it? But always be careful not to overdo any retouching so that it looks artificial.

key close-up. The stock solution (10 grains to 1 ounce) has sufficient strength to be used as an opaque to spot pin holes in negatives or to eliminate entire backgrounds but *should be used with caution*. Three drops of a wetting agent may be added, if desired, to help in applying the solution evenly.

Notice that the dilution amounts are given in drops. This will not seem strange when you find out actually how little is required. Measure the stock solution and the water with an eye dropper, placing the required quantities of each in a small bottle or container. The implements of your craft will consist of either a Q-tip (a bit of cotton wrapped tightly around the end of a toothpick will do as well) or a spotting brush and a retouching stand or viewing box for the negative.

One of the first things to learn about using dye is not to apply it to the emulsion side of the negative. If you do, the gelatin emulsion may swell and soften with the moisture and become extremely susceptible to scratches. An exception is when working with miniature negatives since the solution does not "take" very well on the reverse side. But treat these little fellows carefully!

Dip the brush (or cotton swab) into the diluted dye and, using a twisting motion, wipe it across a scrap piece of blotting paper several times to remove the excess solution. The retouching implement should be fairly dry for best results. Never, at any time, use so much of the dye solution that it is possible to shake moisture out of the swab or brush.

Using a circular motion, apply the brush to the desired area. At first you may see nothing but, after many turns of the brush, the negative will begin to take on a slight pinkish tinge. If you think the brush has deposited all the dye it can for the moment, recharge it but always be sure to keep it quite dry. An actual pool of the solution on the negative is greatly overdoing it and will spoil your results. Build the dye up gradually until the treated part has a decided reddish tinge. Remember that unevenness of application can be prevented only if the dye-charged brush is *kept moving* until all the dye on the brush is absorbed into the emulsion.

Now! Is that enough dye? There are two things you can do to learn your progress at this point: Make a contact proof print (be sure the last application of the dye is dry) or examine the negative with either a blue or green filter, such as either a Kodak Wratten C5 (No. 47, blue) or B (No. 58, green) Filter. Lacking a filter, a piece of blue cellophane will serve because blue is the near-complement of red; you will obtain a fairly good idea of the negative's printing properties. As a matter of fact, you will be seeing the negative much as it will be "seen" by the blue-sensitive paper emulsion! If the retouching seems to be unfinished, return the negative to the retouching stand and add more dye, checking your progress periodically.

If you are dissatisfied with the dye dodging, it is possible to remove all the retouching by soaking the negative in plain water for several hours. A drop or two (no more!) of ammonia added to the water will help speed the removal. The dye may also be removed locally, if you wish, by using a clean cotton swab charged lightly with 28 percent ammonia. *Do not allow this ammonia solution to come in contact with the emulsion side of the negative as it may spoil it.* Remember, too, not to work with the unstoppered ammonia bottle close to you since it is irritating to nasal membranes. Even a faint whiff of ammonia is more than enough!

Some workers believe the dye solution is more easily applied if the negative has been previously soaked and the excess moisture blotted away. However, it is best to practice this technique first with a discarded negative.

Perhaps the best way to practice retouching with a dye solution, until you get the "feel" of the process, is to fix out several pieces of film until clear, wash and dry them, and attach one of the pieces to the edge of the negative with Scotch tape. Apply the dye solution to this blank sheet of film. Then, if any errors are made, simply discard this piece of cleared film and attach another to the negative.

For altering negative details, dye dodging is a valuable supplementary technique to pencil retouching, and a companion technique to the ground-glass work described in the following section. By all means, purchase a bottle of the red dye at once, if you haven't one already. But don't just add it to the collection of bottles on your darkroom shelf—learn how to use it!

GROUND-GLASS PRINTING

Look at the illustrations which accompany this section—quite a difference between the "straight" and the "worked-up" prints, isn't there? What made this difference possible? Only a piece of ground glass and a soft-lead pencil. With these simple materials, the transformation of a mediocre print into one with pleasing quality is possible for any photographer—and at little expense or trouble. The cardinal rule, as for any retouching, is not to overdo it.

Primarily, this method of printing consists in taping a negative in contact with a piece of ground glass on which additional negative details can be drawn with a pencil. The "sandwich" thus produced is then printed simultaneously as a unit, either by contact or by projection.

As might be expected, the work is somewhat easier with comparatively large-size negatives; also, the penciling is less apparent because large negatives require a smaller degree of enlargement than do small ones to produce a print of any certain size. But, this does not mean that the ground-glass technique cannot be used successfully in conjunction with small negatives. In this connection, a good magnifying glass will aid in doing smooth penciling. However, if you use miniature-size original negatives, you may find it expedient to make a large-size copy negative to which the ground glass can be attached.

A piece of *finely* ground glass about 1/16 of an inch thick should be used. Inasmuch as it can be obtained inexpensively from a glass store, it's a good idea to purchase several pieces of the ground glass in the same size as your negatives. This will prevent extra trips to the glass store in case of breakage; or should you at any time in the future decide to make another print in this manner, the materials will be ready and waiting. *The finest ground glass is none too fine.* If you find this to be the case, you can grind your own using emery of No. 1200 grade.

The appearance of the ground glass itself may at first lead you to suppose that it absorbs much of the printing light and may lead to trouble in printing. Fortunately, the loss of light is slight. This is seen to be the case when the negative-ground-glass combination

Several changes were made between the original print at the left and the final print above. Ground-glass retouching accounted for most of the differences. Note how the lighting on the background has been changed and that the objectionable shadow from the glasses has been removed. The retouching tool is a cardboard stump.

is assembled. Negative details are readily discernible, even when viewed from the back and through the glass. Although the appearance of the "sandwich" might indicate it would produce a badly diffused print, the difference in sharpness—even in enlargements of heroic proportions—between a single negative and the same negative after the glass has been added, is not unduly noticeable. However, as might be anticipated, the addition of the ground glass does have a slight flattening effect on the print contrast. For this reason, to maintain normal print contrast, it may be necessary to use the next harder grade of paper than would otherwise be used.

Bind the negative to the ground glass with a piece of transparent Scotch tape so that the negative will be printed emulsion side down in the customary manner. Apply the tape to only the edge and the borders of the negative and the glass, so that it will not interfere with those portions of the image which are to be used in making the print.

Tape the negative to the glass with the ground side of the glass uppermost. The matte surface of the glass will then be accessible for the pencil retouching, and the retouching will be separated by the thickness of the ground glass and the film base from the negative image on the emulsion side of the film. This is important for the following reason:

Because it is practically impossible to incorporate details in the pencil work on the ground glass with definition as sharp as that of the negative image, it is advisable to separate the retouching marks from the emulsion by a short distance so that the retouching will be suitably diffused in the print. Thus, the appearance of the pencil work, which would be rather obvious otherwise, will be minimized when the print is made.

To add the desired negative shading or detail to the ground glass, place the glass and negative combination on a retouching stand so that the work is illuminated by transmitted light. If a retouching stand is not available for this purpose, you can use a contact printer as a light table; or as a last resort, you can work against the glass of a window through which daylight enters a darkened room. You can easily tape the combination temporarily to a clean pane of glass. Position the negative to "look outdoors," while you are doing the necessary pencil work on the ground glass.

The actual retouching may be accomplished by any convenient means, depending on the amount of detail you wish to incorporate in the final scene. The softer the pencil lead, the more density will be deposited, and the choice of pencils may be governed accordingly. The sharpest work is possible with a finely pointed, medium-hard-lead pencil which can be used for adding missing print details or strengthening sharp details which are already present but have insufficient printing density.

Soft-lead pencils are customarily employed in conjunction with an artist's tool known as a "stump." This is simply a tightly rolled piece of cardboard or stiff paper which is used to soften pencil lines by a slight smearing action. This is an ideal combination for working clouds into a landscape or for adding a desirable amount of separation between a portrait subject and a dark-tone background. Probably the majority of your ground-glass work can be carried out most effectively in this manner. Stumps in various sizes can be obtained from artists' supply stores, or they may be made as needed by rolling a small sheet of stiff paper to about the size and shape of a cigarette. They can then be whittled to a fine point with a knife in a manner similar to that used in sharpening a lead pencil, and slightly roughened with a piece of sandpaper.

The next method of retouching is reserved for comparatively large areas of the negative. Graphite is scraped from a soft-lead pencil with a razor blade until a little pile of the powdered graphite is collected on a sheet of smooth paper. (Lampblack or crayon sauce may also be used satisfactorily). The graphite is then applied to the ground glass with a tuft of cotton. Place the cotton in contact with the finely divided graphite so that a sufficient quantity adheres to the cotton. Using a circular motion, rub the cotton briskly onto a sheet of waste paper for practice and to smooth out the pigment. Then rub it lightly on the areas of the ground glass which require treatment. The graphite density should be added gradually, by building up the tones with a series of successive applications rather than by attempting a heavy application all at once.

In order to see how the work is actually progressing, you may want to make one or more proof prints. These need be no larger than contact prints. By examining the results of your retouching, you can readily see, for example, that a pencil line is a bit too prominent and needs subduing with a stump, that a cloud highlight requires slightly more density, or that a shadow detail can be improved. Because the work progresses so easily, it is difficult to avoid undue enthusiasm and consequent lavish applications of pencil. This introduces the danger of adding detail and densities which may lead to an undesirable, artificial appearance in the final print.

One other precaution is to avoid getting finger marks on the ground glass. Oily fingerprints cause a transparentizing action which may lead to almost complete transparency of the ground glass in the areas affected. These areas then transmit light more readily than do the neighboring areas of the glass, and the subsequent print may contain various dark spots caused by this carelessness in handling the ground glass. If you wish, handle the ground glass with lightweight cotton gloves.

On the other hand, this same transparentizing principle can be employed to advantage as a method of dodging. A small amount of Vaseline oil can be placed on the ground glass, directly over a negative area which requires added printing exposure, in order to produce a desirable darker tone in the print. This method of increasing print density in a given area is particularly recommended where it is necessary to subdue brilliant print highlights.

It is possible to remove the pencil marks and oil spots from the glass if you wish to use the same piece of ground glass for other negatives. However, because of the low cost of the materials, and the fact that it is difficult to redraw the pencil work accurately after it has once been removed from the ground glass, it is best to leave the ground-glass negative sandwich intact if there is a possible need for additional prints. Use a new piece of glass for each new negative.

In spite of these recommendations, should it still become necessary to clean the ground glass, this can be accomplished easily by scrubbing the glass with soap and water and a stiff-bristled brush.

PAINTING WITH LIGHT

Next to making good "straight" prints, *local* printing is the most important technique a photographer can learn. Local printing, sometimes referred to as "spot printing," can make a world of difference in the aesthetic quality of a print from a particular negative. It can emphasize important details or subdue unpleasant ones, stress compositional lines, and regulate print contrasts. It offers a simple means of improving mediocre pictures and of enhancing good ones. Yet, local printing is more than a mere trick of the trade. It can be an extremely practical method of control; in deft hands, it is an art in itself as a means of interpretation through painting with light.

Because of its nature, local printing must be learned in the darkroom. No musician ever mastered his instrument by reading in a book how it should be done; it took practice. The same holds true for any craftsman, including the photographer.

DODGING

The first type of local printing with which you should become proficient is dodging, or "holding back" light. Its most common usage is found in lightening objectionable dark shadows which,

Keep a variety of versatile dodging tools ready. These are the light "retarders."

if allowed to print normally, might be devoid of details. Dark shadows are seen in prints of excessive subject brightness range, such as an improperly lighted portrait, a landscape containing brilliant cloud highlights and dense areas of foliage, or a scene with a dark foreground and sunlit distance. The range of tones may have been recorded satisfactorily on the negative, but because of the limited density range of the paper, both ends of the scale have to be controlled individually if we are to expose the print for the *relatively more important middle tones.* Very often such a print may be improved if the light coming from the shadow portions of the negative is partially retarded during the print exposure.

How do you know if a print can be improved by locally retarding the exposing light? The best answer is to try it and compare your result with a straight print. Exactly how much light should be held back? Again, the only way to find out, unless past experience can help you, is to try it and see.

Dodging implements are perhaps best made as the occasion demands them, because probably no two negatives will present exactly the same requirements. In one instance, a tiny ball of cotton on the end of a broomstraw will be the best form of dodger; an oblong piece of black paper stuck onto the end of a wire will suit another particular purpose admirably; or perhaps a sheet of

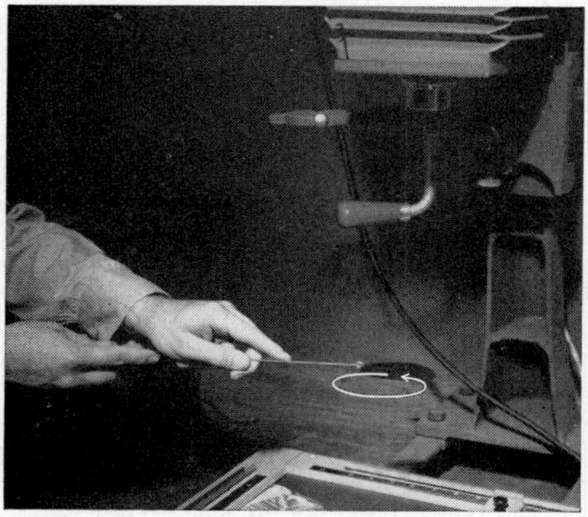

Two important things about dodging tools—don't overdo the effect in the print; keep them in continuous motion.

opaque cardboard may be needed to hold back an entire dark foreground area. It may surprise you to note that a clenched fist can be made to conform to innumerable shadow outlines. But the best dodging implements of all are those cut with a scissors from a proof print of the same subject.

Let's make an example of this point since it is well worth considering. Let's assume you're making a 14 by 17-inch print of a sailboat splashing along at a merry clip. The trouble is, you've decided, that the sky area in front of the boat is too dark and needs to be lightened so the boat can "move into that space a little easier." The problem is, then, to hold back a rather definite area of the sky in front of the boat. This is how to solve it: From an 8 by 10-inch proof print—which can be hastily made just for this purpose—cut out that portion of the sky which you want to print lighter. Then use the cut-out piece of sky area as a dodger. You'll find that an 8 by 10-inch print is just about the right size to use for this purpose when making 14 by 17-inch prints.

In general, hold your dodger up about a third of the distance from the easel to the enlarging lens. The closer it is to the easel, the smaller the shadow on the paper, whereas the farther it is from the easel, the larger its shadow. Although the size of the dodging implement itself may be constant, the area affected may vary considerably by simply changing the distance between it and the paper. Sharp outlines are secured by using the dodger close to the paper.

You may wish to elaborate any of these basic procedures, such as with multiple dodging, to secure a desired effect.

It is important in most types of dodging to keep the dodging implement in gentle but constant motion during the portion of the exposure it is being employed. If this is done, then no definite lines of demarcation will be noticed between affected and unaffected areas. The dodged areas should blend in smoothly and artistically with the adjoining ones. If the shadows appear light or unnatural, you probably overdodged them. Study your faults carefully and try to correct them skillfully when making the next print. If you find you have need for a "third hand" when doing this work, a foot switch control on the enlarger may help considerably.

PRINTING IN

The second type of local printing is known as "printing in," "burning in," or "spot printing." It can darken a distracting portrait background or an excessively brilliant sky, or it can subdue unwanted reflections or highlights of almost any sort. In fact, the possibilities it offers you for exercising your artistic judgement are practically without end. It differs from holding back in that density is intentionally *added* to a specific area instead of being subtracted. Also, printing in takes place after the normal print exposure has been given and therefore is in addition to it. It is generally used to subdue too-bright print areas, either by adding to heavily exposed negative detail which did not record in an undodged print, or by securing added emphasis for the main point of interest in a picture by further subduing subordinate areas.

Without any sensitive paper in the easel, turn on the enlarging light and study the projected image of your negative. See how bright the side of that white house is where the afternoon sun hit it? Now cup your hands midway between the lens and the easel and try to block out all of the picture except just that brightly lighted area. Let only that particular portion of the light *and no more* pass through your fingers or palms. If you can't control the light with sufficient accuracy with your hands, cut a small hole approximately the shape of the too-light area in the center of a sheet of opaque cardboard and hold this over the easel. The card-

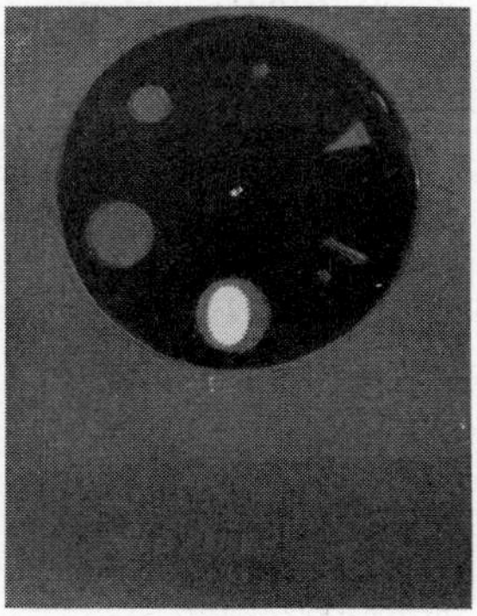

Most enlargements will benefit by careful use of a "printer inner" such as this. A similar implement can easily be cut out from stiff cardboard. Buy it or make it, but be sure to use it!

board should be large enough to cover the paper during exposure. Now you are ready to try a print exposure and the subsequent printing in of the too-bright area.

Note the normal printing time, and also the duration of the additional exposure required to print in the house until it is darkened sufficiently. Then, with this information filed with your negative, it will be a simple matter to reproduce the correct printing technique whenever necessary.

DODGING ON PAPER

There is an amazingly simple method of print dodging that is overlooked by most photographers. This is penciling or smudging directly on the paper before it is exposed. It works like this: Suppose you wish to make a print of a landscape scene. There are several clouds and a road which could be lightened to advantage. Yet, because of the number of areas to be dodged, and because of the approximate outlines of the areas within which the dodging must be confined, it is practically impossible (within the normal exposure time) to treat. So this is what you do:

1. Get the dodging materials ready and put them next to the easel. The dodging material itself can be either crayon sauce (usually obtainable at art-supply stores) or finely powdered graphite. You could even take a soft (2B or softer) pencil and, with a razor blade, shave off some of the graphite into a small pile. Whatever your dodging medium, it can be applied by "smudging" with a ball of cotton, a tuft of cotton wrapped on a wooden matchstick, or an artist's stump (described on page 113).

2. Place the negative in the enlarger, focus it, make the usual adjustments, and determine the exposure time by means of a test strip. This much is regular, routine procedure.

3. Place a red filter over the enlarger lens, position the unexposed printing paper in the easel, and turn on the enlarger.

4. Following the projected red image as a guide, lightly smudge (with the crayon sauce or graphite) the areas which you want to print lighter than normal. For fairly large areas, such as a cloud, a tuft of cotton is ideal for spreading the black powder. Dip the

cotton into the powder, test it on a scrap piece of paper to see that a small amount will be deposited, and go over each cloud in turn. For more detailed work, such as the ruts in the road which you wish to emphasize, use the cardboard stump. And for extremely fine details, use a sharply pointed pencil.

Add the powder gradually, building up the density evenly with successive applications, if necessary. Be sure to use a circular motion so that the powder gets down into the "pores" of the paper texture and is not just deposited on the tops of the tiny bumps.

A sharply pointed pencil—used with *very* light pressure, of course—has a limited "retouching" application in printing portraits with paper dodging. For example, you may wish to place or to emphasize a line highlight down the length of a subject's nose, or you may want the eye catchlights to print bright and clear in spite of a diffusion disc placed over the enlarger lens. In cases such as these, it is very easy to mark the paper by using the projected image as a guide. Incidentally, it may be necessary to round out the catchlights by spotting after the processed print is dry.

5. Let's say that the sensitive paper has been smeared or penciled as desired, the red filter removed, and the exposure given. Next, take a wad of clean cotton in one hand and insert the paper into the developer with the other. As soon as the paper is immersed, rub the emulsion with the cotton to remove the crayon sauce or graphite, as the case may be. Turn the cotton over and over while rubbing the print to pick up all of the dodging medium. It takes only a half a minute or thereabouts to remove the medium, as it comes off quite easily.

Obviously, this system of dodging—like other methods—has both its advantages and disadvantages. On the one hand, it is simple, convenient, and effective, but on the other hand it is not suited to volume print production, particularly where the dodging on several prints must match closely. Also, it is better adapted to use with smooth-surface papers than rough-surface ones which are more difficult to "powder" without overemphasizing the surface texture. This is particularly true in even-tone areas without fine detail which often helps to hide any dodging of this sort which may otherwise be a bit obvious.

PRINT FLASHING

Print flashing is simply a technique of "burning in" without the negative in the enlarger. It is an extremely useful method of controlling print tones and densities, of varying print contrast *locally,* and of subduing or obscuring completely disturbing details or patterns which might otherwise be objectionable in a "straight" enlargement. It is advisable at the outset to point out that flashing is not a substitute for ordinary dodging or burning in but is, in effect, a supplementary technique. Thus, any particular print may be both printed in and flashed, depending on the effect desired. Keep in mind that flashing hides texture and darkens with a "grainless density," while printing in brings out the detail and texture of the picture's highlights.

Flashing is accomplished in either of two general ways. The first is for controlling the tones of comparatively large areas in the print. Let's take a hypothetical example and follow the technique through, step by step:

Suppose that in a back-lighted landscape scene the sun glistens in an objectionably bright manner on a lake which occupies the lower half of the print. Such specular reflections, if printed normally, would appear very disturbing to the print observer since it gives the psychological impression of looking directly at a brilliant light source—something which one would not ordinarily do. In other words, it makes one feel almost as if it were necessary to squint at the print, even though the highlights are not actual reflections of the sun but only small spots of white paper. As you realize, this myriad of minute reflections is represented in the negative by small areas of practically opaque silver, and it would be impossible in printing to darken each and every one of them down a tone or two by ordinary dodging methods. Here is where flashing can save the print. The procedure is to give the print its normal exposure time as predetermined from test strips. Then, without moving the paper or the easel, remove the negative from the enlarger negative carrier. The empty negative carrier should be returned to the enlarger if it will help prevent any serious light leak from the lamp house during the flashing exposure.

Whether one of these pictures is better than the other is not so important as realizing that you can make either one from the same negative if you know how. The version at the right is a straight print. However, the top print required holding back the clouds, printing in the corners, and also flashing the corners. The flashing reduced the print contrast in the corners, helped to concentrate observer's attention in center of print.

After replacing the negative carrier, stop down the enlarger lens at least two or three more stops than was used to make the actual print exposure. It is desirable to reduce the intensity of the light in this manner, since it will mean that the flashing light will more nearly approximate the average brightness of the projected image and will be much more easily controlled than if it were to "blast through" brightly. Establish a level of light where the flashing exposure ranges from 10 to 20 seconds; any flashing time shorter than 10 seconds means that you will have to hurry the procedure, and reproducible effects will be difficult to achieve.

Hold an opaque card at about one-third of the distance from the lens to the paper and, while keeping the card constantly in motion and shielding the upper portion of the print, expose the lake and the sun reflection portion of the scene with the "imageless" light. The amount of flashing exposure is dependent on the effect desired, the height of the enlarger lamp house, and other related factors. Accordingly, it can best be determined by experiment.

The effect of this flashing is to subdue reflections suitably. Strange as it may seem, if the operation is done properly, the middle tones in the shadow areas will not be noticeably affected, the reason being, of course, that a slight amount of fog density is most readily noticeable only in the highlight areas. Since the primary effect of flashing in general is a reduction of contrast and highlights, this fact opens up many possibilities for local control over print contrast. For example, the corners and borders of a portrait subject can be printed lower in contrast by flashing than is the central area where the figure is located and which, of course, can be effectively shielded from the imageless flashing light.

You may wonder how it is possible to control the placement of the flashing light without using the negative projected image as a guide. There are several ways in which this may be accomplished. For instance, let us suppose that in the example of the back-lighted water scene it was desirable to flash only the bottom portion of the print as far up into the scene as the farther shore of the lake. It is a simple matter to place a marker on each side of the easel at the shore line while the negative image is being projected onto the easel. Then, with the negative removed, it is possible to use an im-

The tangle of ropes and the poles were included as a part of the scene. The camera saw too much and confusion resulted.

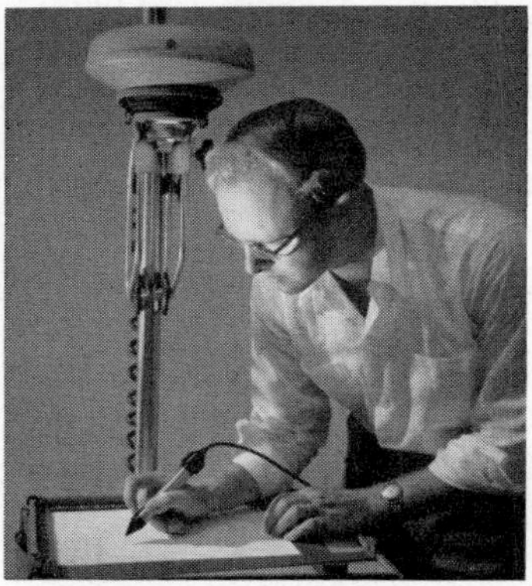

The areas which needed darkening were too small to be printed in so local flashing saved the day. During flashing, a red filter was in front of the enlarger lens.

aginary line between these two markers as a guide to the flashing.

Let's take a somewhat more complicated example in which a portrait is taken of a centrally located subject seated in front of an objectionably patterned background. The object in this case is to subdue (or blacken, if desirable) the background without affecting the subject. Here is how this is done: After the normal print exposure has been given, place a red filter over the enlarging lens so that the projected image can be used as a guide but will not affect the exposure of the paper. Using a soft-lead pencil with a rounded point, lightly trace a guideline about one-fourth inch *inside* of the subject's outline. Then remove the negative and, taking care to keep the flashing light approximately one-fourth inch *outside* or away from the guideline, flash the paper on the easel. By this procedure, you will be sure that the light used for flashing will not strike the pencil line and perhaps cause a light line of demarcation in the print after development. The final step in this procedure is, of course, to develop the print and, while the paper is immersed in the developer, to remove the light pencil guideline by rubbing the surface of the paper lightly with the fingers. True, this is a somewhat tricky operation, and the desired results may not be achieved on the very first attempt. However, a flashing procedure such as this does not require a particularly high degree of manual dexterity.

Flashing in details. The second method of flashing is used for subduing objectionably bright print details. Although holes may be cut into opaque paper or cardboard, and the print details flashed in, in much the same manner as they would be burned in normally, much finer control may be obtained with the use of a specially modified flashlight. An ordinary pen-type flashlight may easily be converted to this use by taping a cone of black paper around its tip so that its light can be projected wherever desired onto the paper through an aperture as small as desired. So that the flashing may be more easily controlled, it may be necessary, particularly with the higher-speed projection papers, to reduce the light intensity of the pen light by taping a suitable number of sheets of tissue paper over the flashlight lens.

Some expert print makers prefer to construct a permanent, and somewhat more convenient, hand flasher which operates from an electric-light socket by means of an extension cord. A plastic socket, such as that used for a small-base, Christmas-tree bulb, is a handy size, and a 7½- or 10-watt frosted lamp will give about the right level of brightness. A cylinder of metal, the adjustable-nozzle "snoot," and a simple off-on switch are all the other parts needed to do a good job of flashing in details whenever necessary. This system has the advantage of not using batteries, and thus assures a constant brightness.

It is helpful, particularly with your first few attempts at flashing in details to flash small test strips and immediately develop them to check the results. Keep track of the flashing time as well as the general negative-exposure time, and alter your reprinting procedure accordingly. Do not try to flash the print while it is developing, even if you notice then that the original flashing exposure was insufficient, because with some papers this subsequently flashed area may have a warmer image tone due to its shorter development time. An area such as this would be especially—and objectionably—noticeable if the print were toned later.

Flashing print frames. Interesting silhouette-type frames can be added easily to a print by an adaptation of the flashing technique, and these frames can be used in many ways to produce unusual poster-type effects. Many subjects can be adapted to various border masks. Silhouetted foreground objects, such as overhanging porch roofs or columns, may be introduced in a landscape; black oval frames can be added around portrait subjects, if desired. Whatever mask outline you select, however, should be simple and easily recognizable.

Suppose you wish to give a water-front scene or a group of sailboats the appearance of having been taken through a porthole. Only five simple steps are necessary: (1) Expose the print as usual, (2) place on the print an opaque paper mask cut to the desired shape, (3) remove the negative from the enlarger, (4) flash expose long enough to blacken the borders, and (5) develop as usual.

Let's elaborate these few operations for the above example of the sailboat scene. After the correct print exposure has been given, place a perfectly round object, such as a plate, of the desired size over the paper in the easel. While the plate is being positioned, the red safelight should be kept over the enlarger lens so the paper will not be further exposed at this time. Remember, this will allow sufficient illumination for you to see the projected image, yet the red light will not affect the blue-sensitive emulsion of the enlarging paper.

After the mask is in position, remove the negative from the carrier, and give the printing paper a flash of light to blacken completely the remaining print area. When the print is developed, the central, unchanged portion of the marine picture will be seen through the artificial porthole. This illusion can be further heightened somewhat by partially blue-toning the picture. The deep blacks of the frame will give the appearance of being relatively unchanged, while the scene "beyond" will take on a pleasing aspect of reality.

Local printing is not always simple to execute properly, so do not be discouraged if you find it necessary to make many prints before achieving the described results. Even the experts had to practice dodging or printing in and especially flashing to become skillful. Remember, next time you print a problem negative, a good print *can* be made; local printing may help you do it.

DODGING WITH MATTE ACETATE

It sometimes is necessary to enlarge a miniature negative which requires a considerable amount of *precise* dodging. If you have ever worked with this type of negative, you will recognize the problem immediately. Ordinary dodging wands and other implements often cannot be used with complete success to dodge areas of odd shapes or contours. Also, if several print areas require simultaneous dodging treatment, how many photographers have the needed five hands to do the job? Use Kodak Crocein Scarlet on the negative, you suggest? Well, that may be a helpful approach (see page 106), but these dodging dyes are difficult to apply to small negatives, particularly where sharp "edge treatment" of dark shadows is required.

The answer lies in using a sheet of matte acetate. The necessary shading is penciled on the acetate sheet which is placed in contact with the enlarging paper. (Recognize the similarity to the ground-glass retouching technique?) Then, when the print exposure is given, the pencil markings and shading are incorporated into the print. The process requires surprisingly little artistic ability, and the materials are inexpensive.

Here are the steps for really precise and repeatable dodging:

Step 1. Compose the projected image and adjust the enlarger height as desired. Then turn the negative over so that the emulsion side is up and, with the negative in this position, make a reversed-image print.

Step 2. After this print has been processed and dried, tape it down on a flat, well-illuminated surface. Now tape a sheet of clean matte acetate over the print so that the diffusing or matte side of the acetate is uppermost.

Step 3. Using a medium-soft pencil and very light strokes, gradually shade in the areas which you want to print lighter than they normally would. The fine tooth of the matte acetate provides an excellent retouching surface and permits either a very light or heavy deposit of the graphite to be made.

In many instances, the pencil lines alone will take care of the retouching or fine-line dodging that is required. In a portrait subject, for example, you can easily emphasize the highlight down the center of the nose or across the lower lip. Also, line-lighting effects can be heightened and separation lines improved; or, perhaps broader areas should be lightened, for example, cloud "fluffiness" brought out, or a country lane lightened. All of these areas require that fine pencil lines be added to the acetate and then that they be smudged or shaded with a tuft of cotton or a cardboard stump. The possibility of lightening broad areas means that you can practically add details where none existed in the negative, for example, a shaft of light from a church window, or a lighter background for a portrait.

Step 4. After you think the retouching or dodging has been completed, turn the negative over in the enlarger to its normal emulsion-down position. Turn on the enlarger and, with the acetate sheet *matte side down* in the enlarger easel, register the retouching with the projected image.

This step is not difficult, but be sure you take sufficient care so that the registration is accurate. This may require a slight adjustment of the height of the enlarger because the reversed-image print may have changed its dimensions as a result of being processed. After the retouching has been lined up with the projected image, tape down one edge of the matte acetate sheet so that the retouching can be swung like a page of a book into or out of position.

This is the most contrasty print that could be made from an underdeveloped negative. But it lacks punch and contrast.

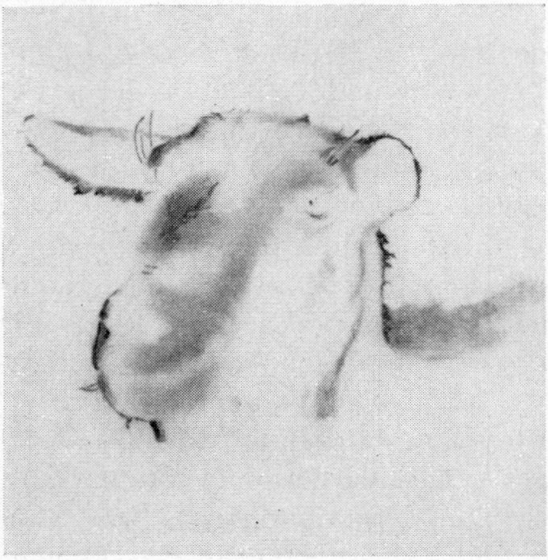

At the left is the handiwork which made the difference in the print below. This retouching is simply pencil work on a sheet of matte acetate placed in contact with a reversed-image enlargement made the same size as the final print. With the matte acetate on the easel, the retouching was incorporated automatically when the final print exposure was given.

Step 5. Now you are ready to make the dodged print. Hold the acetate sheet up out of the way and insert a sheet of sensitive paper in the easel. Lower the acetate sheet onto the photographic paper and, to insure good contact between the two, place a clean sheet of glass over them. Make the exposure, process as usual, and the job should be done.

Be sure, however, that the print is dodged exactly the way you want it to be, since it's easy to change the degree or placement of the dodging if you feel it could be improved. Perhaps you will want to regard this first print as a "progress proof." It may be that some borders of dodged areas on the acetate sheet need to be cleaned up with an art-gum eraser or that more density needs to be added to give just the desired effect. Once these changes have been incorporated on the matte acetate, obviously any number of prints with exactly the same dodging can be made.

Because the matte surface of the acetate sheet is an effective light diffuser (and, in fact, makes an excellent diffusing material for use over flood-lamp reflectors), it must be kept in contact with the paper surface or else diffused images will result. It is for this reason that the glass plate is absolutely necessary and that the matte side of the acetate must be down, immediately next to the printing paper. For this reason also, the technique of dodging with matte acetate works best with smooth or fine-grained paper.

If the matte acetate sheet is in contact with the printing paper, its use does not increase the print exposure appreciably. It does lower slightly the contrast of the resultant prints, but this is not serious since the amount is equivalent to only about one-half a paper contrast grade. Just be sure that the print receives full development, and if the soft results still bother you a little, try using the next higher paper contrast grade.

Matte acetate sheets, under the trade names of Kodapak Diffusion Sheets and Matte Kodapak Sheets, are available from photographic dealers. Perhaps it will have to be ordered for you, but it is available. Matte acetate in rolls is obtainable from Kodapak dealers who are located in most of the largest cities. In addition, Kodatrace, which is a blue base matte acetate handled by Kodak Industrial Dealers, can also be used for print-retouching purposes.

"DODGING" WITH THE DEVELOPER

It's happened to all of us: a sheet of photographic paper has been exposed, dodged with utmost care, and immersed in the developer; then, as the print image first began to appear in the early stages of development, you realized that a particular area did not receive quite enough local exposure. Was this sheet of paper for which you paid good money destined for the wastebasket? Not if you're prepared for such emergencies and know how to "dodge with the developer." The technique of salvaging a partially processed print such as this is, admittedly, best suited to fairly large-size prints in which the subject is composed of rather broad masses and areas rather than of fine details. However, the day will probably come to every photographer when he can use this technique to advantage, so here it is.

Let's suppose you are developing Kodak Opal Paper in the recommended developer, Kodak Selectol. The developer dilution is 1 to 1 (one part of Selectol Developer stock solution to one part of water) and the development temperature is 68 F. The control solution is *undiluted* Selectol stock solution, preferably warmed to about 75 to 80 F. A tuft of cotton will serve as an applicator.

After the general print image has just become visible, quickly remove the developing print, and rinse it off in a stream of running water. After rinsing the print, dip the cotton tuft into the concentrated developer and apply it to those areas of the print you feel will not develop normally to sufficient density. Keep the print flat to avoid having the developer run down into adjacent areas. Also keep the cotton moving in small circles. Wait a few seconds to give the control solution time to "take hold," and then replace the print in the tray of the normal diluted developer and *agitate it briskly* for the next few seconds. The cycle can be repeated two or, at the most, three times before the print is fully developed and placed in the stop bath. This technique will be satisfactory for general shading. For more detailed work, it will be necessary to wipe the print surface free of water after rinsing and apply the developer with a brush if necessary.

There are a few do's and don'ts which, if heeded, will lead to better results: Keeping the print out of the tray too long and failing to agitate it when the print is returned to the tray may result in stains and/or developer streaks. Do not mix developers, that is, do not use one type for the control solution and another in the developing tray, since they may not produce an image tone of the same color and can increase the possibility of development streaks. For example, although individually each is an excellent developer, do not use concentrated Kodak Dektol Developer as a control solution and diluted Kodak Selectol as the primary developer in the tray. Keep in mind, also, that the degree of density control is fairly limited and does not approach the degree of control possible with ordinary dodging which controls the relative exposure times of local print areas. Never try to rub the developing print with your fingers to "heat" the developer in local areas; while it has been done with small success, this is inefficient and only invites stains.

P.S. *You now have a résumé of the most common techniques used to control print densities. The realization that control possibilities during printing are practically* unlimited *should help remove any mental barrier you may have had in deciding how to get into a print all the attractive interest you saw in the subject when it was photographed. Why not find that problem negative, take it into the darkroom, and say something like this to yourself: "Since a photograph is only a design formed of different tones ranging from light to dark, and because I can alter the value of any or all of these however I wish,* I have absolute control over the appearance of my final print."

Once you are in this frame of mind, it should help you go a long way toward improving your print-making ability.

Chapter 9

Tricks in Enlarging

Tricks of the trade—that's what any craftsman needs. And the more tricks in enlarging you know, the better enlargements you'll make! So let's examine briefly the special printing techniques concerned with diffusion, combination printing, texture screens, vignettes, and others. All set? Let's go!

DIFFUSION

Back in the early 1850's, when exposures were long and enlargers but a dream of a mad photographer, one chap had an idea about print diffusion. From the front of his camera to the floor he stretched a violin string. Then, while his subject sat immobilized in the posing chair during the camera exposure, the photographer sawed vigorously on the string with a violin bow. Diffusion indeed! "Mush" might be a better word for it!

That was in the 1850's. Today? Print diffusion is still with us and, from all appearances, always will be. But fortunately there are easier methods than our grandfathers first imagined for utilizing the diffusion principle.

Print diffusion is the effect presented by an image that is not quite sharp. Why, you might ask, would anyone—after spending a considerable sum for precision-made, top-quality, coated camera and enlarger lenses—want to diffuse a print intentionally? Paradoxically, there are several good answers to this question. For example, diffusion will minimize the effect of minor negative defects, such as coarse grain and scratches, which may be particularly evident in prints made from comparatively large "blowups" from miniature negatives. Coarse retouching marks on portrait negatives can also be "hidden" in the same way. Furthermore, it is occasionally desirable from an aesthetic viewpoint to slightly diffuse subjects, such as portraits of women or "atmospheric" landscapes, to create a more pictorial impression rather than a quite literal one.

Diffusion may be divided into two general types, depending on the time at which it is introduced into the picture. The first is negative-type diffusion, generally obtained by placing a diffusion disc over the camera lens at the time of exposure. The actual diffusion disc or other type of diffuser, such as an adjustable portrait lens, which is used depends on the degree of diffusion desired. Because the highlights of a subject reflect the most light toward the camera, the corresponding areas in the negative will be affected (diffused) the most. Of course, this is not a printing technique, but you should be at least familiar with it as a commonly used method of altering the appearance of a scene.

In the second, or positive-type diffusion, the diffuser is placed in front of the enlarger lens. This time it is the shadow areas which will receive the greatest exposure (from the clearer portions of the negative) and therefore will be the areas of greatest print diffusion.

There are advantages in each method. Although it is a matter of personal choice, generally negative diffusion is considered the more desirable. Back-lighted, wet-pavement bricks, back-lighted blond hair, sparkling reflections in a winding stream—all of these and many more are improved by a slight diffusion of the highlights. As a general rule, all specular reflections (the most brilliant) are more pleasing when thus softened. Psychologically, you will find less "strain" on the eyes in viewing a diffused photographic reproduction than would be the case with an undiffused one. Of course, the disadvantage of the negative-diffusion method is that, even if desired, an absolutely sharp print cannot be made from a diffused negative. This can be overcome, however, by making two film exposures, one with and the other without the diffusion disc in place.

The advantages of positive diffusion are readily apparent. The original negative still may be as "sharp as a tack," and the degree of diffusion readily controlled and easily accomplished in a variety of ways. Diffusers can vary from a piece of nylon stocking, some ordinary plastic window screening, or a sheet of cellophane that has been slightly wrinkled, to optical-glass diffusers made especially for this purpose. They all render the print less sharp and, of particular importance, "gray down" the highlights by partially scattering the light of the projected image. The advantage of optical-glass diffusers is that highlights tend to remain more brilliant because the scattering is confined more closely to the shadow areas.

The technique preferred by many print experts is to diffuse the image for only a portion of the total printing time, the remainder of the exposure being completely undiffused. This technique results in a combination "sharp-plus-diffused" image which helps to keep the highlights clear and sparkling but, at the same time, to hide coarse grain, retouching marks, etc. The proportion of diffused to undiffused exposure time will naturally depend on both the light scattering properties of the diffuser and the effect desired. As a general guide, a moderate diffuser might be used for 25 percent of the exposing time while the remaining 75 percent would be undiffused. A hint in regard to a diffused portrait print is to sharpen the eye catchlights with a spotting brush.

As you have probably surmised, any type or degree of diffusion will lower the print contrast. With slight diffusion the lowering of contrast is not appreciable. However, with moderate-to-heavy diffusion, it may be necessary to use a higher grade of paper contrast in order to achieve normal print contrast.

Better too little diffusion than too much. Excessive diffusion leads very quickly from degraded print quality to grayish mush. Several years ago the degree of diffusion in both landscapes and portraits did border on mush. Fortunately, much of this fad has now disappeared, and the modern tendency is to use diffusion only if it is necessary or will add artistically to the desired effect.

Speaking of artistic effects, sometime try *local* print diffusion. This is easily done with a dodger of wrinkled cellophane or, for a "diffused vignette" effect, with a hole cut in a sheet of cellophane which would diffuse the print corners but not the center.

The key to success is extremely careful masking with the aid of cut-out paper masks. This is how to print clouds in a blank sky, step by step:

Step 1. Support a piece of clean plate glass about halfway between the enlarger lens and the easel. Do this by laying it across two up-ended blotter rolls, cigar boxes, or anything else which will give about the right height and is reasonably steady. The right height is about one-third the distance from the easel to the enlarger lens.

Step 2. Insert the foreground, or subject, negative. Focus it on the easel and stop down the enlarger-lens diaphragm to where it will be during the print exposure.

Step 3. Next, lay a large, discarded print or a piece of white or light-tone paper face down on the plate glass so that it will intercept all of the light from the projected image. Fasten this paper lightly in place with Scotch tape.

Step 4. With a sharp pencil, trace the horizon line, or the edge of the area to be masked, onto the paper. Remove the paper.

Step 5. With a *very* sharp knife, such as a surgeon's scalpel or an etching knife, cut just *inside* the traced line—into the foreground part of the mask—so that the projected edge of the foreground will extend slightly beyond the edge of the mask. This will prevent the formation of a white line at the juncture of the two images, as might be the case if you were to cut directly on the traced outline. The diffusion caused by the light passing the edge of the mask during the print exposure keeps this line from showing in the print.

The mask is now in two sections. The part corresponding to the foreground will be used to shield the bottom part of the paper while the sky is being printed; the top section will, in turn, be used while the foreground is being exposed. If the negative has a sky area so dense that it does not print, no masking of this area is necessary while printing in the foreground.

Step 6. Trim the sky section of the mask along the cut edges so that just a little of the sky image will "spill" over it during projection. The amount to be trimmed away is very small—1/16 inch or less if you are making an 8 by 10-inch print and up to 1/8 inch for a 16 by 20-inch print.

Step 7. Project the image onto the easel; place on the glass the section of the mask corresponding to the sky, and tape it down. Get this mask into EXACT position—the glass can be shifted slightly to do this after the mask is taped in place.

Step 8. Determine and make the foreground exposure.

Step 9. Mark the top and bottom lightly on the edge of the printing paper, and place the paper in a light-safe place.

Step 10. Remove the sky mask. Do not move the foreground negative just yet. Then, using the projected image of the foreground negative as a guide, put the foreground mask in position on the glass. Be sure the mask is adjusted ACCURATELY, and then tape it down.

Step 11. Remove the foreground negative, insert the desired cloud negative, and readjust the enlarger if necessary. Do NOT MOVE EITHER THE MASK OR THE EASEL.

Step 12. Replace the printing paper in the easel PRECISELY as it was during the previous operation and print in the clouds, the exact exposure time having been predetermined.

Step 13. Remove the paper and process it according to the manufacturer's recommendations.

Your result should be a perfectly blended combination of the two negatives. If the two sections of the print do not match in some way, the cause of the trouble should be readily apparent and a new print made. Or, if there was only a slight misfit, the error can be concealed by careful spotting on the print.

That is all there is to it. After one or two attempts, it won't seem so difficult because, really, it is a simple procedure. Just be sure, before you start, that the direction of the main light in both scenes is the same. It's rather disturbing if, for example, a cloud negative is printed with a landscape foreground, and the sun position is different for each one. If you are further interested in combination printing—the fancy name is *Montage*—look up some of the references given on this subject on page 249.

TEXTURE SCREENS

Suppose that, just before exposing a sheet of paper on the easel, you placed a sheet of tissue paper on top of the paper, and a sheet of glass on top of the tissue to hold it flat. Then you made the exposure, giving a little extra time to allow for the light absorbed, scattered, and reflected by the tissue paper. This is the simplest way of making a texture-screen print. The print image will be broken up somewhat, or "texturized," according to the textured pattern of the tissue paper. The effect is, of course, more suitable for some subjects than it is for others.

Texture screens can be improvised from many translucent materials or screenings which can be used in one or more thicknesses and for all or only a portion of the total print-exposure time. Or, you can make texture screens from opaque objects that have a textured surface, such as cloth or grained plywood sheets. To do this, glance a spotlight obliquely across the surface of the subject and make an underexposed negative of it with your camera. This texture-screen negative can either be combined with the subject negative and printed with it or enlarged separately onto a large sheet of film. In this latter case, this film can then be handled as a true texture screen and printed in contact with the enlarging paper in the same manner as the sheet of tissue paper.

A final word about using texture screens: Use them as often as you wish, but be sure they improve the final print or give the exact result you are seeking. The photographic process has enough merit to stand on its own two feet; to look good a photograph doesn't have to be disguised like an etching!

VIGNETTES

A vignette is, of course, a print in which the edges of the subject—usually a head-and-shoulders portrait—fade gradually into the surrounding area of the printing paper. There's no mystery about it: An image of the head and shoulders is simply projected through an oblong hole in an opaque cardboard held underneath the enlarger lens so that the print borders remain unexposed. Keep the cardboard in continuous motion during the exposure so that the "fade out" between the exposed and unexposed portions of the print will be gradual. The best vignetting effects are usually obtained with high-key portraits of women and children. It's far too delicate a treatment for a man!

However, if you have lost your enthusiasm for plain-vignetted prints, here's an idea: Try making a vignetted print that has a *gray* tone instead of a white tone surrounding the image. It's a little harder to make but, with the right subject, it may be more artistic.

The gray-tone background is produced exactly as though an ordinary vignette were to be made, except that the edges of the paper are flashed after the vignetted subject exposure has been given. One of the most convenient ways to do the flashing is this: After the subject exposure, take out the enlarger lens board but leave the negative in place. Have ready a dodging wand of about the same size as the oval through which the subject image was projected. Take the exposed paper out of the easel and mark it so you can tell which side is the top and which is the bottom. Now place a test-strip paper on the easel, and with the usual test-strip exposure technique, find out how much exposure will produce the desired shade of gray on the print borders. Replace the paper with the portrait image oriented as it was previously. Turn on the enlarger, using the dodger to protect the paper area exposed to the subject from the flashing light and giving the borders the amount of exposure as indicated by the test strip.

It will probably take a few trial prints before you get the exact effect desired, but it'll be worth your while when you do. Just don't start to make a vignette with your last sheet of paper!

THE EMMERMANN PROCESS

If you enjoy print making at all, you ought to make at least one print by the Emmermann Process just for the fun of it. The method is easy to follow and requires no additional equipment or special solutions. Its real purpose is to condense or flatten the scale of an extremely contrasty negative. In effect, it enables you to retain all possible shadow detail of a contrasty negative when printing for the highlights. Have you "lost" some shadow detail recently? This is how you can "find" it:

Soak the paper in the developer, place it on the easel, and give the paper two separate exposures, one for the shadows and the other for the highlights. Due to the action of the developer already in the emulsion, the shadow details appear during the interval between the two exposures. This silver density then acts as an automatic mask or shield which prevents further shadow exposure while the highlights are being printed. The paper is finally developed in a tray for the usual time. Sounds easy enough, doesn't it? A bit messy perhaps, but surely not difficult.

To familiarize yourself with the technique, make a few practice prints and compare them with a print made in the normal way from the same negative. You will quickly learn to detect the reduction in print contrast and to know when this method of so-called "tonal expansion" should be used.

Before you start, however, two words of caution: Not all enlarging papers are suited to the Emmermann Process since the double-exposure treatment may tend to reverse them. Secondly, be sure to use *fresh* developer to help keep the print from staining, since the total development time is somewhat longer than normal. With fresh developer, you should experience no difficulty with staining; if you do, add ¼ ounce (8 ccs) of 10 percent potassium-bromide solution to each quart (or liter) of the developer working bath. A final suggestion is to keep the safelight illumination rather dim since the paper will be handled under darkroom conditions longer than ordinarily.

Here is the Emmermann Process in detail: Select one of your negatives that has a very long density scale—for instance, a negative with adequate shadow detail and excessively dense highlights. This negative may have been normally exposed but overdeveloped; or the extreme contrast range may be due to extreme differences in subject brightness. If this negative were printed in the usual manner, chances are that the shadows would have to be retarded by dodging and/or the highlights "burned in" with extra exposure. Even then it would probably be a difficult job to squeeze the tonal extremes together sufficiently. The important consideration is, however, that the negative *does* have the shadow detail you wish to retain. Even this process can't make something out of nothing!

This is an example of a scene with brilliant highlights and deep shadows which has benefited by an expansion of the tonal scale. But the negative MUST have adequate shadow detail if these areas are to record satisfactorily in the print. Fresh developer is necessary for stainless prints made by the Emmermann Process.

With your long-scale negative in the enlarger, make the best print you can in the usual way, carefully noting the exposure time and the contrast grade of the paper. Then take another sheet of paper *of the next harder grade* and soak it in a tray of fresh developer for 1½ minutes. To help prevent the faster enlarging papers from being fogged by the safelight, soak the paper either emulsion side down, or with the safelight turned off. Place this paper face up on a sheet of glass or the bottom of an upturned tray, and with a cloth or rubber squeegee remove the excess developer from both sides of the paper.

To help keep the easel dry, cover it with a large sheet of celluloid or acetate. Now position the developer-soaked paper on the easel. The limp (it shouldn't be dripping!) paper will be a little stubborn when it comes to its lying flat on the acetate sheeting. An oblique glance at it will show you that the trouble is caused by air bubbles which can be eliminated easily with a small roller or squeegee. Work rapidly at this point because the longer the developer-soaked paper is out of the tray, the more chance there is of encountering stains from oxidized developer.

The masking, or shadow, exposure should receive about half the exposure time required for the normal print. If, for example, the normal print requires 10 seconds' exposure, make the first exposure only 5 seconds. After the enlarger has been switched off, *do not move the paper;* just let it develop on the easel for 1½ minutes. When the shadows have developed, expose for the highlights by giving 1½ times the normal print exposure. In this hypothetical example, the second exposure will be 15 seconds. Remove the print from the easel and develop it for no longer than 1½ to 2 minutes in the tray of fresh developer.

Now compare the two prints you have made. There is little difference in the highlight areas and middle tones. But notice the blocked-up shadows in the normal print and the full shadow detail in the one produced by the Emmermann procedure. Of course, the difference is due to the "automatic" mask formed by the first exposure and development. This thin, top veil of masking silver protects that portion of the paper emulsion underneath it from further exposure. Because the second exposure does not penetrate to the lower levels of the emulsion, both extremes of the negative's tonal range are preserved. Incidentally, this masking principle is the same as that involved in making contact prints on the printing-out paper often used for temporary proofs by portrait photographers. These reddish-purple prints are notable for their excellent shadow detail which is produced by the density being built up and masking the shadow areas as the exposure increases.

The ratio of ½ the time of the normal print exposure for the first exposure to 1½ times for the second exposure will serve as a guide for your trial Emmermann print. In most cases this will produce satisfactory results, but the ratio may be varied as necessary. The clue to the proportion of the total exposure time that should be allotted to the masking exposure depends on the characteristics of the negative. Contrasty negatives having little shadow detail should receive proportionally less total exposure than high-contrast negatives in which the shadow detail is adequate.

Oh, yes, when you're through printing in this manner, don't forget to wipe off the easel with a damp cloth and then dry the easel thoroughly.

MATCHING THE FIRST PRINT

Here's a problem that occurs quite often in the printing experience of most photographers: Suppose you have made an excellent print and then wish to make several more just like it. The duplicate prints may be wanted for gifts or for sending out simultaneously to several salons. Or perhaps you are a professional photographer and have had a customer reorder additional prints from a portrait sitting. In any case, probably no permanent record was kept of the enlarger lens stop, the exposure time, and the development time used in making the first print. Obviously, the first attempt at duplication will have to be on a trial-and-error basis. One of the best ways to do this is to place the sample print you are trying to match in a tray of water (provided it hasn't been mounted, of course!) next to the developing tray. If necessary, arrange the safelight so that the developing print and the finished print will receive the same amount of illumination. When wet, the sample print will have the same reflection characteristics as the one wet with developer. This allows a much closer match to be made than if you attempted to compare a wet print with a dry one. The system is, then, to expose the new print and develop it until its density matches that of the wet comparison sample. When the two are judged as identical, *quickly* remove the developing print and immerse it in the stop bath.

There is one thing to watch for, however, in matching prints in this manner. Some enlarging papers have in their emulsion a yellowish sensitizing dye which quickly becomes colorless when the print is placed in the fixing bath. In addition, the portions of the light-sensitive emulsion not used to form the image partly "veil" the image while the print is in the developer and in the stop bath. This "veil" also quickly disappears shortly after the print is placed in the fixing bath. Thus these two "temporary" effects—the yellowish-dye tinge and the slightly veiled image—may mask the subsequent appearance of the fixed print. The natural tendency is to let the print in the developer go too dark, particularly if you are watching (and comparing) the shadow details. The clue is, then, to match the highlights since they are least affected by either of the above paper characteristics.

Regardless of whether the job at hand is matching a previously made print or making the first print itself, it is quite desirable to know whether the paper being used exhibits the tendencies described above. It helps in judging the depth to which any given print should be developed. A simple test to find this out can be made as follows:

Expose in succession two moderately sized test strips, taking care to include the same shadow area in each of them. Develop them together, and place them both in the stop bath, *but carry over only one of them into the fixing bath.* Now turn on the white light and compare the two pieces. Is the fixed image darker than the unfixed image? Leave the white lights on and immerse the unfixed strip in the hypo. Watch to see if the action of the hypo darkens it appreciably. If the fixing bath changed the visual appearance of the image, you will know about how much of the haze to discount when judging prints on that particular paper while they are in the developer.

ENLARGEMENTS FROM COLOR TRANSPARENCIES

Have you ever wondered whether to take two cameras along on a vacation trip—one loaded with black-and-white film and the other with color film? This discussion may help you decide since it is easily possible to make excellent quality black-and-white prints from good color transparencies.

The out-of-the-ordinary step is to make a film negative by enlarging the color transparency, just as you would an ordinary negative, but using a sheet of film on the enlarger easel instead of a piece of paper. The resultant negative is enlarged just like any ordinary negative.

There are a few recommendations to note that will be helpful: Place the transparency emulsion side *up* (toward the light source) in the negative carrier so that the final paper print won't come out

Why not try making black-and-white prints from color transparencies? The results are perfectly satisfactory if the intermediate negatives are made properly. Here's a sample.

reversed; mask off the rest of the negative carrier so that no stray light will lessen the projected image contrast; cover up any light leaks from your enlarger lamp house so as not to fog the sheet of film. The exposure will probably have to be determined by the usual test strip method (see page 70) until after you have performed the operation a few times and are familiar with the conditions. If you have the Kodak Flurolite Enlarger A or the Kodak Hobbyist Enlarger, a three-diameter enlargement on Kodak Panatomic-X Sheet Film will be about 25 seconds at *f*/8. Panatomic-X Sheet Film is, incidentally, a good choice of film materials for this job and should be developed for about 5 minutes in a tray at 68 F in Kodak Developer D-76. Of course, other film-developer combinations can be used, but the important thing is not to get the negative too contrasty.

As you would suspect, some color slides make better black-and-white prints than others. First, select one that is absolutely sharp, scratch-free, and normally exposed. A *slightly* dark transparency will also reproduce well but a light transparency will never make a really good print. Next, be sure that the transparency is clean and dust-free. In most cases light fingerprints or oily smudges can be removed by breathing on the transparency, then wiping it gently with a soft cloth. Kodak Film Cleaner or carbon tetrachloride *may* cause streaks or spots by removing some of the protective lacquer with which the emulsion side of the film is coated. If this occurs, the lacquer should be removed completely, and Kodak Film Lacquer applied.

You may want to consider using a colored filter over the enlarger lens when exposing the film. A filter here has about the same general effect as the same filter on the camera lens when photographing an actual scene. For example, if you want a contrasty dark-sky-white-cloud effect in the final print, use an orange (G) filter over the enlarger lens. If you want to lighten the greens, use a green (X1) filter. With panchromatic negative materials, the Kodak Wratten Filter X2 (No. 13) is suggested for improved rendering of flesh tones. However, no filter at all will keep the tone relationships about the same as you see them in the color transparency and for general work no filter is required.

ENLARGING FROM WET NEGATIVES

Only if it is absolutely necessary, a satisfactory enlargement can be made from a wet negative. And when is it necessary? Well, it depends entirely on the circumstances, such as a news break or some other instance when a deadline must be met and there is not time to wait for a negative to fix, wash, and dry normally. This technique isn't something you'll need very often, but it is handy to know in case of an emergency.

Let's pick up the process at the point where the negative is in the fixing bath and you have just turned on the white light. Incidentally, if you're in a real hurry, you'll be using one of the concentrated liquid fixing baths, such as Kodafix Solution, instead of one of the ordinary hypo baths.

As soon as the negative has cleared, i.e., has lost its "milky" appearance, give it a quick rinse under a stream of running water. Then, depending on the kind of negative carrier you have, there are two general techniques which can be used.

To enlarge a wet negative in a glass negative carrier, the trick is to combine negative and glass without air bubbles between them. Doing this under water helps.

For glassless negative carriers. Place the negative on a sheet of glass and lightly squeegee all the excess water off both the front and back surfaces of the negative. Check the negative carefully for water droplets since, if present, they will show up as objectionable "blobs" in the print.

For glass negative carriers. Use only the bottom glass of the carrier. If this glass isn't easily removable—and it isn't in some carrier types—wet the negative and quickly "roll" it emulsion side down on the glass. This "rolling" must be done by starting with one edge of the negative and proceeding evenly so that no air bubbles will be trapped between the emulsion and the glass. Wipe off the bottom of the glass and the top of the negative—careful, don't move it—and make whatever prints are necessary.

If the bottom glass of the carrier *is* removable, you may prefer this variation of the above method: Place both the negative and the glass in a tray of water and bring them together *underneath* the surface of the water. Draw them out together and dry off the bottom side of the glass and the top side of the negative. Do not place the top glass on the negative—just put the bottom glass and the negative in the enlarger without breaking the moisture seal between them. Another, perhaps superfluous, "don't" is: Don't use glycerine or any similar viscous liquid to try to keep the negative from drying out. If you do, hordes of little air bubbles will plague you. Who wants to goop up an enlarger with glycerine, anyway?

In each of these two techniques for printing from wet negatives, it is easy to see why the enlarger should not be heated before starting, and why speed in working is imperative: The negative must not begin to dry out due to the heat from the enlarger. If this happens, the negative may stick to the glass or curl up out of the focal plane. Make those exposures and get that negative back into the fixer as soon as you can.

P.S. *That's all there is to it; hurry up and make the enlargement!*

Chapter 10

Add a Dash of Color

IF YOU haven't already done so, next time you're near a photographic exhibition take a close look at the number of toned prints on display. Besides the obvious sepias and blues, you'll find a large percentage of quality prints have been altered in tone, from almost imperceptible hue shifts to bold color effects quite suited to the mood of the picture.

Smart toning improves the appearance of most prints. We're used to *cool* snow and water, *sun-bathed* landscapes, the *warm* tone of flesh in portraits. The expert photographer recognizes the subconscious stamp of approval most people place on well-toned prints, and he uses toning *whenever it will contribute to the effect he wishes to portray.*

BLUE TONES

Pictorialists and salon exhibitors regularly use blue tones for creating mood pictures of such subjects as night, fog, coldness, mystery, rain, etc. A great variety of tones is not available with the usual gold chloride toner. The familiar slate-blue is similar in all papers which will tone in this solution and is effected primarily only by the depth of image tone in the original print and somewhat by the type of development prior to toning.

Brilliant blue tones are possible with iron toners such as the Kodak Iron Toner T-12. Such toners are quite likely to produce inferior tones and stained highlights, however, unless special precautions are taken to insure complete removal of hypo and residual silver salts.

In general, use a blue toner for fog, rain, night, marine, and snow scenes.

RED TONES

Red tones are appropriate for such subjects as sunsets, fires, and certain industrial operations. Pleasing reddish tones can be obtained by using a gold chloride toner such as Kodak Blue Toner on prints which have previously been sulfide toned. Thorough washing for at least 30 minutes is necessary before placing the sepia-toned print in the Blue Toner; otherwise, stains may result.

Strange but true, reddish tones are produced by blue toning a sepia print. Use red for sunsets and fire scenes.

Browns are most popular of all the toning colors for portraits and landscapes.

BROWN TONES

Although almost any color can be produced by some type of toning process, brown tones are by far the most common. Virtually all toned portraits are some shade of brown. Most portraits which are to be hand-colored are given a basic brown tone to save the colorist much time and effort. The pictorialist generally selects brown tones for exhibition photographs of landscape, architectural, and similar subjects.

Brown tones can be classified into three broad groups—the characteristic reddish-to-purplish-brown tones produced by selenium toners, the colder-toned chocolate browns of the single-solution sulfur-reacting toners, and the warm brown (somewhat yellowish-brown with the finer grained papers) of the bleach and redevelopment sulfide toners. In addition to these pronounced toner differences, the papers themselves vary considerably in their image characteristics, and by selecting the proper combination of toner and paper, tones ranging all the way from a decidedly cold brown to a very reddish-brown or yellowish-brown can be obtained.

TONING PROCEDURES

Toning is easy. Many excellent toners are available from manufacturers in concentrated package form, ready for dilution or simple mixing. Most of them will keep for months or even years, take up little storage space, can be used at room temperatures, and work rapidly, usually as single solutions.

There are many ways to tone a print. Here are several which have been used with varying degrees of success, as indicated:

Metal salts combined with potassium ferricyanide. Such metals as cadmium, uranium, copper, iron, cobalt, molybdenum, and tungsten have frequently been incorporated with potassium ferricyanide to form the colored ferrocyanide of the metal. A great variety of colors is possible but this type of toning is not generally suitable since highlight stain is usually present and the toned images are generally unstable to heat and light.

Dye mordanting. If an ordinary black-and-white print is treated with certain ferrocyanide, thiocyanate, or silver iodide-potassium iodide complexes, the silver image is converted into complex compounds which have the power to attract certain basic dyes. Greens, reds, blues, browns, yellows—in fact, almost any hue can be obtained in this manner. The resulting dye mordanted images have good light stability but, unfortunately, highlight stain is almost always present. The toning process is somewhat lengthy and involves the use of two solutions which are expensive to prepare and which usually have poor keeping characteristics. So if "any possible colors" with dyes interest you, be sure to read the next two sections.

Monochrome dye printing. A monochrome dye print of superb print quality can be made using a monochrome or "single-dye" Dye Transfer technique. In fact, there is so much to be said in favor of this new control process that a detailed discussion of it is presented in Chapter 12, starting on page 190. Don't overlook this discussion if you are really interested in *top* print quality.

Variations of the Flexichrome Process. Practically any desired color can be obtained by making your print via the Kodak Flexichrome Process. The procedure is the same as for an ordinary Flexichrome print up to the point where the gelatin relief image is dyed in the modeling agent, stripped from its support, transferred to the final support, and dried. The details of this procedure are fully explained in the Data Book entitled "The Kodak Flexichrome Process," which is obtainable from most photographic dealers.

After the gelatin relief image has dried firmly in contact with the final support paper, it can be colored with any single dye solution desired, or a mixture of two or more dyes, for that matter. It's best to use a soft sponge, rather than a large brush, for the coloring since it is more convenient and less time consuming. Apply the dye solution evenly, blot the print surface gently, rinse it with a 2 percent acetic acid solution, and then gently blot it dry. That's all there is to it.

Of course, you will want to be careful not to replace completely the modeling agent since without it, the shadows would be lacking in depth and the general print quality would suffer, particularly for medium-to-low-key subjects.

There are three additional advantages to a monochrome Flexichrome print beside the obvious fact that the print can be made in tones from pastel pink to a sickly cyan to a deep, rich, velvety, chocolate brown. The first is that the image is composed of dye particles and, therefore, has a very long density scale or "tonal range." In turn, this means a very high print quality is possible. Secondly, much local reduction can be done with a finely pointed brush and plain water. Simply dip the brush into water and carefully paint over any areas you wish lightened. Thirdly, you *cannot* make a mistake with Flexichrome. If the print does not turn out the desired hue the first time, just redye it again and again until you're satisfied. Wait a year and change it again!

Hypo-Alum (Kodak Hypo Alum Sepia Toner T-1a formula). One of the most highly regarded toners in the trade consists of a hypo and potassium alum solution with a silver salt added to reduce any tendency to bleach. Most papers will tone to a rich pleasing brown in about 15 minutes when the solution is used at 120 F. The silver image reacts directly with the colloidal sulfur in the toner to form a very stable image of silver sulfide. Although no packaged form is on the market, the solution is fairly easy to prepare from bulk chemicals, quite economical, and has high capacity and good keeping characteristics. It is not necessary to wash prints thoroughly before toning and the highlights are free from stains.

Bleach and sulfide redevelopment (Kodak Sepia Toner—packaged; Kodak Sulfide Sepia Toner T-7a formula). Any paper can be toned in a bleach and sulfide redevelopment type of toner. Even the pure bromides, which resist practically all other types of treatment, fall easy prey to the action of this old stand-by. It generally gives the most satisfactory results with inherently cold-toned papers. The warmer papers have a tendency to form rather yellowish-brown images.

The black-and-white print must first be treated in an acidic solution of potassium ferricyanide and potassium iodide. The silver ferrocyanide image which is formed is converted almost instantly to stable silver sulfide in the dilute sodium sulfide redeveloping solution. The entire toning process, including bleaching, rinsing, and redeveloping, takes less than five minutes.

Prints to be treated in Sepia Toner should receive 10 to 20 percent more than normal exposure to compensate for the definite bleaching action which takes place. If the prints are washed well before toning, this bleaching is a repeatable effect which can be corrected. Small traces of hypo left in the print from insufficient washing will cause the bleach to act like Farmer's reducer, and excessive or irregular bleaching may occur.

The bleaching solution should not be used in chipped enameled trays or allowed to come in contact with metal objects containing iron. Iron reacts with ferricyanide to form Prussian blue, and blue spots are quite likely to form on the prints. Even the water supply from old rusty pipes may be a source of trouble.

The sulfide redeveloper must be used near an exhaust fan or preferably under a well-ventilated hood. The hydrogen-sulfide fumes given off are both disagreeable and very poisonous. It is advisable to use print tongs or to wear rubber gloves since the solution is strongly alkaline.

Tone control—i.e., partial or incomplete toning—with Sepia Toner is not practical. The bleaching process does not proceed uniformly, and if the action is incomplete, spotty tones will result.

Polysulfide (Kodak Brown Toner—packaged; Kodak Polysulfide Toner T-8 formula). Solutions containing sodium carbonate and mainly sodium polysulfide will react directly with silver images to form silver sulfide. Toning is complete in 5 minutes at 100 F or 20 minutes at 68 F. Inexpensive and simple to use, polysulfide toners are well suited for large-scale toning operations. Partial toning is not satisfactory. The toning action is not uniform, and if the print is removed before completely toned, irregular tones will result.

As a general rule, warm-tone papers, such as Kodak Opal, Illustrators' Special, and Ektalure, should be developed in a cold-tone developer if they are to be subsequently toned in Kodak Brown Toner. The reason is that polysulfide toners produce a yellowish-brown result when the original image is comparatively fine grained. Although this yellowish-brown color is preferred by many photographers who wish to oil color their prints, it is not a tone that is usually pleasing by itself. In addition, these toners lessen both density and contrast, the effect being most pronounced on fine-grained images.

However, it is easily possible to compensate for density and contrast losses and, at the same time, to produce a more pleasing (less yellow) image tone by changing the time of development for papers that are inherently warm toned. Do it this way: Determine the exposure to obtain a print of normal quality with a 2-minute development time. This can be done with a small test strip if desired. Then, for the final print, give the same exposure time but extend the development time to 3½ minutes. As a black-and-white print, it will look a little dark, but the toning process will bite it back so that the end result will look just right.

Highlight stains may result unless the print is washed thoroughly before toning. A Kodalk bath, as described on page 78, will reduce the tendency to stain. A fresh fixing bath and a short fixing time will also help to improve the washing.

These sulfide-type toners should be used near an exhaust fan or preferably under a well-ventilated hood. The hydrogen-sulfide fumes given off are both disagreeable and poisonous. It is advisable to use print tongs or to wear rubber gloves since the solution is quite alkaline.

Selenium (Kodak Rapid Selenium Toner—packaged). Selenium toners contain sodium selenite as the principal toning agent. The silver image is oxidized by the selenite to reddish-brown silver selenide. The toning proceeds rapidly at room temperature.

Both the contrast and density are increased *slightly* by the toning process. If the original print is to be fully toned, it should receive normal exposure but about 10 percent less development time.

A Kodalk prebath is recommended to neutralize any acid from the fixing bath. Otherwise, traces of acid remaining in the print will cause decomposition of the toner; finely divided selenium will then be deposited on the print and cause an objectionable pink highlight stain.

The extent of dilution of the stock solution is not critical. At a 1 to 3 dilution, a print is completely toned in 3 minutes. Partial toning is satisfactory at a dilution of 1 to 10. The action progresses uniformly and the print may be removed at any time.

Nelson Gold (Kodak Gold Toner T-21 formula). Kodak Gold Toner T-21 for inherently warm-tone papers consists of a mixture of hypo, potassium persulfate, silver chloride, and a small quantity of gold chloride. The silver image is converted primarily into silver sulfide, with traces of gold probably present in the image.

No one yet has been able to package it successfully but, nevertheless, it is an excellent toner for papers yielding warm-tone prints. It yields a rich pleasing brown tone unlike that of any other toner. Furthermore, with this toner prints can be partially or completely toned as you desire. This gold toner is a great favorite among both salon workers and professional portrait photographers.

Prints should be prepared with normal density and contrast. Toning proceeds evenly at from 105 to 110 F and is complete in 20 minutes. Partial toning is satisfactory at shorter times. Toning at temperatures below 100 F is unsatisfactory; the required time increases rapidly until, at room temperature, there is no visible effect.

Kodak Gold Toner T-21

STOCK SOLUTION A

	Avoirdupois / *U. S. Liquid*	*Metric*
Warm water, about 125 F (50 C)....	1 gallon	4.0 liters
Kodak Sodium Thiosulfate (Hypo)...	2 pounds	960.0 grams
Kodak Potassium Persulfate.........	4 ounces	120.0 grams

Dissolve the hypo completely before adding the potassium persulfate. Stir the bath vigorously while adding the potassium persulfate. If the bath does not turn milky, increase the temperature until it does.

Prepare the following solution and add it (including precipitate) slowly to the hypo-persulfate solution while stirring the latter rapidly. *The bath must be cool when these solutions are added together.*

Cold water	2 ounces	64.0 cc
Kodak Silver Nitrate, crystals........	75 grains	5.0 grams
Sodium Chloride..................	75 grains	5.0 grams

NOTE: The silver nitrate should be dissolved completely before adding the sodium chloride.

STOCK SOLUTION B

Water	8 ounces	250.0 cc
Kodak Gold Chloride..............	15 grains	1.0 gram

For use, add 4 ounces (125 cc) of Solution B slowly to Solution A while stirring the latter rapidly.

The bath should not be used until after it has become cold and has formed a sediment. Then pour off the clear liquid for use.

Pour the clear solution into a tray supported in a water bath and heat to 110 F (43 C). During toning the temperature should be between 100 and 110 F (38 and 43 C).

Prints to be toned should be washed for a few minutes after fixing before they are placed in the toning solution. Dry prints should be soaked thoroughly in water before toning.

Keep at hand an untoned black-and-white print for comparison during toning. Prints should be separated at all times to insure even toning.

When the desired tone is obtained (5 to 20 minutes), remove and rinse the prints in cold water. After all prints have been toned, return them to the fixing bath for 5 minutes, then wash for 1 hour in running water.

The bath should be revived at intervals by the addition of Gold Solution B. The quantity to be added will depend upon the number of prints toned and the time of toning. For example, when toning to a warm brown, add 1 dram (4 cc) of gold solution after each fifty 8 by 10-inch prints or their equivalent have been toned. Fresh solution may be added from time to time to keep the bath up to the proper volume.

Remember that, after toning in Kodak Gold Toner T-21, prints should be refixed in a fresh fixing bath to insure the removal of excess silver salts. They should then be washed thoroughly. The toned image is quite stable, but it should be protected from excessive heat or intense light. If image-tone changes do occur from either of these causes, storage in a cool, dark area will usually restore the original brown tone.

Thiourea Gold (Kodak Blue Toner—packaged). Kodak Blue Toner contains thiourea and gold chloride as the principal reacting agents. Although the mechanism of reaction has not been fully explained, apparently the silver image is etched slightly by the thiourea and finely divided metallic gold is deposited on the silver grains.

Although both the visual contrast and density of a print are increased by this toner, the effect is slight and the necessary exposure decrease in making the original print will vary from none to not more than 10 percent for low-key subjects. Thorough washing before toning is very important. Traces of residual hypo may cause uneven toning.

Toning progresses slowly but uniformly at room temperature.

The time may vary from 10 to 45 minutes. Any intermediate tone in high-key prints can be obtained simply by removing the print when the desired depth of tone is attained, but *it is advisable to let low-key prints tone to completion.* The toned image is more stable than the silver image alone.

Red image tones can be produced by first toning prints in Kodak Brown Toner or Kodak Sepia Toner and then placing them in this Blue Toner.

PREVENTION OF TONING STAINS

Selenium, sulfide redeveloping, and polysulfide toners are quite likely to produce definite highlight stains if the prints are not properly prepared for toning. The intensity of the stain is usually proportional to the residual amount of silver salts and hypo in the black-and-white prints. Undesirable concentrations of these contaminants are present in prints treated in exhausted or nearly exhausted fixing baths or in prints which have not been washed properly.

Residual hypo and silver salts can be kept at a minimum by observing the following precautions: 1. Use a fresh or nearly fresh fixing bath. 2. Rinse the prints for 2 minutes in a 2 percent solution of Kodalk Balanced Alkali immediately following the fixing bath. 3. Wash thoroughly.

The importance of using a Kodalk bath can not be overemphasized. Kodalk causes the hypo and silver salts to wash out more easily, while under conditions of imperfect washing, the residual alkali serves to retard the fading action of the residual hypo. The alkalinity also prevents the formation of pink highlight stains caused by the precipitation of metallic selenium when an acid-reacting print is treated with a selenium toner.

These precautions are particularly important to prevent highlight stains when using the packaged Kodak Rapid Selenium, Brown, and Sepia Toners, and the formula toners, Kodak Polysulfide T-8 and Sulfide Sepia T-7a. Kodak Hypo Alum Sepia Toner T-1a, Gold Toner T-21, and Blue Toner are generally free from any tendency to form highlight stains. Irregular toning may result when using Blue Toner, however, if hypo is still present.

THE EFFECT OF PROCESSING VARIATIONS
(PRIOR TO TONING)

Image tone is primarily a matter of silver grain size, so that variations in development which influence particle size have a marked effect upon the tone. These differences are usually magnified by the toning process.

Adding bromide to a developer, or using warm-tone developers such as Kodak Selectol and Selectol Soft in place of a colder tone developer like Kodak Dektol, will give a warmer black-and-white image. Most of the brown toners will give a corresponding or greater increase in warmth of the toned image, some becoming quite yellow-brown, while Kodak Blue Toner will tone with greater ease and produce bluer tones.

A somewhat similar effect is observed if the original development time is decreased. This latter procedure is not recommended, however, for making marked changes, since it usually degrades the image and produces inferior tones.

Incidentally, the surface of the paper selected has a slight effect on the brightness of the resultant image tone. Matte surfaces generally produce somewhat colder or less bright image tones than the luster surfaces.

Although quality in a print is difficult to define, it is largely dependent upon the scale of values reproduced, and skimpy development results in a reduction of the number of distinguishable tones. For highest quality, all prints to be toned should receive full development.

Many toning failures can be traced to improper fixing. Traces of silver halide left in the emulsion from insufficient fixation will react with most toners to produce muddy tones. Complex silver salts left in the print from an exhausted fixing bath are difficult to wash out, and will form stains when the print is toned. A fresh fixing-bath treatment is recommended for all prints to be subsequently toned.

For many years some photographers have recommended that prints should be fixed in a non-hardening fixing bath if the prints are to be toned subsequently. The belief that improved toning results will be obtained by this technique is largely a myth, perhaps fostered by armchair experts. There is no perceptible difference in the color of the toned prints, regardless of the hardening properties of the fixing bath, and almost no difference in the time of toning. In fact, it is generally advisable always to use a hardening hypo bath since otherwise there would be the danger of scratching a physically unhardened print emulsion.

The importance of proper washing cannot be overemphasized. Traces of hypo may react with certain of the toners to produce staining or muddy tones, while with those containing potassium ferricyanide, a dilute Farmer's reducer will be produced and part of the image may be permanently destroyed. If the toning bath contains hypo it is, of course, not necessary to wash the prints thoroughly before toning.

Whenever the prints are to be dried before toning they must be thoroughly washed before drying. It is difficult to remove complex salts from the paper once the print has been dried, even with extended washing.

P.S. *As a final word, don't think that all prints have to be toned. Some toned prints are accepted in salons in spite of their tones, not because of them! Just remember the principle: toning should* contribute *to the total effect you wish to portray in your print.*

Chapter 11

Reducing and Intensifying

REDUCTION

Punch! That's what you'll learn about in this chapter. It's more than print quality; it's print punch, carrying power, brilliance. You've probably heard about making dark prints lighter with Farmer's reducer. However, it's not the mere ability to salvage an overexposed or overdeveloped print that makes this technique so famous; what counts is *how* the appearance of a reduced print differs from that of a normally made print.

First, before discussing print reduction, let's clarify its purpose. Reduction merely means bleaching or lightening the picture. However, let's not regard it primarily as a salvage technique for prints that were accidentally made too dark. Print reduction has a more noble purpose—that of making a good print better. It can do this by either of two means: by local area reduction or by total print reduction. Or, you can combine the two.

Print reducers, such as Farmer's reducer, have two simultaneous results on a print—the print is made both lighter and more contrasty. With these end results in mind, probably you already see several useful applications of print reducers to your own work. And, you're right. There are several ways in which a print reducer can help you. For example, typical situations are:

PROBLEM 1. *You wish to print a low-contrast negative on Kodak Opal Paper which is available only in a normal printing grade, not the grade 3 or 4 which you need.*

Answer: Intentionally overexpose the print, process it normally, and then reduce it back to normal density.

PROBLEM 2. *You have printed for the highlight or middle-tone portion of a long-scale negative, and the print shadows have become somewhat dense and "blocked up."*

Answer: Locally reduce just the print shadow areas, making them as much lighter as you desire.

PROBLEM 3. *You have a portrait of a rugged old character, which prints normally on the No. 2 grade of Kodak Opal Paper, for example, but it lacks extra carrying power and punch.*

Answer: Intentionally overexpose the print, reduce the entire print slightly, and then work locally on the highlight areas which need special emphasis.

FARMER'S REDUCER

Probably the most widely used print reducer is Farmer's reducer. This reducer can be obtained in a convenient packaged form, Kodak Farmer's Reducer, or you can make it up yourself from only two inexpensive and easily obtainable chemicals, sodium thiosulfate, which is ordinary hypo crystals, and potassium ferricyanide. Mix up a stock solution of each chemical as follows:

STOCK SOLUTION A

Water	16 ounces
Sodium Thiosulfate (Hypo)	4 ounces

STOCK SOLUTION B

Water	8 ounces
Potassium Ferricyanide	2 ounces

For normal print reduction, mix the following working solution:

Solution A	6 ounces
Solution B	½ ounce
Water	50 ounces

Stock Solution A will keep indefinitely; Stock Solution B will keep about six months in a well-stoppered brown bottle. However, the working solution will keep only about *ten minutes* before its activity deteriorates. Obviously, you will have to prepare the working solution immediately before use; furthermore, after you have reduced two or three prints, you'd better mix a fresh solution so you'll have a better idea about the speed with which the reducing action will take place.

Step by step, this is the procedure:

Step 1. Intentionally overexpose the prints by about 20 to 60 percent. Naturally, the amount of overexposure is an individual matter with each subject. It depends on such factors as the original subject contrast, the type of subject, the lighting contrast, and the contrast grade of paper which you are using. For example, low-key prints lend themselves to reduction better than do prints of average key, whereas high-key pictures in general are entirely unsuited to this treatment. Also, character studies of middle-aged-to-elderly people, as a subject group, can be reduced with more pleasing results than can, say, prints of either babies or glamour girls.

Step 2. If the print dries, resoak it in water for no less than 15 minutes so that the reducing action can proceed evenly. Washing for only 15 minutes after normal fixation is sufficient before reducing the print.

Step 3. Completely submerge the thoroughly soaked print in the working solution and agitate the print continuously.

Step 4. At the end of ten seconds, quickly remove the print from the tray and place it under a stream of running water. *Do not wait for the reducer to react on the print before taking it out of the tray.* The reason for this is that the reducer has a slight continuing action even after the print is placed in the running water. It naturally takes a short while before the water can displace the reducing chemicals from the print emulsion.

Step 5. After a few moments of rinsing, inspect the print for changes in image density. Keep your eye on the print highlights, where the reducing action will be first noticed. If the print has not been lightened sufficiently, return it to the tray of reducer for another brief "bite." The cycle of reducing and then rinsing can be repeated as many times as you desire. Just be careful not to overdo it—don't let the highlights be "eaten away right down to the bare paper." Remember, it's just like getting a haircut; it's easy to take it off, but putting it back on is another matter! Each print will, of course, require a different time of treatment. In general, prints having a warm image are reduced slightly faster than prints with a neutral or cold image tone.

Step 6. The final step is to wash the reduced print for one hour in running water to assure complete removal of the chemicals.

Both of these pictures were made on the same grade of paper but notice the higher contrast on the large illustration at the left. This added contrast was a result of intentional overexposure plus total print reduction in Farmer's reducer.

LOCAL AREA REDUCTION

This same general technique can be used to reduce local print areas. Sometimes you may want to emphasize a highlight or middle-tone area.

Have you ever noticed how the inclusion of a bright object helps to "pep" up an otherwise dull scene? Well, local reduction often works the same way. Perhaps all that some of your overexposed prints need is a few lighter areas to save them from the wastebasket. But often even a well-planned and carefully made print can be bettered.

Take that old print of yours of the road winding through the countryside, for instance. Although you yourself have always been fond of that shot, somehow it didn't seem to win the interest and praise you thought it deserved. The next time you are waiting for a batch of prints to wash, why not get out the reducing materials and try to make that road a shade or two lighter? Maybe that is just what it needs. After all, the "S" curve of the road is really the structural backbone of that print. If it were emphasized, the road would stand out from way across the room, whereas now it merges confusingly with adjacent details in the scene.

A surprising thing about removing silver from the darkest print areas is that often hidden shadow details are uncovered—details which could not be seen when viewed by reflected light. What causes these shadow details, once given up for lost, to appear, seemingly from nowhere? It's due to that fact that shadow details often extend "below" the visual level of a print's darkest tone. Sometime take one of your prints in which the shadow details are too dark to be seen clearly and hold the print up in front of a bright light source. Now, with the light transmitted *through* from the back of the print, can you see those shadow details any better? You bet you can! If you want them to be more apparent when the print is viewed by reflected light, locally reduce those areas. When enough "top" silver has been removed from the dense areas and the local contrast has been stepped up a little, there will be your shadows, luminous and full of detail.

To reduce a print locally with Farmer's reducer, soak it well, place the print on an upturned tray bottom, and with a towel wipe off the surface moisture from the print. Apply the reducer with a piece of cotton or a brush, with a light, circular motion, to the desired print areas. At no time leave a pool of the reducing solution standing on the face of the print. This may cause uneven or splotchy reduction, with the outline of the pool showing plainly in the finished print—which *would* finish it! Lighten each area a little at a time, rinse, wipe dry, apply more reducer, rinse, and so on until the desired effect has been achieved. Time and patience will see you through and it will be definitely worth while—if you don't overdo it.

Farmer's reducer, however, has one serious disadvantage. Unfortunately, as a result of its action, it has a tendency to stain the picture image a pale-yellowish color. Don't misunderstand—it is still a very helpful and widely used print reducer. In the first place, the stain, which varies in intensity, depending on the degree of reduction, is not very noticeable in many instances where the print is reduced only slightly. Secondly, with cream tint or old ivory paper stocks, the color of the stain nearly matches the tint of the paper, and the stain thus passes unnoticed.

There are, however, other reducer formulas which have the added advantage of not staining the print. Two of these are given here, one being recommended for total print reduction, and the other for reduction of local print areas and of fine details.

FOR TOTAL PRINT REDUCTION

An excellent print-reducing formula is the Kodak Non-Staining Reducer R-14. In fact, there is no reason—if the ingredient thiourea is available—why this reducer should not be used in all instances where Farmer's reducer might otherwise be employed. The two solutions are made up as follows:

Kodak Non-Staining Reducer R-14

STOCK SOLUTION A

	Avoirdupois U. S. Liquid	*Metric*
Water (125-140 F) (50-60 C)....	16 ounces	500 cc
Thiourea	½ ounce	15 grams
Sodium Thiosulfate (Hypo).......	1½ pounds	700 grams
Water to make.................	1 quart	1 liter

STOCK SOLUTION B

Water (about 125 F) (50 C).....	12 ounces	375 cc
Potassium Ferricyanide	5 ounces	150 grams
Water to make.................	16 ounces	500 cc

These stock solutions will keep indefinitely in separate bottles, particularly if Solution B is stored in a brown bottle away from continued exposure to a strong light source.

The two stock solutions are mixed immediately prior to use according to the following reduction purposes:

For chemically de-specking prints

Stock Solution A..	2 parts
Stock Solution B..	1 part
Water	2 parts

Just a touch of a pointed brush charged with this solution will eat the silver away to white paper in a matter of seconds.

For local print reduction

Stock Solution A..	10 cc
Stock Solution B..	5 cc
Water	300-500 cc

Use a brush or a cotton-wrapped toothpick dipped into the working solution but blot or wipe away most of the excess from the brush before applying the reducer to the print. Keep the brush moving with a continuous "retouching-stroke" manner on the area to be reduced. Immediately flush the print with running water after any noticeable lightening of the treated area has occurred. Blot off the print and repeat the applications of reducer until the desired effect has been attained.

For total print reduction

Stock Solution A. .	10 cc
Stock Solution B. .	5 cc
Water	1-2 liters (or quarts)

This may seem to you like quite a weak solution but, remember, the stock solutions are extremely strong-acting and the weaker the working bath, the easier it will be for you to stop the reducing action with precisely the right amount of density removed. Furthermore, the slower acting a reducer is, the less tendency there is for any "continuing action" (of the reducer, even though the print has been placed in the wash water) to overdo or spoil the result. Agitate the print continuously while it is in the reducer to help insure even reduction. In fact, the same procedure outlined previously to be used with Farmer's reducer should also be followed with this reducer.

As with Farmer's reducer, any print reduced with the Kodak R-14 Reducer should first be soaked for not less than fifteen minutes in a tray of water. The prints should be completely immersed during this time and the water should be about room temperature. Mix the working bath at the end of the soaking time, not before, since the mixture is rather short lived. When active, the reducing solution is a pale straw color; if it turns green to blue-green (depending on the dilution), it is no longer effective and should be replaced with a fresh bath. After reduction, wash the prints just as though they had come from a fixing bath, for one hour in running water.

What's so wonderful about this particular formula and why is it recommended? It's, simply, the excellent non-staining properties due to the thiourea. This chemical prevents the appearance of the yellowish residual stain image during reduction. If you have worked at all with Farmer's reducer, you will appreciate this advantage without doubt. Although thiourea is not a common chemical, it is not difficult to obtain. A drugstore or small photographic store probably will not have it on hand. However, it may be readily ordered from your photographic dealer, and stain-free reduction will make any wait well worth while. Incidentally, another name for the same chemical is thiocarbamide. Probably the reason photographers don't make wider use of the R-14 Reducer is that it is recommended primarily for graphic arts purposes.

In all fairness, it should be mentioned that thiourea is a strong fogging agent for sensitized photographic materials. As a result of handling the chemical, some few particles of the dry powder may remain suspended in air for some time and will cause black spots on film or paper emulsions if it comes in contact with them. Obviously, the work should be done away from rooms where photographic materials are usually handled. It is also difficult to remove traces of thiourea from the hands and some types of containers by washing in water; therefore, if the hands are contaminated, they should be rinsed in a dilute sodium hypochlorite solution, and then washed thoroughly in warm water. Containers, such as trays used for reducing prints which will be later used to hold paper developers, should also be cleaned in this way. The dilute hypochlorite solution can be prepared by adding one ounce of any commercial hypochloride solution, such as Clorox or Sunny Sol, to one quart of water. These simple precautions, of course, apply to the following "dry" reducer which also contains thiourea.

SMALL-AREA REDUCTION

Let's spend just a bit more time in this department since it is here that much work can be done to make good prints better. First of all, buy enough chemicals to make the following solutions, plus a small bottle of methyl alcohol, and you will be all set. No need to get any more, a little of these solutions will go a long way.

Solution A

Iodine	20 grains
Methyl Alcohol.............	1 ounce

The iodine is a little stubborn about dissolving, but placing the components in a capped bottle and shaking it will hasten the solution.

Solution B

Thiourea (Thiocarbamide)....	40 grains
Water to make.............	1 ounce

These are your stock reducing solutions which will keep indefinitely. To use them, mix equal parts of A and B with an equal part of methyl alcohol. An assortment of small brushes, a bit of cotton wrapped around a stick, and an additional wad of cotton will complete this inexpensive equipment—a small price to pay to obtain sparkling results in your prints.

The advantage of this reducer is that it is known as a "dry" reducer, so called because the print is worked on while in a bone-dry state. Then, too, the active reducer ingredients are dissolved in alcohol which has a tendency to evaporate rapidly—so much so that the print quickly becomes dry after each application of the solution. Therein lies the success of this particular method; it allows exceedingly fine work to be done without staining the print. Furthermore, most other solutions for the same purpose are water-soluble. When used on a damp print, as they must be, it is more difficult to confine the action of the reducing solution to fine print details. This method eliminates that difficulty.

Let's suppose that you wish to improve the roundness of a cloud. The dry print is placed on a flat, well-lighted surface, with the prepared working solution in a small glass beside it. Also have ready a medium-size cotton pad and the bottle of alcohol. Dip one of the brushes into the reducing solution and carefully apply it to the cloud area to be lightened. Since, at this dilution, the reducer works fairly rapidly, do not allow the tiny pool of solution to stand on the print for very long. Saturate the pad with the alcohol, and quickly wipe it over the area just reduced with the brush. As with Farmer's reducer, it is better to remove the silver a little at a time, so that the reduction may be controlled more easily. Now repeat the process, applying the reducer and then wiping it away with the cotton pad containing the alcohol.

When working up lighter print areas, such as a cloud highlight, be sure that you do not over-reduce the whole cloud down to the white paper base. Of course, that's going too far. Keep in mind that areas of least density are acted upon sooner than are the shadows. If the density seems to go down a little too fast for accurate control, try either one or a combination of both of these alternatives:

(a) Do not wait quite so long to remove the reducer after each successive application, or (b) dilute the working solution with another part of alcohol.

In portraits, this method of controlled local reduction affords an excellent way of adding eye catchlights if they are missing. Just place a tiny drop of the solution in the desired place and let the reducer eat the silver completely away. If you make the catchlights a trifle large or irregular, they may be rounded easily later when the print is spotted.

After the print has been reduced to your satisfaction, place it in a bath of plain hypo for a few minutes and then wash it in running water for the usual length of time. Immersion in the hypo bath is very necessary because the active ingredient in the reducer is the iodine which becomes "neutralized" in the hypo. Thus the possibility of the treated print areas becoming lighter or slightly stained by small amounts of residual iodine is removed. Rinse out the brushes you used, as well as the wad of cotton, so that they will be ready for some other purpose next time you need them.

Before actually starting to work on one of your good pictures, it is definitely advisable to practice on a few old or discarded prints, so that you may first attain some degree of proficiency. It would be unfortunate to over-reduce a lovely 14 by 17-inch print, and then accuse this method of spoiling it for you. So, by all means, practice a bit—it's not hard to learn.

INTENSIFICATION

Do you recall the story in Hale's *Peterkin Papers* about the fellow who accidentally put too much sugar in his cup of coffee? His entire family tried adding vinegar and several other things to make it taste like good coffee again, but without success. The problem was finally solved by a friend who suggested that they throw it away and pour a fresh cup!

Well, intensifying a print is much like adding vinegar to remedy sweet coffee. If the print had been made right in the first place, intensification wouldn't be necessary. And, furthermore, it would probably take less time to go back and make a good new print than to intensify one which had been accidentally underexposed.

Nonetheless, the process does have some merit. It can salvage a light or weak print, and the resulting image is a pleasing brown-black color that is as permanent as the original silver image. In addition, the degree of intensification can be easily controlled over a somewhat limited range. Just don't try to intensify a print locally, because, if you do, the intensified tone will not match the rest of the print in image color.

Among the various intensifiers for negatives, chromium is the only one that can be recommended for use on paper prints. This is because many solutions owe their intensifying properties to a staining action, or else their effect depends on the production of an image that may not be permanent, as does that of the mercuric-chloride intensifier. Potassium bichromate (the "chromate" signifies chromium) overcomes these difficulties. The two stock solutions may be prepared in advance, and each will keep well.

Stock Solution A
10% solution of potassium bichromate

Stock Solution B
10% solution of hydrochloric acid

The degree of intensification may be partially controlled by the percentage of hydrochloric acid present in the bleaching bath. The more acid used, the less the intensification, and vice versa.

Although the action will depend somewhat upon the image tone of the original print, the following table will serve as a basis from which to start. This bath should be made up just prior to use.

	Slight Intensification	*Medium Intensification*
Stock Solution A.........	20 units	20 units
Stock Solution B.........	40 units	10 units
Distilled water to make...	100 units	100 units

All operations directly concerned with the intensification may be carried out in normal room light. In order to avoid any reversal of the silver chloride image, intense sunlight, however, should be avoided.

Place the print in a tray of water for about 15 minutes so that the gelatin emulsion can expand fully. This is necessary if the bleaching and subsequent operations are to act uniformly over the entire surface of the picture. Then bleach the print until the traces of the black silver image have been removed. This will occur in about 5 minutes. However, do not fail to allow the print to remain in the bleach as long as necessary to remove *all* traces of the silver image.

Next, place the print in running water for not less than a half hour and at least until the orange coloration has been *completely* removed. Immersing the bleached print in a 2 percent solution of Kodalk Balanced Alkali (which causes the gelatin to swell slightly) will facilitate the removal of the bichromate.

The print is now ready for redevelopment with any normal paper developer. Packaged developers are, of course, very convenient to use. The redeveloped image appears in a normal developing time. There is no need to place the print in a stop or fixing bath; just wash it for about half an hour in running water, and dry. Do not use blotters for drying—the emulsion is quite soft at this point and would probably pick up considerable lint.

It is best to wait until the print is dry before finally appraising the darkening effect of the intensifying treatment. If the intensification does not appear to have been sufficient, the procedure may be repeated, but there is little to be gained by intensifying prints more than twice.

Chapter 12

Control Processes

THE TERM "control process" has a sort of aura about it, hasn't it? But there need be no mystery. By "control process" we mean a process for regulating or modifying strictly "mechanical" results, particularly with regard to *local* print areas. Thus, ordinary dodging is a simple control technique. When the average photographer speaks of a control process, however, he usually means something on the order of the bromoil, paper-negative, or gum printing processes. In spite of the fact they occasion awe or reverence among pictorialists, very few of these processes seem to be surviving the test of time. The modern photographer neither tolerates the extra fuss and bother nor desires the somewhat "fuzzy" results usually obtained with the old processes. So, since we're modern, you and I, we can skip most of these techniques. And yet a few controls are worth considering; for instance, let's take a look at the paper-negative process.

PAPER-NEGATIVE PRINTS

"If it were not for the paper-negative process," said pictorialist Cecil B. Atwater, "many of my negatives would be worthless. The nature of my business is both an advantage and a disadvantage. I see a lot of country, but I have to be constantly on the move. I cannot come back tomorrow, when the light will be better, or when there may be clouds in the sky. I have to make my pictures now, and if there are flaws and defects due to factors beyond my control, I have to correct them in the paper negative."

Of all the known control processes, the paper-negative is perhaps the best known, the easiest, and the one which permits the greatest control. Certainly it is the oldest; as long ago as 1835 Fox Talbot made successful photographs using light-sensitized sheets of "best quality" writing paper.

Is making paper negatives a lost art? Let's hope not! How else could you easily remove a shiny, incongruous car from a photograph of an otherwise picturesque country lane? In other words, the paper-negative technique is a wonderful way to rework a picture which cannot be retaken under ideal circumstances. It doesn't take much skill by means of this process to move, add, or delete telephone poles, tin cans, clouds or nearly any small details which, either by their presence or absence, detract from an otherwise pleasing composition.

Equipment. You will need only one item of equipment in addition to that found in almost any darkroom for making enlargements. This is a contact printing frame the size of your final print. Since large paper negatives up to 16 by 20 inches in size are exhibited in salons, it is recommended that a 16 by 20-inch frame be obtained if you are interested in this phase of print making, then you will be able to handle practically any size of print the occasion may demand. It would be unfortunate, for example, to buy an 11 by 14-inch frame and then wish to make a 14 by 17-inch print.

Procedure. Starting with a normal negative—usually of a landscape or seascape—here, in brief, are the steps involved in making a paper-negative print:

Step 1. Make an enlargement, cropped and dodged as you want the final print to be. Use a pencil or artist's stump to *darken* any detail or area which needs to be subdued.

Step 2. From this enlargement, make a contact paper negative. The usual retouching tools and technique can be used to alter details on the negative. Remember that any pencil retouching on the negative means that the final print will be *lightened* in the corresponding places.

Step 3. From the retouched paper negative, make the final print by contact. That's all there is to it—almost.

Let's take a look at some of the finer points in the process.

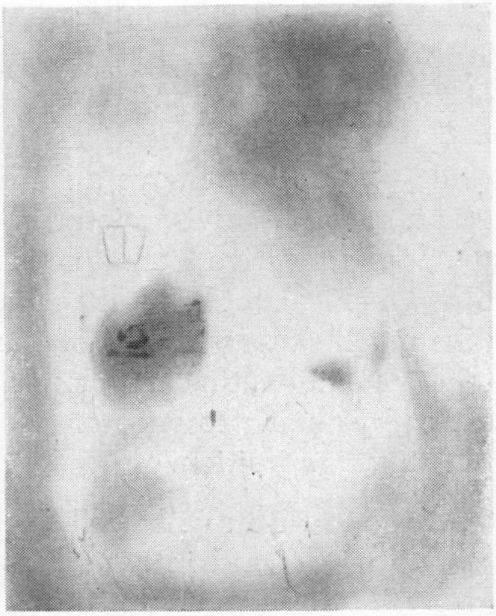

First step in the paper-negative process is to make a low-contrast print on single-weight paper. This print is then retouched with a pencil on either the emulsion or reverse side of the print. This retouching is shown at the right.

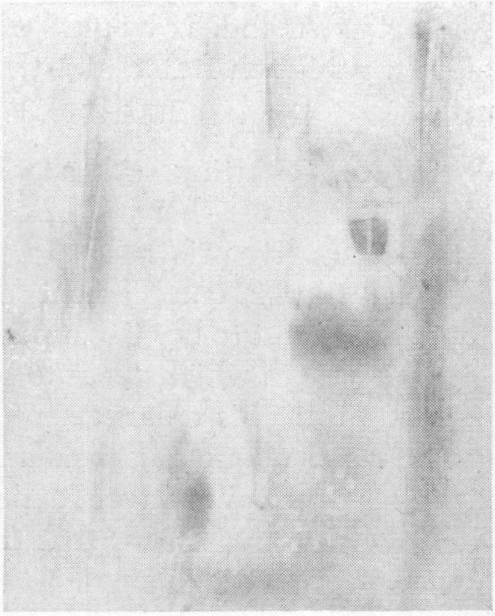

The retouched positive is then used to make a paper-negative print with an ordinary contact printing frame. The paper negative can also be retouched with a pencil. This pencil work on the reverse side of the negative is shown at the right.

The final print is a contact print from the retouched paper negative. Compare this version with the straight print and notice how the automobile was eliminated and the street-light detail was restored. Final print is on a rough-textured paper.

As in any artistic technique, there are some pitfalls to be avoided—any artist knows it isn't difficult to paint a poor picture!

In the first place, you want the contrast and the shadow and highlight details of the final paper-negative print to match those of a carefully made, top-quality "straight" enlargement from the same negative. There's no point in being evasive about it—this close match is not easy to achieve. If you have had any experience in making copies, you probably know it's generally advisable to make both of the intermediates low in contrast and fairly heavy in density. Since they actually are used as *transparencies*, by all means judge these intermediates by *transmitted* light, not by reflected light as you do an ordinary print.

Viewed by reflected light, each intermediate will seem far too dark, almost beyond redemption. But hold each dark positive or negative up to a fairly bright illuminator, and even the darkest shadow areas will appear luminous with full detail—or at least they should. Your aim should be a *transparency* that appears normal in density, but has easily discernible detail in both highlights and shadows and is very low or flat in contrast. The lower the contrast, particularly in the positive, the easier it is to retain the details at both ends of the tonal scale. Consequently, the softest grade of paper—usually designated as No. 1 contrast—should be used as a general recommendation. Don't be concerned at this point about the flat appearance of the picture; in going from step to step, the process has a tendency to gain contrast and, unless the intermediates are kept intentionally at a low contrast, the final print will be so extremely contrasty as to be completely unusable. Then, too, it's an easy matter to make any necessary adjustments in contrast in the final print by simply choosing an appropriate grade of printing paper.

Grain in the paper-negative print. In contact printing both the paper negative and the final print, the exposing light has to penetrate the paper support. The diffuse outline of individual paper fibers in the stock are, therefore, also recorded in the negative and final print emulsions as a textured pattern superimposed on the actual subject. In some instances this texture, or grain, as it is more commonly called, is fairly desirable. If it is not excessively heavy, it can lend a pleasing aspect of "pictorial diffusion" which often enhances some types of subjects, such as atmospheric landscape scenes, crumbling buildings, and the like. It certainly hides any graininess of the negative.

Generally speaking, however, one of the problems in the paper-negative process is not to let the paper grain become too pronounced. These are modern times when sharp, clear pictures are more in vogue than are the overdiffused, mushy prints of the mid 20's. For this reason, it is always advisable to use a smooth-surfaced, single-weight paper, such as Kodabromide N or A (and, of course, No. 1 contrast) for both the paper positive and the paper negative. To help hide excessive paper texture, a rough-surfaced paper such as Kodak Opal R, S, or Z is suggested for the *final* print. Rough surfaces also help to hide any rough retouching!

Another alternative for eliminating much of the grain is to use a film positive. This is particularly feasible if much retouching does not have to be done on the positive.

Retouching the intermediates. Any retouching in the paper-negative process should be applied only while the intermediates are viewed as *transparencies,* i.e., by transmitted light. For viewing the print as a transparency while this work is being done, a retouching stand is ideal, a negative viewing box is satisfactory, or, lacking either of these, the print may be taped by its borders to a windowpane so as to "look outdoors." Daylight will usually provide adequate illumination for the work. It helps to mask off with opaque paper any light from the illuminator not covered by the picture. Otherwise, this bright stray light will "stop down your eyes" so that you cannot see the details of the scene so readily.

First, using a pointed pencil, clean from the positive intermediate print all small white spots, such as might be caused by dust on the film negative. Then, tone down any objectionably bright areas by gradual shading with the pencil. If the areas are large and of comparatively even tone, they may be treated with a tuft of cotton and a small quantity of powdered graphite or crayon sauce. Blend any unevenness with an artist's stump; a few stumps of different size will be helpful. Build up the density gradually, and blend it in smoothly with the neighboring print areas. Both an art-gum eraser and a kneaded rubber eraser are handy tools for correcting minor mistakes and for general "touching-up" purposes.

The most common error in paper-negative making is over-retouching so that the result appears artificial. Better no retouching at all than too much.

All in all, retouching either the positive or the paper negative is very similar to the technique described on page 128 for retouching and dodging prints with pencil work on matte acetate.

Any retouching which should be sharp, such as lines and other details, should be drawn on the emulsion side of the positive or the negative, as the case may be. Retouch larger areas, such as those which require general smudging, on the reverse side of the intermediate.

The use of transmitted light, the retouching implements, and the general recommendations are the same for retouching both the positive and the negative. The key difference is this: Whereas every mark you make on the positive will be recorded as added density in the final print, the retouched negative areas will be lighter in the final print. The negative, then, is the place to lighten cloud or portrait highlights, or catchlights in the eyes; also, to brighten teeth or to emphasize reflections in water or back-lighted scenes, and so on.

Again, be careful about over-retouching. However, don't let this precaution keep you from making tone alterations if they are needed, because this is the reason for making a paper-negative print in the first place.

A new technique. With the advent of two products, Kodak Selectol-Soft Developer and Kodak Opalure Print Film, an increased degree of control has been made available to the photographer interested in the paper-negative process. Opalure Print Film is a material designed for producing warm portrait prints. Its emulsion is similar to that of Kodak Opal Paper, but an important difference is that it is coated on a white film base. This film base, unlike paper, is homogeneous. This means that light will be diffused in passing through this base but will form no perceptible pattern which will be recorded by the adjacent light-sensitive emulsion. Thus Opalure Print Film is an ideal material for use in making the intermediate positive and negative if no texture is desired in the final print. Furthermore, because its surface is ideal for accepting pencil work, any desired retouching or corrections can be incorporated easily. To help reduce expense, an ordinary film positive and an Opalure Print Film negative can be used as the intermediates.

In order not to build up excessive contrast, and because Opalure Print Film is available only in one (normal) grade of contrast, Kodak Selectol-*Soft* Developer should be used for *both* the positive and the negative. This developer yields very soft images in the recommended development time of 2 minutes at 68 F, diluted 1 to 1, and at the same time builds up contrast gradually with continued development. Consequently, it is important to develop both the Opalure Print Film positive and the subsequent negative for about 1½ to 2 minutes, but no longer. Immerse the exposed film *face up* in the developing solution, being careful to have the developer cover every portion of the film quickly and evenly. Agitate the film *continuously* during development to help avoid streaks which, if present, might be incorporated in the final print.

All during processing, keep in mind that the emulsion of Opalure Print Film is physically soft—more so than that of photographic papers—and that the film must, therefore, be handled with care. To help avoid scratching or otherwise abrading the emulsion, processed films should be hung up by one corner to dry. Do *not* place the film between blotters to dry or the emulsion will stick to the blotter next to it and be ruined.

The final print is, of course, made by contact with the paper negative in the contact printing frame. Good contact is imperative during the exposure, as it is also when making the paper negative. If necessary, sheets of blotting paper may be placed behind the printing frame to help secure good contact.

The paper-negative process is at its best for landscapes or other scenes where the print benefits by de-emphasis of details, and a misty-morning or old-world-charm effect is desired.

Diapositive-master negative control. Would you rather spend all evening making one *good* print than one mediocre print with enough time left over to watch television for an hour or two? If you're after the super print, then these next few paragraphs are for you.

This control process is similar to the paper negative process except that both the intermediate positive and the duplicate negative are made on film. In brief, the steps are as follows:

Step 1. From the original negative make a print by enlargement onto an 8 by 10-inch sheet of film.

Step 2. After processing this film, which is a positive transparency called a diapositive, retouch it as desired.

Step 3. Place the retouched positive on an illuminator and copy it onto the largest size sheet of film that your enlarger takes.

Step 4. Process this film normally to make the master negative and retouch it as desired.

Step 5. Use the master negative to make as many super identical enlargements as you need.

Now, it sounds like some extra trouble to go through these extra steps so there must be some excellent reasons for doing it. And there are. For instance, you have absolute control over the contrast and density of the master negative regardless of the contrast and density of the original negative. Also, you can retouch to your heart's content—by means of reducer, pencil, ground glass, or dye—on either or both of the film intermediates, and without any danger of spoiling a valuable original negative. It's this control in retouching, of course, that appeals to the master pictorialists, such as Fassbender, Shigeta, Underwood, and others. It's a nearly ideal method of lightening or darkening any area of a picture without resulting in a textured or fuzzy print a la carelessly made prints by the paper negative process.

The two most important retouching tools are Crocein Scarlet for dye dodging and Farmer's reducer for chemically reducing either or both the diapositive and the master negative. Just remember the principles that: dye on the diapositive or reducer on the master negative will make the final paper print correspondingly darker; dye on master negative and reducer on the positive will make the final print lighter. Look up the technique of using dye, on page 106, and the technique of using reducer, on page 170. Farmer's reducer works the same way on film as it does on paper except that film requires a somewhat stronger solution.

Copying the retouched diapositive presents no particular problem: Use an ordinary illuminator or printing box but be sure that the lighting is suitably diffused with opal glass so that the illumination is evenly distributed. Mask off any area of the illuminated surface not covered by the diapositive. Scan the entire transilluminated diapositive with an exposure meter to obtain an average reading and expose the master negative film as indicated. Don't neglect to take the bellows extension factor into account when calculating the exposure. Obviously, a view camera with a ground glass back is the most convenient type of equipment to use for making the master negative.

Kodak Commercial Film is suggested as a film material to be used for both the diapositive and the master negative. It has a comparatively low speed (A.S.A. Index of 6 for tungsten light) which is a help in controlling the exposure when used for this purpose. In addition, it is a blue-sensitive film which means that the development may be carried out under a red safelight (Kodak Safelight Filter, Wratten Series 1).

To help preserve all possible tonal range and detail of the original, the diapositive should be exposed so that even the brightest highlights should have a slight density and the development should be slightly less than normal. This will result in a transparency that is fairly dense and flat in contrast: It is not, in other words, a transparency that has the same characteristics as one intended only for viewing. In addition, the master negative should be a *trifle* more dense than an original negative of normal density.

This should be sufficient information to get started with this technique of techniques. As a final word, plan out all the steps *before* you start: know exactly what part of the picture you are going to make lighter, what part darker, and exactly how and at what stage of the process it is going to be done. It's work to make a print this way but well worth it if you do a good job.

DWARFED BY A. UNDERWOOD, FPSA

The longer you look at these two pictures, the more different they become! Compare the sky, the pattern of the rapids, the rocky foreground, and the tone of the figure.

DWARFED

BY A. UNDERWOOD, FPSA

The differences between these pictures were made with Farmer's reducer and with dye either on the large intermediate film positive or on the final duplicate negative.

MONOCHROME-DYE PRINTING, A NEW CONTROL PROCESS

If there were only some way to make a print with "velvet" black shadows and "beaded-screen" highlights, then you would have *quality!* It is a fact, of course, that the blacker the black it is possible to obtain, the better the print quality will be, provided the gradation is satisfactory. The silver in an ordinary photograph can be only so black and no more. But a photograph with a *dye* image can possess a depth of shadows which extends even beyond that of silver. In other words, dye particles can produce a *blacker* black than can silver particles, probably because of the higher reflectance (they're shinier) of the tiny silver particles themselves. For the technically minded, this fact can be readily checked with a reflection densitometer.

All this is quite important *to you*. It means that here is a convenient printing technique whereby *you can obtain better print quality than you ever had before*. But that's far from all: Here is a new control process by which prints can be made in any shade or tint of color desired, from jet-black to elephant-pink to seaweed green! And with perfect control over a range of contrasts.

Monochrome-dye printing is based on the Kodak Dye Transfer Process. If you are at all interested in this undreamed-of print quality, obtain from your photographic dealer a copy of the book entitled "Kodak Dye Transfer Process," which contains complete details on dye printing in natural colors. However, keep in mind that making a *monochrome*-dye print entails less than one-third of the time, materials, and difficulties involved in making a full-color print by the same process. For example, there are no problems of registration or color balance. The fact is that making a monochrome-dye print is considerably easier than might first be imagined after glancing through the book mentioned above.

Let's say it again, the process of producing monochrome-dye prints is not difficult. In fact, the first portion of the work follows the steps used in making an ordinary enlargement. The remainder of the procedure is no more difficult than the first part and requires neither much practice nor particular skill to make beautiful prints. At least, read this through to see if you're interested.

In outline, the process is as follows: From an ordinary black-and-white negative an exposure is made on a sheet of Kodak Matrix Film in the desired print size. This film can be handled in much the same manner as enlarging paper, the outstanding difference being that it is placed emulsion *down* on the enlarging easel. After exposure, it is developed in a tanning developer and then is given a hot-water treatment which produces an image composed of a gelatin relief.

By way of a brief explanation, a gelatin relief image is composed of gelatin of varying thicknesses, the actual amount in a given place being directly proportional to the "blackness," or amount of silver, in that place. Thus the print shadow areas, which received a heavy exposure and are very dense, are represented in a relief image by a comparatively thick layer of gelatin. On the other hand, highlight areas, which received considerably less exposure and have very little silver, are comprised of a fairly thin layer of gelatin. A gelatin relief image might be considered as a topographical map with high, "mountainous" shadows and low, "valley-like" highlights.

Since gelatin is a porous, moisture-absorbent substance, a gelatin relief image immersed in a dye bath absorbs the dye in proportion to the amount of gelatin in a given area; therefore, shad-

The Matrix Film is exposed through the back and processed in a developer which hardens the exposed parts of the emulsion.

ows contain relatively lots of dye, whereas highlights contain only small amounts. A gelatin relief image of this type is commonly known in the trade as a "matrix" since "matrix" means literally a mold for use in casting.

After this matrix is dyed in a (monochrome) dye solution, the surface dye is rinsed off, and then the dye image is transferred to a sheet of mordanted paper—the mordant locking the dye particles firmly in place and preventing them from "running." If desired, the matrix may be redyed and retransferred until as many prints as necessary are produced.

Throughout the entire process, the many controls inherent in the Dye Transfer Process, in addition to ordinary photographic techniques, such as dodging and flashing, can be applied.

Equipment and materials. Most of the equipment required for monochrome-dye printing is standard darkroom equipment. Here is what you will need: an enlarger, three trays, a printing easel, a large squeegee (such as a Kodak Rubber Squeegee or a Kodak Professional Print Roller) which is at least as wide as the maximum-size print you plan to make, and a surface such as that provided by a flat table top on which to make the actual transfer. The surface should be flat and smooth; if convenient, a sheet of plate glass, Carrara glass, Bakelite, or any other material with a

After development, the film is given a hot-water treatment which removes the unhardened parts of the emulsion making a relief image.

similar surface may be used. It should be several inches larger than the prints to be made and should be mounted on a worktable of convenient height. The Kodak Dye Transfer Blanket is a convenience, but not an actual necessity. Incidentally, the transfer technique is described on page 200. Kodak Matrix Film and Kodak Dye Transfer Paper comprise the print-making materials.

Solutions. The complete list of solutions required includes Kodak Tanning Developer A and Kodak Tanning Developer B, Kodak Matrix Film Fixer, Kodak Dye Transfer Paper Conditioner, Kodak Matrix Highlight Reducer, glacial acetic acid, sodium acetate, and monochrome dye. These solutions, except the monochrome dye, are the same as those required for the Kodak Dye Transfer Process and are available in individual packages and are simple to prepare for use.

A suitable monochrome-dye solution. There are at least three different, convenient sources of obtaining a satisfactory monochrome dye. Probably the best is the Kodak Black Matrix Dye Set, a product intended for use in making Dye Transfer "derivations" or in other special Dye Transfer applications. This is available in an inexpensive, two-solution kit, one bottle containing the black-dye stock solution, and the other, a buffer solution. The

After processing, wipe off only the reverse side of the film and hang it up to dry. Be careful of the wet emulsion since it scratches easily.

directions which should be followed for mixing and using the two solutions are contained in this kit. About one quart of dye working solution is a convenient amount to mix at one time, and this much will accommodate matrices up to 16 by 20 inches in size. The dye can be re-used to make many prints, and has a good storage life.

The second source of the monochrome dye is the Kodak Flexichrome Color Set. To make a working solution, simply dissolve the contents of a jar of any Flexichrome Color of the desired color in 1 quart of 2 percent acetic acid. Two or more Flexichrome Colors may be mixed together to form practically any combination of printing color. For example, the Kodak Flexichrome Modeling Agent may be mixed with a jar of the dark-brown color to form a selenium-like print tone.

A third technique for preparing a monochrome-dye solution is simply to mix the three Kodak Dye Transfer Dyes in a suitable proportion. Use with the buffers and acetic acid, as described in the instructions included with the Dye Transfer Dyes for making a normal-contrast stock solution. For example, a brownish "portrait" tone may be obtained by adding the three dyes together in the ratio of 3 magenta, 4 cyan, and 6 yellow. It should be noted that a mixture of Dye Transfer Dyes has somewhat less printing

While the matrix is dyeing, condition several sheets of Kodak Dye Transfer Paper and squeegee one of them onto a smooth surface.

density than the dye in the Kodak Black Matrix Dye Set and, accordingly, the matrix exposure should be somewhat on the heavy side if Dye Transfer Dyes are to be used for monochrome printing. Let's briefly follow the process through, step by step, to see the exact technique of monochrome-dye printing:

Step 1. With a Kodak Safelight Filter, Wratten Series 1A, as the darkroom illumination, place a sheet of Kodak Matrix Film, *emulsion side down,* on a sheet of black paper on the enlarging easel.

Step 2. The relative speeds of Kodak Matrix Film and Kodabromide Paper, No. 2, are approximately the same and, therefore, the photographic paper may be used for making hasty test-strip exposures if desired. Developing time for the film in a tray of the tanning developer is 2 minutes at 68 F with constant agitation.

Step 3. Pour out the developer and rinse the film quickly for 20 to 30 seconds in cold, running water.

Step 4. Transfer the film to the Kodak Matrix Film Fixer bath for about 1 minute. Room light may be turned on after ½ minute in this solution.

Step 5. Prepare a tray of hot water at about 120 F, and place the film in this water for 1 minute with constant agitation. Repeat

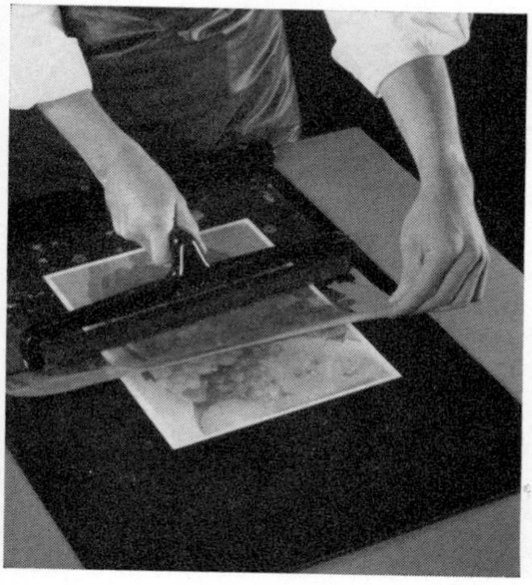

Rinse the dyed matrix in a 1 percent acetic acid bath and then roll it with one firm stroke into contact with the Dye Transfer Paper.

with three other fresh hot-water baths for ½ minute each or until all the soluble gelatin has been removed from the film. (Note that the film is backed with a gelatin coating. Be certain that this, too, is dissolved away.)

Step 6. Place the matrix, emulsion up, in a tray of cold water to chill it for ½ minute. At this point, the film should be hung up to dry. Do not insert the matrix directly into the dye solution, because, when an undried matrix is dyed, it is more susceptible to abrasions and may tend to pick up solid particles in the various solutions.

Step 7. Place the film in the dye solution for not less than 10 minutes *with intermittent agitation.* During the time the film is dyeing, soak one or more sheets of Kodak Dye Transfer Paper in the Kodak Dye Transfer Paper Conditioner solution for about 20 minutes; longer soaking will do no harm.

Step 8. Prepare a solution of 1 percent acetic acid, remove the matrix from the dye bath, and rinse it in the acetic acid solution for 1 minute. It is convenient to mix a gallon or so of 1 percent acetic acid because a fresh first-rinse bath is used for each print.

Step 9. The matrix can then be placed in a second tray of 1 percent acetic acid, called a "holding bath," until ready for transfer.

It is important to dry the finished print as quickly as possible to help prevent diffusion of the dye image. A blotter roll is a help.

Step 10. Place a sheet of conditioned Dye Transfer Paper on the flat transfer surface and squeegee it firmly with a flat rubber squeegee to remove excess surface moisture.

Step 11. Remove the matrix from the holding bath, drain it for only 2 or 3 seconds, and then put it, emulsion to emulsion, on top of the Dye Transfer Paper. Immediately roll the two into contact and cover them with a blotting paper, the Dye Transfer Blanket, or a sheet of plastic for about 5 minutes.

Step 12. After the dye has completely transferred from the matrix to the paper, remove the matrix, rinse it in warm water, and dry it. Or, after rinsing, the matrix may be redyed if additional prints are desired.

Exposure latitude. The exposure latitude of the Matrix Film is moderately wide—particularly on the overexposure side of normal. The correct exposure just covers with a thin veil of gelatin the highest diffuse highlights in which detail should be retained. It may be helpful in determining the exposure to lay a coin or some other small, opaque object over a highlight area during a test-strip exposure. After hot-water development, the area covered by the coin should be perfectly clear and, by comparison, the adjacent highlight area should have a very light gelatin deposit.

If, by accident, the matrix should be overexposed, this can be corrected after the matrix is completely dyed. To do this, the matrix is simply placed in a tray of plain water and agitated until dye has washed out until only enough is left in the matrix to produce an image of normal density when transferred. Keep a record of the amount of water used and the time of immersion so that the results can be repeated with subsequent prints if desired. *Go easy here:* the water causes the dye to bleed out very rapidly, and a 15-second rinse, for example, will make quite a difference.

After the water treatment, the matrix is rinsed in a tray of 1 percent acetic acid and the dye image is ready for transfer. Large amounts of "wash-back" should be avoided because an overexposed but washed-back matrix may tend to increase transfer time and the sharpness of the transferred image may suffer. Then, too, the gradation is not so satisfactory.

Contrast control. Kodak Matrix Film is available in only one normal grade of contrast. However, the process can accommodate a considerable range of negative contrast in any or a combination of several steps throughout the process. The first contrast control is the selection of the correct filter for use on the enlarging lens. With a negative of average contrast, printed in a diffusion enlarger, use a Kodak Wratten Filter No. 2B over the enlarging lens. This light-yellowish filter controls the degree of light penetration in the yellowish matrix emulsion, and its use helps to maintain normal print contrast. A Kodak Wratten Filter No. 35 (violet) will result in decreased contrast, whereas a yellow filter, such as the Kodak Wratten Filter No. 6, will increase the contrast.

The second place in the process where contrast can be controlled is in the mixing of the matrix developer. In fact, this is where the major degree of control *should* take place. The developer for the Kodak Matrix Film is a two-solution, ready-mixed type of developer which needs only to be mixed with water for use. The contrast of the print is controlled by adjusting the relative amounts of the two developer components according to the following table:

MATRIX DEVELOPER PROPORTIONS FOR CONTRAST CONTROL

Type of negative	*Kodak Matrix Developer* Part A (in cc)	Part B (in cc)
Low-Contrast	75	75
Normal-Contrast	50	100
High-Contrast	20	130

This table assumes that a diffusion or cold-light enlarger (such as the Kodak Flurolite Enlarger) will be used. For a condenser enlarger, do not use a yellow filter over the enlarger lens for the first few trial prints unless you are printing a negative of abnormally low contrast.

For each of the types of negatives included in the above table, the total quantity of developer recommended is 150 cc; this is sufficient for one 8 by 10-inch matrix. For each matrix of larger size, the quantity of developer must be increased as follows:

Matrix Size (in inches)		*Total cc of Developer*
11 x 14	....	300
14 x 17	....	450
16 x 20	....	600

Contrast can be increased slightly by adding a small amount of 28 percent acetic acid to the first acid rinse bath. Be sure to measure and keep track of the exact amount. This works as follows: After dyeing the matrix in the usual manner, the matrix is removed from the dye bath and transferred directly, without draining, to the first rinse bath containing the excess acid. The matrix should be agitated continuously for from 1 to 5 minutes in this bath, depending on the amount of contrast needed. The acid "drives" more dye into the shadow areas of the matrix, and thus increases the contrast. If the contrast of an initial monochrome-dye print is thought to be excessive, the contrast of successive transfers can be reduced by adding a small amount of 5 percent solution of sodium acetate solution to the first acid rinse bath. From 1 to 5 cc of the sodium-acetate solution can be added to 150 cc of the standard rinse.

Highlight control. Many pictorialists, in making ordinary black-and-white prints, intentionally make excessively dark prints and then "bite them back" with a cutting reducer, such as Farmer's reducer, in order to insure that their prints will have both brilliant highlights and deep shadows. Some careful workers may perhaps swab excessively dark shadow areas with a solution of Farmer's reducer to lighten them suitably. Similar control can be exercised by means of Kodak Matrix Highlight Reducer, which can be used to lighten the highlights of intentionally overprinted matrices or to salvage prints in which the highlights are somewhat too veiled. The procedure is simply to add from 1 to 5 cc of the Kodak Matrix Highlight Reducer to 150 cc of the first acid rinse. The control takes place in the dyed matrix, remember, and not in the finished paper print. Shadow areas can be rinsed locally with water in order to lighten them. A good-quality camel's hair brush may be used for this work.

Transfer technique. A clean, positive transfer technique is essential to good results and, accordingly, a brief description is in order: Lower the dyed and rinsed matrix so that one end is in contact with one end of the transfer paper. Some of the excess acid rinsing bath should drain down the matrix to form a long narrow "bead" or pool at the juncture of matrix and paper. Place a heavy length of glass or some other suitable weight over only about one-half inch of the matrix so that the matrix and paper are held together at this point. Then, using only a single sweep of the roller, squeegee the remainder of the matrix into firm contact with the transfer paper. The "bead" of moisture rolling along just ahead of the squeegee will help to keep air bubbles from being trapped between the matrix and paper.

The Kodak Dye Transfer Blanket will be a convenience in making the transfer, and its use is particularly recommended if many prints are to be made by the monochrome-dye method. Its use is quite simple: Grasp the left corner of the transfer blanket, pull it taut, and place the matrix, gelatin side up, on the blanket. Swing the blanket over close to the paper, keeping it taut so that the matrix does not touch the paper. Lay the roller on the blanket near the hinge and then roll it over the blanket *once,* with a smooth, uniform stroke to bring the matrix into contact with the paper.

Prints in any color. Do you have trouble in toning silver-print snow scenes just the right shade of blue? Or a portrait the desired hue of rich chocolate brown? With monochrome-dye printing, finding the exact hue to use is simple. Prints may easily be made orange, green, pink, blue, or even black. Just select from a Kodak Flexichrome Dye Set, whatever color of dye you wish, or mix up your own combination of Kodak Dye Transfer Dyes. Add about 20 cc of 28 percent acetic acid, plus all the color from one "button" or jar of Flexichrome Dye, to one quart of water. This should make a normal working dye solution. If more contrasty results are desired, add a little more acid to the solution.

Probably the best way to work is to use the Kodak Black Matrix Dye as a neutral base, and then to tint it with a small amount of either a Flexichrome Color or one or more of the Dye Transfer concentrates. Keep a record of the exact proportions of the dye components used, since this will permit prints of a particular color to be duplicated at a later date.

Ordinary color-mixing techniques are used in preparing a dye working solution of the desired hue. Suppose, after making an initial transfer, you think that the tone of the print is too cold. Simply add a few drops of magenta and yellow dye concentrate to the working solution and, after transferring the redyed matrix a second time, check the image tone of the second print against that of the first. In a similar manner, cyan dye will neutralize a print that is too reddish, and yellow dye will neutralize one that is too bluish. This process offers limitless possibilities of hue variation and, furthermore, for the first time enables the photographer to mix the *precise* color he wants for a specific subject.

Variations and double printing. Ordinarily, photographers shy away from anything which sounds as complicated as "double printing." But the monochrome-dye process offers many interesting—and simple—possibilities of this sort. Suppose you wanted to print a snow scene in which the middle-to-highlight areas would be neutral in hue, but the shadows would be a decidedly bluish color to simulate a sunlight-reflected skylight lighting condition. This could be accomplished easily in a monochrome-dye print by making the first transfer with a dye of a neutral hue. Without disturbing the freshly made print, the matrix could then be redyed in a bluish dye bath. The unwanted blue dye in the highlight areas would be washed out by simply agitating the matrix in a tray of plain water. When enough blue dye had "bled" away, the matrix would be rinsed in the ½ percent acetic-acid holding bath and then transferred a second time to the imbibition printing paper. Of course, the two transfers would have to be made in register, but this could be accomplished in one of several convenient ways. The one requiring no extra equipment whatsoever simply entails placing clear Kodapak Sheet over the print and registering the redyed matrix with the print image. The purpose of the Kodapak Sheet is, of course, to prevent any premature transfer of the dye in the matrix to the gelatin of the paper. With the two images in register, one side of the matrix is held securely in place, and the Kodapak Sheet is slipped out of the sandwich. The print roller is then used to squeegee the two images into perfect contact.

Using this general double-transfer technique, many variations of double-toned images can be made. However, the second transfer could also be used as a means of introducing a second image from a different negative. Thus, "Drink No-Thirst Cola" in cool, blue-green letters could appear in the sky area over a blazing, orange desert scene. Or a black, palm-tree silhouette could be added easily to a moonlight, ocean-beach picture taken in Maine. Again, the process offers limitless opportunities for the imaginative photographer.

Monochrome prints from Kodak Ektacolor and Kodacolor negatives. Another advantage of the monochrome-dye process is the possibility of making top-quality, black-and-white prints from color-film negatives. This is often impossible with ordinary contact papers which are not sensitive to red light. And ordinary enlarging—particularly with an enlarger using a "cold" light as the illumination source—may not only mean fairly long exposures but also distorted monochrome tonal relationship. For example, red lips might appear much too dark, and a bright, blue-green area (represented by a reddish area in the complementary-colored negative) might appear nearly white. However, all these troubles are immediately solved by making a "no-filter" exposure from the negative in an enlarger onto a sheet of Kodak Pan Matrix Film. Note that this is a *panchromatic* film and therefore is quite different from Kodak Matrix Film. This panchromatic film should be processed exactly according to directions and then printed by the monochrome-dye procedure described in this chapter.

After treatment of dye prints. Monochrome-dye prints, just like full-color dye prints, can be spotted or retouched with the customary techniques. They can be ferrotyped in the normal manner and mounted by any ordinary mounting procedure.

If you're a connoisseur of print quality, it is practically guaranteed that, after seeing a monochrome-dye print, you will never be completely satisfied with prints made by the "old-fashioned" silver method. Keep in mind that the biggest difference in print quality will be in prints of average or low key and those with a long density range. The shadows will not have a tendency to "plug up" when a moderately high density is reached, but will range on down and down, retaining detail until an unbelievable depth of tone is reached. This means that original subject lightings can be somewhat more contrasty than you might otherwise dare to use and, if printed in monochrome dye, the details in the shadows will still be apparent. It can be said without qualification that monochrome-dye prints are capable of producing the finest quality possible in a print viewed by reflected light.

If you are interested in making monochrome-dye prints, be sure to consult the Kodak Data Book, "Kodak Dye Transfer Process."

USING POSITIVE AND NEGATIVE MASKS

Many sorts of odd print effects can be achieved by combining positive or negative masks with the original negative when making an enlargement. The most interesting of these effects are:

1. Posterizing, in which the final print is composed of only three or four different tone values.
2. Bas relief, in which the subject is presented as a line image.
3. Highlight emphasis, in which a light, high-contrast negative is printed with the original negative.
4. The Persson "tone-separation" process, in which the original negative is divided up into two "separation" negatives, one containing the highlights and the other, the shadows.

P.S. *Because these processes have such little practical value in everyday print making—"mostly bas and no relief," as someone put it—information about them will be found only on page 250 in the references under masking.*

Chapter 13

Let's Finish the Print

IN BUILDING a new bookcase for your living room, would you consider it finished and ready to show your friends after all the rough pieces had been fastened together? Well, it's the same with a print after it has been processed and dried. It, too, needs those final, finishing touches before it is ready for delivery or for exhibition.

SPOTTING THE PRINT

No matter how careful you have been with regard to dust, scratches, fingerprints, etc., a few unsightly spots often appear—even on the experts' prints. Generally, there are two kinds of spots that must be dealt with before a print can be considered finished: black, and white.

A black spot, which is caused by an undeveloped "pinhole" in the negative, usually results from dust on the film at the time of exposure. The speck of dust, which may have settled on the film from the camera interior, prevents the light of the image from affecting the sensitive emulsion in that particular small area. Thus, when the film is developed, this tiny spot will be transparent. Prints from this negative will record the tiny, transparent spot as a small, black dot. If the pinhole happens to occur in a deep shadow area of the subject, it may pass unnoticed in the final picture; if it should fall in any middle tone or highlight, the defect will, of course, have to be removed. To do this, silver density has to be reduced in the dark spot to match the tone of the surrounding print area. This can be accomplished either by chemical means (a silver reducer) or physical means (an etching knife).

Chemical etching. A suitable solution for reducing the black spots is about a 5 percent solution of sodium hypochlorite which is available in some ordinary household bleaches, such as Clorox. The bleach is applied with a pointed toothpick or a small spotting brush to the print surface. The solution can be used directly out of the bottle or, to permit better control of the reducing action, it may be diluted with an equal part of water. The spot should normally be cleared within a few seconds, and then should be blotted with a piece of damp cotton. By carefully controlling the reaction time, it is possible to reduce the spot to match exactly the density of the surrounding area and make further work unnecessary. Sometimes, that is.

If prolonged action of the bleach reduces the black spot to white, whereas the surrounding area is some tone of gray, slight further correction will be necessary, as explained on page 208. This is not serious; it is much easier to take care of spots which are lighter than the surrounding area than those which are darker than their surroundings.

After the objectionable dark spots have been bleached, wash the print for a few minutes in running water to remove any bleach which may remain in the print emulsion.

Another method of "de-specking" prints is a modification of the local reducing procedure described on page 171 using the Kodak R-14 Non-Staining Reducer.

An easy way to remove dark spots from a print is to touch them with a bleaching solution, such as Clorox.

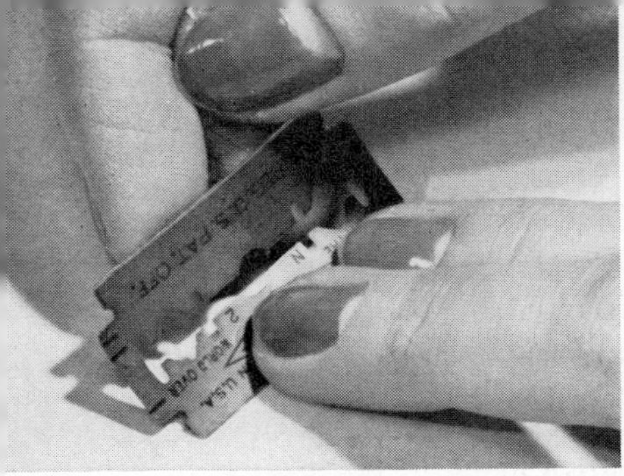

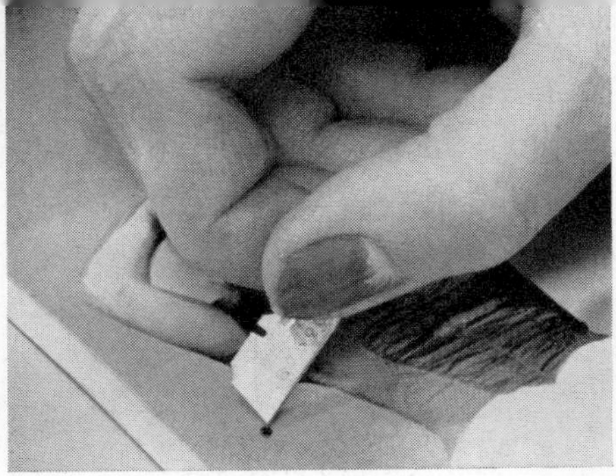

Physical etching. An etching knife, such as that used by professional negative retouchers, offers another means of eliminating black spots from prints. A satisfactory substitute for an etching knife can be made from a discarded razor blade. Break a double-edged blade in two the long way, and then break these pieces in half, crosswise. Any jagged edges along the break should be honed smooth on an oilstone or else they may tear the emulsion. The important thing about an etching knife is that it should be as sharp as possible; do not hesitate to use a new razor blade whenever you suspect that the old one is becoming dull.

The objectionable dark spots in the print are now removed by carefully scraping or etching, with the blade held at right angles to the surface of the print. "Right angles" means just that—otherwise pieces of the emulsion will come up—not unlike the action of a pickaxe pulling up asphalt pavement! The secret of successful etching is to remove the silver densities *gradually* with a light stroke, trying to shave off tiny layers rather than to accomplish the job all at once or with only a few strokes. Go back and forth lightly over the spot again and again, with the point barely touching the print. Continue this etching until the spot is no longer visible and matches the surrounding tones of the picture. Should the etching be carried further than intended, and the spot consequently made lighter than the surrounding tones, a slight amount of correction with a spotting brush may be needed.

If a particular print has necessitated a considerable amount of etching with an etching knife, the print surface may assume a slight "excavated" appearance when viewed obliquely. This can be remedied by waxing matte-print surfaces with any one of several preparations available for this purpose. (See page 213.) If the print is glossy, referrotyping should help solve the problem.

Spotting. White spots are perhaps the most common type of print defect. They are caused by dust or small dirt particles on the negative or negative carrier during the print exposure, or, less likely, by foreign matter which may have settled on the sensitive paper emulsion just before the print exposure was made.

As with black spots, the white variety is best prevented by keeping the darkroom and all items of equipment scrupulously clean. Once the white spots have appeared on a print, however, they can be removed with a small brush and a bit of spotting color.

Spotting media may be divided into three different types: pigments, pencils, and dyes. The choice is largely a matter of individual preference, but to some extent it is governed by the type of work to be accomplished.

Pigments for spotting prints are available either in the form of a stick of black India ink or as a pad of spotting colors containing daubs of black, brown, and white water-soluble pigment, such as the Kodak Spotting Colors. Either can be used satisfactorily, and both are recommended for all-round spotting work. Incidentally, if you find the India-ink stick relatively insoluble, rub it lightly on a piece of ground glass. The granular ink particles can easily be taken off the glass surface which serves as a miniature palette.

The pigment is taken up on a water-moistened brush, and a few trial strokes with the brush are made on a piece of scrap paper or on the white margin of the print, later to be trimmed away. The black pigment (use brown for spotting sepia-toned prints) should be deposited in a fine "stipple" of gray tone that is neither excessively moist nor dark.

Practice strokes should be a trifle lighter than the tone you wish to match on the print. If the marks are too light, remoisten the brush slightly, give the tip another light twirl in the spotting medium, and test the brush once more on the white paper. The primary purpose of the practice strokes is to remove excess moisture from the brush so as not to leave droplets of moisture on the print when the brush is lifted from the print surface. If a dark tone is to be matched, the brush should be well charged with the pigment, whereas if a light tone is to be duplicated, a comparatively small amount of pigment should be used. It is helpful to start first with the dark print areas and then proceed to the lighter areas since the pigment deposited on the spots will get lighter and lighter as the brush becomes dryer.

When all is ready, shape the end of the brush to a very fine point. About brushes in general: a small brush does not necessarily mean a fine point. Large spotting brushes should have a fine point also. A brush that is too small will not hold sufficient pigment and means that excessive time will be spent recharging the bristles and wiping away the excess. Now bring the brush lightly in contact with the white spot. Touch the spot several times with just the very tip of the brush until a sufficient amount of pigment has been deposited to match the surrounding print area. It is far better to add to the density a little at a time, building it up gradually, instead of trying to hide the spot all at once. Should the pigment be deposited too heavily, it can easily be removed with a tuft of moist cotton. Then, after the print has dried a moment, another try can be made.

Spotting prints with pencils is the easiest method of all to learn and consists only in touching lightly the objectionable white spot with a sharply pointed pencil until the spot has disappeared. This method also has the advantage of speed; when a brush is used, it requires occasional dampening and recharging with pigment.

When a pencil is used for spotting prints, a light stroke should be used so as not to dent the comparatively soft surface of the emulsion. The degree of pencil hardness best suited to a particular job should always be used.

The use of a pencil is *not* recommended when a fairly large spot is to be filled in and/or if the surrounding print tones are of a fairly heavy density. A heavy deposit of graphite on a print has a metallic sheen that possesses an entirely different type of reflectivity from that of the rest of the print surface. It can therefore be easily detected. This is particularly true if either the pencil used is quite hard or too heavy a retouching stroke is used so that the pencil point flattens the natural texture of the paper. The proper way to darken a light—and consequently prominent—ear or collar in a portrait is by chalking the print, a procedure which will be explained on page 210.

Glossy paper is perhaps the most difficult of all surfaces to spot. A ferrotyped, glossy surface presents no "tooth" which can break off minute particles of pencil lead. Many photographers prefer pigments but, in general, pigments are usually quite dull unless a small quantity of gum arabic is mixed with them to impart added glossiness.

One of the best ways to avoid these difficulties is through the use of spotting dyes, such as those manufactured by the Webster Company. Kodak Flexichrome Colors and Kodak Matrix Dyes can also be used for this purpose. The advantage of using dyes is that they sink into the emulsion without otherwise altering the appearance of the print (except to increase the density in the areas treated). However, spotted glossy prints may need referrotyping to be uniformly glossy after application of considerable dye.

Another advantage of using dyes is that practically any image tone can be matched by mixing only a few drops of dyes of different colors. For example, a wide range of sepia tones can be produced by mixing black, brown, and yellow dyes, and diluting this mixture with water if necessary. A warm-tone dye can be used to spot a warm-toned print or, with a little blue dye added, to produce the colder tones of a blue-black image-toned print.

The application of the dye to the print is somewhat similar to that used in pigment spotting except that you should use a "dryer" brush. Always test the charged brush on the margin of the print and then work up the spot gradually. Repeat this procedure until the spot has assumed the desired tone. Let's repeat for emphasis: *Do not use an excess of dye on the brush.* If the color has been applied too liberally, the spot can be reduced by gently swabbing the spot with a brush and warm water containing a few drops of dilute ammonia, and then blotting with a tuft of dry cotton to remove the excess moisture. The print should then be dried before continuing with any further spotting in that area.

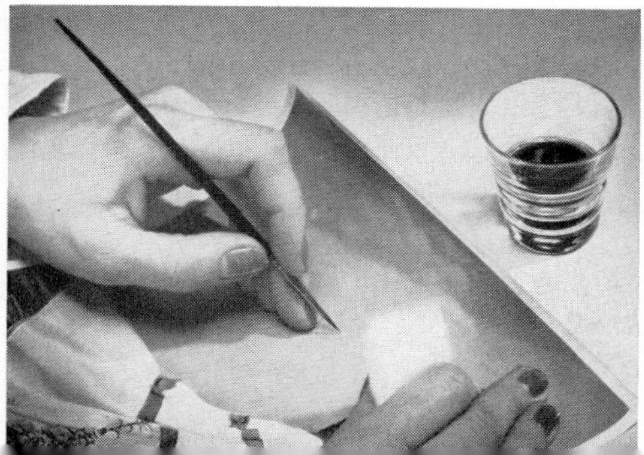

White spots disappear with careful applications of dye. Easy does it here!

CHALKING THE PRINT

We all make mistakes. Suppose, for example, the highlights in a rainy-night street scene were not darkened sufficiently by spot flashing as described on page 124. Sometimes, if the highlight is small, it can be spotted down into "unobtrusiveness" with ordinary spotting techniques using dye or water color.

For larger highlights which need toning down, do *not* try to pencil them in and blend the graphite by smudging. It is difficult to do this on papers which have any sort of surface texture—and most of them do—because the penciling objectionably emphasizes the paper texture by darkening the "hills" and not penetrating to the "valleys." On close inspection, a print so treated looks messy and smudged. Then, too, the graphite deposit seldom matches the image tone of that print. In fact, it is often more reflective than the rest of the print and therefore forms a conspicuously glossy spot if much pencil density is added.

Well, now that you know what *not* to do, let's get busy and do something with those excessively bright highlights. At an artist's supply store, buy a small amount of the finest pumice they have and about three or four sticks of artist's chalk. This chalk is inexpensive, will last indefinitely, and is available in many, many colors. To start, you'll need only black, blue, reddish-brown, and yellow. While you're there, buy a half-dozen assorted cardboard stumps if you don't already have some for use in matte-acetate dodging and ground-glass printing, discussed on page 113.

Chalking a print is simple. With a razor blade or knife, scrape off a little pile of chalk dust from the piece of black chalk onto a piece of glass or any other suitable palette material. If the print is blue-toned, as it might well be for a night street scene, add a bit of blue chalk dust to the pile, and mix it in thoroughly with the black until the color approximately matches the image tone of the print. Obviously, the other chalk colors will be used with the black if you want to match the tone of sepia prints. To this pile, add just a pinch of the pumice and mix that in also. If you don't have the pumice handy, try a bit of household scouring powder as a substitute. The pumice helps to give the chalk a desirable "tooth" which in turn helps you to work the chalk into the print surface better than by using chalk alone.

Is it all mixed thoroughly? Good. Place your print on a flat, well-lighted surface. Next dip one of the cardboard stumps into the pile of chalk dust and rub it around a bit to pick up a sufficient quantity. Don't worry about carrying too much chalk dust over to the print. Now, with the stump, begin to rub the chalk onto those highlights which need to be darkened. Start from the center of the highlight and work outward in ever-widening circles. When you think you have added enough density to the highlight, dust off the excess chalk from the print with a soft-bristled brush and inspect your work carefully. Add more chalk if necessary.

While this work is in progress, have on the stove a teakettle of water heated to the boiling point. After the print highlights have been darkened to your satisfaction, blow the excess chalk dust off the print surface. Then hold the print, emulsion side down, and pass the print through the steam from the kettle. Be careful to steam the treated areas thoroughly. Then immediately plunge the print into a tray of cold water and hang it up to dry.

The steam-and-cold-water treatment is intended to soften the emulsion enough to allow the chalk to sink into the surface slightly and then set the gelatin firmly around the chalk particles. Thus, the chalk dust becomes a part of the emulsion and cannot be rubbed off.

All in all, chalking a print is a neat trick which today is almost a lost art. But its ease of application and the considerable improvement which judiciously applied chalk can effect make it well worth while for you to include it among your print-finishing techniques.

LACQUERING AND WAXING THE PRINT

How would you improve the looks of a dingy, dull-looking pair of shoes? Shine them, of course. If you've been observant throughout the print-making process, it shouldn't be news to you that waxing and lacquering can do much the same for a matte-surface print.

Let's see how it does it: When a beam of oblique, incident light strikes a print surface, most of the light bounces off at the same angle. But a small part of the beam is reflected up toward the observer's eye by the surface irregularities, that is, the "texture," of the print. These irregularities, while they may seem small, are nevertheless huge when compared with the wave length of light. From this you can easily see that the rougher the surface, the more the light beam will be deflected or scattered into the observer's eye. Light-tone print areas don't suffer very much by being diluted with this stray light, but shadow areas which should be quite dark are "grayed down" considerably by it. The way to keep shadow areas dark is to provide them with a smooth surface from which the oblique, viewing-light beam can bounce off easily without interference from the paper texture. A smooth surface is exactly what waxes, lacquers, and plastic finishes supply. The smoother its surface, the greater the range of densities a print will have. *And the greater its available maximum density, the higher the quality it is possible for a print to attain.*

An after treatment, such as lacquering, can also help in protecting the surface of prints. Let's talk about this aspect for a moment.

An application of Kodak Print Lacquer to a print affords protection against moisture, finger marks, and grease by producing a thin, waterproof, almost invisible coating over the print. *This solution is perfectly matte when dry, so it cannot be used to increase print reflectivity.* Before the lacquer is applied, clean the print of all dust or grease with a cleaner, such as carbon tetrachloride, and dry the print thoroughly.

An unmounted print may be treated by briefly immersing the entire print in a tray of lacquer. A few seconds' immersion time is all that is necessary, but during this time be sure to agitate the print to remove all small air bubbles from the print surface and so permit full access of the solution. Immediately following this dipping process, the print should be hung up to dry, and the rest of the lacquer returned to its original container for subsequent use.

Apply the lacquer with a soft brush or lintless cloth to mounted prints. Less of this highly volatile fluid will be lost through evaporation by this method of application. Depending, of course, on the

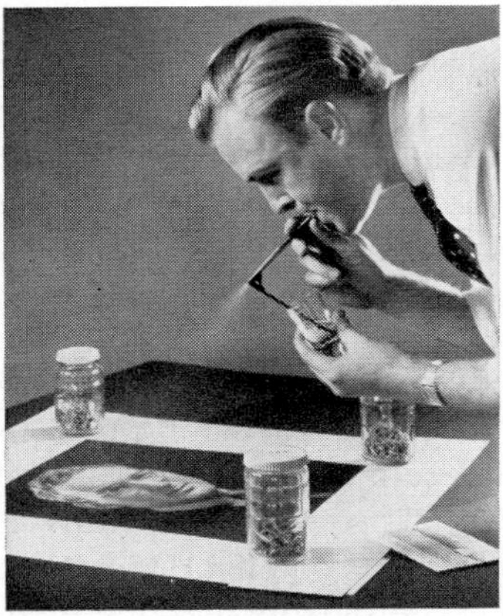

To prepare a print for lacquering, mask off the mount and weight down the masks. Keep a blotter handy to remove moisture droplets from the print. Then BLOW!

thickness of the coating, approximately 1700 square inches of print surface may be covered by sixteen ounces of the lacquer. Kodak Print Lacquer Thinner may be added to the stock solution if the latter becomes too viscous due to evaporation losses.

Heat should not be used to speed the drying process, which normally occurs in a few minutes. If a thicker protective layer is desired, a second coat can be added after the first application has dried *thoroughly,* that is, usually, after a few hours. Prints protected by this lacquer can be washed gently with a mild soap and water if they should become soiled from handling or continuous display, as may happen to photomurals, for example.

Waxes. Nearly any good furniture, floor, or automobile wax can be used to brighten up slightly a dull, matte print. The wax is simply taken up on a cloth, such as a pad of folded cheesecloth, and evenly applied to the print surface, preferably after the print is mounted. The wax surface is then rubbed with a clean cloth until the print has a uniform luster, and that's all there is to it.

High-luster surfacing. For higher print gloss than can be obtained by waxing, Kodak Print Luster is recommended. Apply this material to a mounted print by pouring a small pool in the center of the print, spreading it out evenly with a pad of lintless cloth, and then polishing it lightly. The treated print should be left flat until the

Print Luster is completely dry.

The highest print gloss which can be given to a matte print is obtained with commercial lacquers or plastic-type surfacing preparations, such as the Plastic Finish (wipe-on type) supplied by Sears, Roebuck, and Company. Although it is possible to wipe on a finish such as the Sears' product as directed on the container, a much easier method of application is with inexpensive paint-spray equipment.

Since this treatment adds considerably to the quality of a matte print and is an increasingly popular technique for salon prints in particular, it is worthy of a detailed description. First of all, the print should be mounted, spotted, and etched; in other words, it should be completely finished except for this one final operation. Lay the print flat and protect the mount borders by masking them with brown wrapping paper and masking tape. Pat the tape down lightly or it will stick to the mount perhaps causing the mount surface to split and peel when the tape is pulled up. It's a good idea to make sure the print surface is cleaned of any grease marks by wiping it (don't saturate it!) with a cotton pad moistened with film cleaner. The plastic finish should then be sprayed on from a distance of about one foot from the print, using a technique similar to that of an artist using an airbrush. Start at the top of the print and work down with a series of even, horizontal passes with the spray gun toward the bottom of the print. By all means, do your print spraying in a well-ventilated room. Also remember that many lacquer-type finishes and their solvents are inflammable.

To some extent, the degree of gloss can be varied with the method of application. A moderately high gloss can be achieved by standing somewhat farther back from the print while spraying, thus giving the print only a medium application. Conversely, by decreasing the spray-gun-to-print distance, thus giving a fairly heavy application, a gloss comparable to that of a ferrotyped, glossy print can be obtained. Leave the print flat for at least the next 20 minutes, or until it is "touch dry," and do not handle it roughly for at least two hours—preferably overnight—until the plastic coating is *thoroughly* dry and hard.

After spraying all the prints to be treated in one group, by all means clean the spray equipment if you ever expect to use it again. Turpentine will serve as a satisfactory solvent for this plastic finish; other lacquers may require other solvents.

Because there is a knack to applying high-luster finishes, and the technique varies somewhat with the spray and the spray equipment being used, *practice first on a few discarded prints.* In fact, to amaze yourself, mask off a diagonal half of a low-key print, and lacquer the other half. Pull away the mask and compare the treated and the untreated portions. This, in brief, is what you'll find:

1) The blacks have become blacker, extending the tonal range (density scale) of the print.

2) Shadow details are much more easily seen because the separation between them has been increased.

3) The color of a toned print has been considerably improved because of increased color saturation.

4) If you are going to lacquer the print, you won't need to compensate in exposure for the annoying tendency of a matte-surface print to "dry down," because the brilliance of a lacquered print is about what it was when the print was wet during processing.

5) If you are going to lacquer the print, you can use any favorite print surface, from "A to Z," and still make a print of "glossy" quality.

Some photographer friends of yours may insist that the gloss of a plastic-finished print is too high. Well, lower the gloss and sacrifice some degree of the above advantages of a high-gloss surface. That's what makes horse racing!

Seriously, it is no more advisable to put a high-gloss finish on every subject than it is to print all subjects on glossy paper. Portrait customers do not want glossy prints, and neither do a good many other people. But, aside from a consideration of personal likes and dislikes, there is no "photographic" advantage in adding a high surface gloss to high-key prints or to those of atmospheric fog scenes, both of which have a relatively short tonal range. On the other hand, take a marine scene or a street scene shot in the rain, tone it a gold-chloride blue, apply the glossiest plastic finish you know how, and then just try to keep it out of the salons!

Chapter 14

Print Mounting Methods

IF ALL the photographers who left their prints unmounted were laid down end to end, it would probably be a good thing! A mounted print not only looks obviously better than an unmounted print, but it also lasts longer, because cardboard mounts act as stiffeners and help keep prints from being bent or torn.

Since print mounting is so worth while and easy, let's have no more prints which might have been framed or entered in a salon, except for not being mounted. There are several choices of adhesives and mounting methods, but here are the most dependable and convenient to use.

KODAK RAPID MOUNTING CEMENT

This material is made especially for mounting prints rapidly and permanently to any clean, dry surface. The cement is colorless, moisture-resistant, and non-staining to prints, album pages, or mounts.

Suppose you want to mount some vacation pictures in an album. Arrange the prints on the album page in their desired order. Take the first print and lay it face down on a clean sheet of paper. Squeeze the tube of cement gently and touch the nozzle to the back of the print, drawing a line of cement around all four sides. Keep the line about 1/8 inch in from the edge of the print so that the cement will not squeeze out when the print is mounted. Now put a single drop in the center of the print and let it set for a few minutes. While you are waiting, if you wish, you can be applying cement to the next print.

After the cement has set slightly, mount the print in the desired place by positioning it and applying moderate pressure. Rub the print from the center outward to avoid wrinkles. If excess cement should ooze from the edge of the print it should be removed by wiping with a pad of ordinary cleansing tissue.

A handy trick to know is that prints mounted in this way can later be removed, if necessary, without damaging the print. To do this, place a sheet of clean, heavy paper or cardboard over the print and heat it with a warm (not hot!) electric iron for 10 or 15 seconds. Then remove the cardboard and the print as quickly as possible. Too hot an iron might scorch the print, whereas too cool an iron will not melt the cement.

KODAK THERMOUNT TISSUE

At room temperature this material looks like a piece of glossy tissue paper, but it contains a thermol-adhesive which melts at 175 to 220 F and forms a permanent bond between the print and the mount. A thermostatically controlled electric hand iron is necessary for mounting prints by this method. The iron can be of the ordinary household type, or one, like the Kodak Thermount Iron, designed for this purpose in that it will not heat over 220 F.

To mount a print, only a few simple steps are necessary:

1. Attach the tissue to the back of the print by touching the tissue quickly with one corner of the hot iron.
2. Trim the print and tissue to the required size.
3. Position the print on the mount and cover it with a sheet of clean paper, such as ordinary brown wrapping paper. Do not let the print slip out of position. If necessary, lift the edge of the print gently and tack the tissue to the mount by touching the tissue with a corner of the iron.
4. Press on this paper with the hot iron, allowing about 30 seconds for lightweight prints and smooth mounts, or slightly longer for double-weight prints and/or heavier mounts. For large prints, move the iron back and forth over the entire surface, using moderate pressure.
5. Immediately after ironing, place a weight, such as a heavy book, on top of the print until it has had a chance to cool and stick firmly to the mount.

KODAK DRY-MOUNTING TISSUE

This is a material very similar to Kodak Thermount Tissue except that it is generally used for large-size (8 by 10-inch and larger) prints and requires a mounting temperature of from 185 F to 250 F. The same technique is used in mounting prints as with Thermount Tissue except that a large dry-mounting press and a tacking iron are usually employed. Nevertheless, a home-type electric iron can also be used successfully. In other words, if you have available a dry-mounting press and a tacking iron, so much the better, but these implements are not essential.

The first step is to tack a sheet of dry-mounting tissue to the reverse side of the print, starting from the center and working out toward the corners. Then trim the edges of the print so that the borders of the print will coincide exactly with the dimensions of the mounting tissue. Working on a flat surface, position the print as desired on the mount, tack it in place, and then, with a double overlay of wrapping paper or a thin sheet of cardboard to protect the print emulsion, iron the picture to the mount, using heavy, continuous strokes. If a dry-mounting press is used, the pressure should be applied for 15 to 20 seconds and then released. Time must be allowed for the heat to penetrate the overlay, the print, and the tissue to effect a proper seal. If a thick cardboard is used for the overlay, times up to 45 seconds may be advisable.

The temperature of the iron or press is critically important. If it is not hot enough, the adhesive will not melt; if the temperature is too high, the adhesion will be only temporary. Since excessive heat may also scorch the emulsion, a household iron should be tested for approximate temperature by touching it *lightly* and *quickly* with a wet finger before beginning the mounting operation. If the moisture just sizzles, the temperature is about right. Actually, the ideal temperature is in the neighborhood of 200 F, which corresponds approximately to the setting, indicated on an adjustable electric iron, for ironing silk garments. Should you find that, after mounting, the picture has a slight concave curl, this may be easily remedied by ironing the entire reverse side of the cardboard mount.

DRY-MOUNTING DIFFICULTIES

DOUBLE-WEIGHT PRINT NOT ADHERING FIRMLY TO MOUNT

Cause:

Contraction of gelatin surface in press, causing print to curl away from mount before tissue has solidified.

Prevention:

Immediately after removing print from press, place it under pressure until adhesion is complete.

MOUNTED PRINT IS WARPED OR SLIGHTLY CURLED

Cause:

Damp prints or mounts.

Prevention:

Keep both print and mount in a dry, warm atmosphere for an hour or two before mounting.

NARROW BORDER OF MOUNTING TISSUE SHOWING AROUND PRINT EDGES

Cause:

Contraction of damp print in hot press.

Prevention:

Print should be thoroughly dry before mounting.

PRINT DOES NOT STICK TO MOUNT

Cause:

Temperature of the press is too low, print and mount placed in press upside down, or insufficient pressure of platen or iron.

Prevention:

Temperature for single-weight prints should be about 150 F; for double-weight prints, 180 F to 200 F.

Dry-mounting pressure should be about 1½ to 2 pounds per square inch.

PRINT EMULSION IS STICKY AFTER MOUNTING

Cause:

Melting of damp print emulsion from the heat of the press.

Prevention:

Dry prints thoroughly before mounting. Also keep overlay cardboard or paper dry to prevent sticking.

PRINT HAS TENDENCY TO BECOME DETACHED FROM MOUNT

Cause:

Dry-mounting temperature probably too high (250 F or over), causing tissue to remain in melted state after being removed from press.

Prevention:

Ascertain that print-mounting temperatures are correct. As soon as mounted print is removed from hot press, place it under pressure until adhesion is complete.

MOUNTING WITH RUBBER CEMENT

Another method of print mounting is with rubber cement. But there's a big "if" in using rubber cement: Many brands of rubber cement contain either sulfur or compounds of sulfur. Unfortunately, there is no convenient sure way, including the price, of telling which rubber cement is free from this impurity. Although the quantity of sulfur may seem small (not over .1 of one percent), it is, nonetheless, enough to discolor the print, eventually staining the image yellowish, in much the same manner as a print that had not been fixed or washed adequately. How long before the stain becomes apparent is, of course, dependent on the amount of sulfur, the storage conditions, and the character of the print itself, fine-grained or warm-toned images being most susceptible.

However, in spite of this shortcoming, mounting prints with rubber cement is a very useful technique *if print permanence is not important*. For instance, prints are often mounted in this way when they are to be copied or retouched or reproduced photomechanically. So, if rubber cement can help you, here is how to use it:

The most systematic method of application is first to position the trimmed print on the mount and with a sharp pencil draw a light line as close as possible to the edges of the print. Remove the print and cover its reverse side with a thin, even layer of rubber cement. A stiff brush or your finger will do the job satisfactorily. Then, in the same way, coat the mount with rubber cement, *taking the utmost care not to let any of the adhesive get outside of the rectangular area to be occupied subsequently by the print*. Allow no small "balls" of cement to accumulate on either of the tacky surfaces or they will appear underneath the print as undesirable bumps. When both surfaces are covered evenly, place the print *exactly* on the outlined portion of the mount and rub the print surface with a soft cloth, always working out from the center to insure perfect adhesion. The word "exactly" is emphasized because once the print is on the mount, it is almost impossible to move it even a trifle to compensate for placement errors. When it is down, it is down for good! Rub the cloth lightly back and forth along the print borders to pick up any of the cement which may have oozed from between the print and its mount. It is a good idea to place a pile of magazines or some other convenient weight on top of the print overnight to help insure good adhesion of the print edges.

AFTER THE PRINT IS MOUNTED

There are many variations in the presentation of a print that can be used to enhance its final effect. One is the use of a submount as a narrow border. This creates a size illusion and is particularly helpful with small prints. Dark submounts are advisable for use with high-key pictures, and light submounts for dark pictures.

Of the many suggested ways of drawing lines around print borders to "help contain the picture," the best seems to be accomplished with India ink and a Speedball-type pen at the juncture of the print edges and the mount. By all means, avoid complicated designs or multiple lines drawn on the mount. Signing and titling at the right and left, respectively, are optional but, if present, the lettering should be small, neat, and fairly close to the bottom edge of the print.

One of the best ways to mount a print is with Kodak Thermount Tissue. Recommended mounting temperature is from 175 to 220 F. The iron can be of the ordinary household type, or the Kodak Thermount Iron which will not heat over 220 F.

Chapter 15

The Art of Framing and Hanging

No landscape painter would permit his paintings to be exhibited without first being framed. Neither would a portrait photographer dream of delivering a finished picture to a customer unless the print were enclosed in some sort of a mount or folder. So, even though you have produced an excellent picture with your camera, the final step in the entire print-making process is its presentation.

Exactly why is framing so important? One reason may be found in the definition of art which likens it to "holding a mirror up to nature." Since nature is essentially an "out-of-doors" phenomenon, the frame on a landscape photograph, for example, is analogous to the frame on a house window. The mount and frame provide a desirable separation between the picture and its immediate surroundings ("setting it off," as some people say) and help the mind to accept the picture as a substitute for reality. Of course, other types of pictures and their frames are purely for decorative purposes; for example, an abstract design, such as a photogram, in a bizarre frame may lend itself admirably to a modernistic interior.

The presentation of a photograph depends, of course, on the purpose of the picture, its size, shape, subject, tone, surroundings, and your own preference in the matter. Although vacation snapshots may entail nothing more than pasting them in an album with art corners, the mounting and framing of pictorial enlargements is a matter worthy of discussion.

There are two distinct approaches to the problem of framing enlargements. The first is to frame an already existing picture, and the second is to choose the frame and then make the enlargement accordingly. Actually, from a photographer's standpoint, it is generally easier to start with a frame of a size and style that suit the room's other furnishings, and then to fit the mat and picture dimensions to the frame. In a relatively short time, of course, a photographer can make an enlargement in almost any size he wishes from a given negative. In this respect he has a tremendous advantage over a painter, for whom the frame selection comes last. For example, antique shops furnish a treasure trove of unusual frames that can be refinished, sometimes to outstanding advantage. But, if you're looking for unique frames of rosewood, burled maple, or frames finished in gold leaf, or what have you, you'd better find the frame first and then make your print to fit it.

Let's assume, however, that you are starting with a beautiful, unmounted photographic print and the desire to display it in your home. The first two steps in getting it hung are to make the mat and the frame. The mat is the mount or border inside the picture frame and is usually made of light-tone paper or lightweight cardboard. The picture itself is either mounted directly on the mat or behind it if the mat is of the cutout type which has an opening for the picture to "look through."

Photographic custom has, for the most part, standardized on a 16 by 20-inch mount size for enlargements varying from 8 by 10 inches up to nearly 16 by 20 inches in size. This standardization is undoubtedly due to the influence of salons which, for the purpose of uniformity, usually specify that entries must conform to these dimensions. But there is no reason to adhere rigidly to this size of mount if you wish to display your masterpiece in your own home or use it otherwise for decorative purposes. For example, if your print size is 14 by 17 inches and you want to hang it on a heavily patterned wallpaper, a mat larger than 16 by 20 inches will probably be required to separate the photograph sufficiently from the background.

Consider, for a moment, the shape of the picture and ask yourself these questions:

1. Is it rectangular in shape? If so, it needs a mat with the top and the two sides of equal width and the bottom slightly wider than the sides. This is generally true for both horizontal and vertical pictures.

2. Is the picture an unusually long rectangle? If horizontal, this print requires a mat with the two sides narrower than the top and bottom. If vertical, of course, it requires a mat with wide sides and a narrow top and bottom.

3. Is the picture square? Generally, square prints are mounted with mats having sides wider than the top and bottom. At your discretion, the bottom may be somewhat wider than the top.

To anyone who has readied an enlargement for camera-club or salon exhibition, making a mat and mounting the print on it is a familiar procedure. However, the use of a cutout mat may be a new experience. Cutout mats are very attractive and, in fact, are generally considered more artistic than mats which have the prints mounted on them.

Making a cutout mat is very easy, and no practice is necessary to do a good job. All the materials are inexpensive and readily available at art-supply stores. Here is a list:

1. Matboards. Remember that thin mats are easier to cut, less expensive, and available in more surfaces than thick ones.
2. Newsprint boards (the cardboard for backing the print).
3. A roll of gummed paper or Scotch tape.
4. A T square.
5. A razor blade in a holder, or any *sharp* knife with a thin but strongly backed blade, such as an etching knife, scalpel, or linoleum knife.

The steps in making a cutout mat are as follows:

Step 1. Place the print on the *reverse* side of the mat in the desired position. Square up the sides of the mat and the picture with the T square. Then, while holding the print firmly in place, lightly draw a pencil line around the print. Remove the print and, with the help of the T square, draw a line on the mat ¼ of an inch inside of the print-border lines. These are only guidelines on the reverse side of the mat, so don't worry about erasing them.

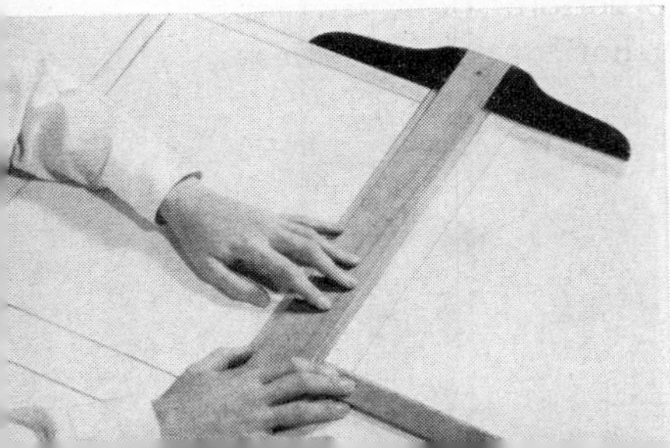

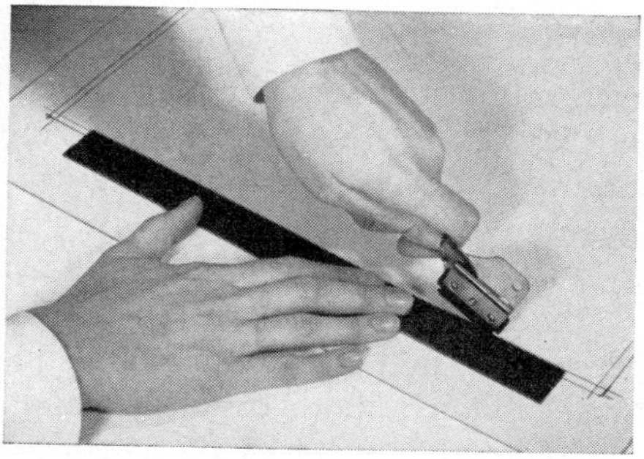

Step 2. Place the mat on top of a smooth worktable that has been covered with a pad of newspapers or cardboard to protect its surface, and cut along the sides of the inner rectangle.

A steel-edged ruler to guide the knife blade in a straight line will be a big help. To get a desirable beveled effect, hold the knife blade at a constant angle toward the center of the mat.

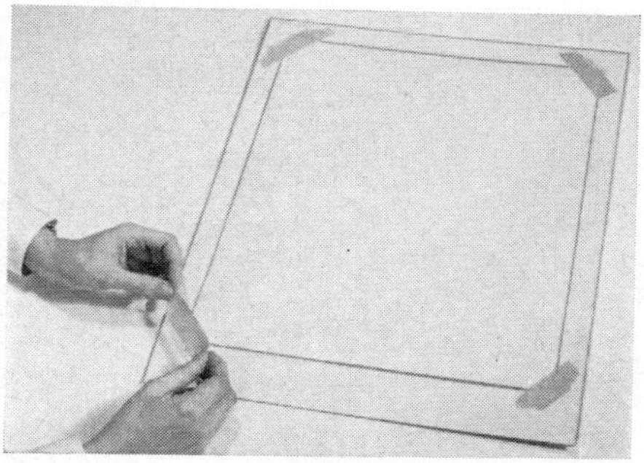

Step 3. After the opening in the mat has been cut, position the print over the opening from the reverse side of the mat and tape it to the mat across each of the four print corners.

Step 4. Next, with the tape, hinge the newsprint board (which can be slightly narrower than the mat) to the reverse side of the mat. Do not put any tape where it will show from the front side of the mat. Finally, swing the newsprint board over the picture so that it will hold the picture firmly against the cutout edges of the mat and keep it flat.

MAKING A FRAME

If you can buy a frame for a standard 16 by 20-inch mounted photograph, and have it suit the mood of the picture, harmonize with the surroundings where you plan to hang it, and please your personal taste, you are unusually fortunate. Buy it quickly! Commercial frames in this large size are seemingly available only in black, which is the simplest, quickest, cheapest, and probably least satisfactory type to find at the framing shop; or in a heavy, ornate, gold finish which is both expensive and probably best suited to a lush oil painting hung in a Victorian décor.

Another alternative is, of course, to have the picture framed professionally in a molding of your own choice. The main difficulty here is that you will probably have to pay a professional's price for the work.

Making one's own frame is a possibility overlooked by many

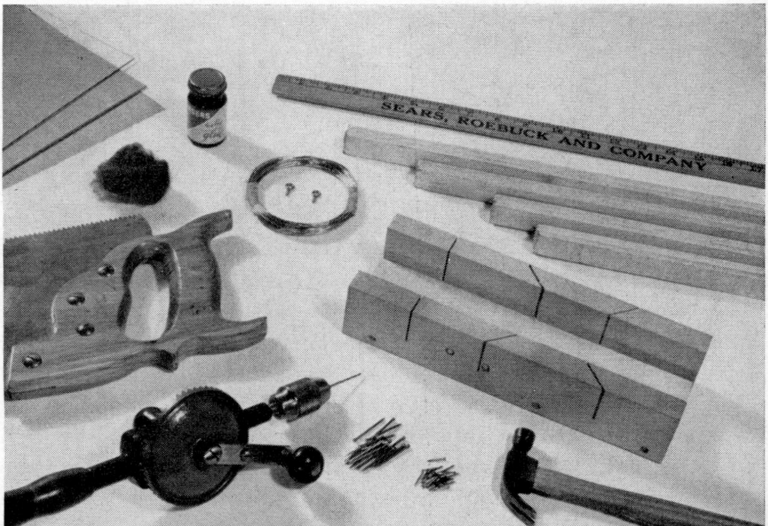

These are all the framing materials needed. You probably have most of them now.

photographers probably because they do not realize how easy it is. Actually, too, it saves money and is fun. What more could any hobbyist ask?

The materials necessary for making a frame are both few and inexpensive:

1. Wood molding. At some lumber yards doing millwork, moldings of various shapes, designs, and widths can be purchased. Some of these are suitable picture framing if the molding is rabbeted, that is, grooved, to provide a space to hold the picture mat and the glass. Most art-supply stores and picture-framing establishments have unfinished moldings for sale. In figuring the length of molding you will need for a frame, add together the length of the two sides and the top and the bottom. Then add to this eight times the width of the molding. The total will now include the amount needed for mitering, since there will be eight 45-degree angles to be cut for each frame.

There are, in addition, wood specialty companies who can furnish catalogs and price lists of the various moldings they manufacture. If a search through the classified pages of your own telephone directory does not disclose the names of such companies, your library undoubtedly has a copy of the *Thomas Register*, in which almost all American manufacturers are listed according to their products.

Although many woods are suitable for frame moldings, a good choice is thoroughly seasoned and dried basswood or clear white pine. These woods are relatively free from grain which might rise with the application of certain finishes or be distracting in itself in a natural or stain finish.

For salon-type, mounted photographs which are usually standardized at 16 by 20 inches, the proper molding width will be from ¾ inch to 2 inches. As a guide to selecting the correct width, keep in mind that the wider the mat border, the narrower the molding. Thus, an 11 by 14-inch print on a 16 by 20-inch cardboard mount might require a 1-inch molding, whereas a full 16 by 20-inch print with no mat border around it would probably look right in a 2-inch molding. In addition, high-key pictures usually look better in narrower frames than do low-key prints which naturally take heavier frames.

2. A saw and a miter box. There is no need to buy an expensive, all-metal, calibrated miter box. All you want is a simple guide for your saw that will enable you to cut the molding at a 45-degree angle. If you haven't a miter box already in your tool chest, it will take only a few minutes to make a simple one, as shown, from three 1-foot lengths of ¾-inch by 2-inch pieces of wood. Or, you can invest in a simple miter box at a local hardware store. It can, of course, be used to cut moldings for innumerable pictures, and its cost per picture eventually will be only a few cents.

3. Glue. Any good wood glue will be satisfactory. Although some frame makers prefer white-flake glue, this has to be heated before use, and in this respect is somewhat of a nuisance and less easy to handle than cold-water casein glue, fish glue, or other ready-to-use types.

4. Brads, screw eyes, and picture wire. Brads are used to help hold the pieces of the frame together. They should be "finishing"-type nails with small heads. The average length of those needed will be about 1½ inches. Get also a few ½-inch brads or ¾-inch frame points.

The screw eyes need be only about 7⁄16 inch or ⅝ inch long. Only two will be used for each picture.

5. Brown paper. Store wrapping paper of the type that comes in rolls will be fine to serve as a final covering for the back of the framed picture. If you don't need an entire roll, a large paper sack from the laundry or dry cleaners will be more than enough for two framing jobs.

6. Glass. Flat picture glass is ideal, but ordinary window glass from the hardware store is less expensive and generally satisfactory. You'd better wait until the frame is actually assembled before obtaining the glass, so the measurements will be accurate. The store will cut the glass for you to exact size, and the edges need not be ground.

Are you ready to begin framing your mounted print?

Step 1. Measure the dimensions of the mat (or mount, if you want to call it that) and mark off on a piece of wood molding the exact length of the frame's four sides. Be sure to mark the molding with 45-degree angles, that is, for each dimension first mark off a 45-degree angle on the molding; then start the measurement at the point where the molding is at its full width. In other words, be sure that no part of the 45-degree angle is included in any of the dimensions.

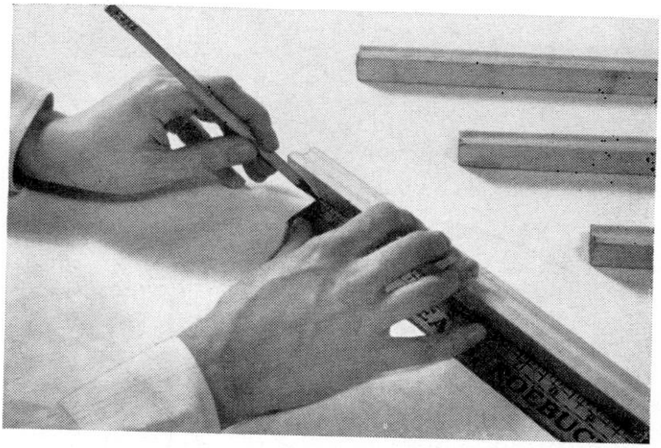

Step 2. After the molding is marked off, cut as indicated, using a saw and the miter-box guide. Frame finishing should begin at this point but will be taken up in a subsequent paragraph.

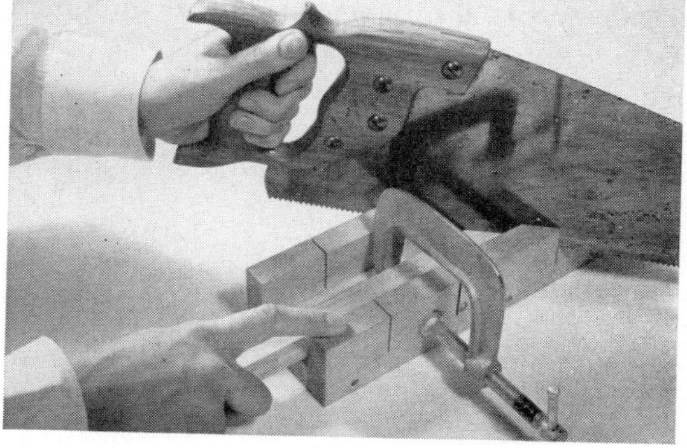

Step 3. Put glue on all of the corner cuts and nail each pair of corners together with two brads, one from each direction of the frame. It is a good idea to drill into the frame corners holes slightly smaller than the diameter of the brads so that the brads will not split the molding when the frame pieces are being assembled. If you are using a vise to steady the frame while nailing it, pad the molding with rags so that the jaws of the vise won't injure the molding. The glue should be fairly dry before proceeding further, and thoroughly dry before hanging the picture.

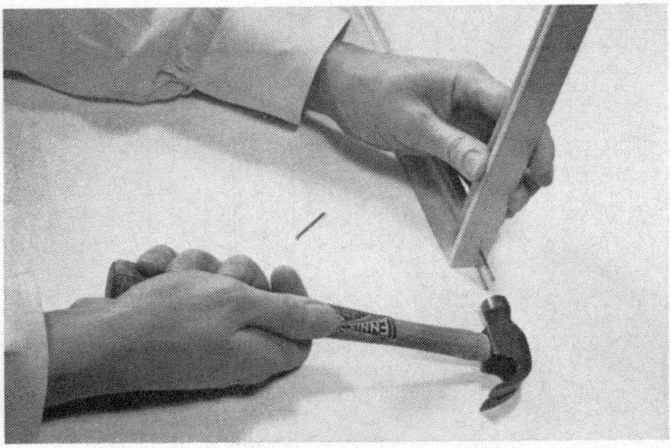

Step 4. Place the frame face down on a table and insert the cleaned sheet of glass. On top of the glass, lay the mounted print also face down. On the back of the mount put first a pad of folded newspaper and then a cardboard the same size as the mount, to hold the picture flat against the glass. Secure the last cardboard in place with ½-inch brads or ¾-inch frame or "glazier's" points driven flush against the cardboard into the frame at about 6-inch intervals. The brads or frame points can easily be put in place with the help of wide-jawed pliers, one side of which is padded to keep it from biting into the frame.

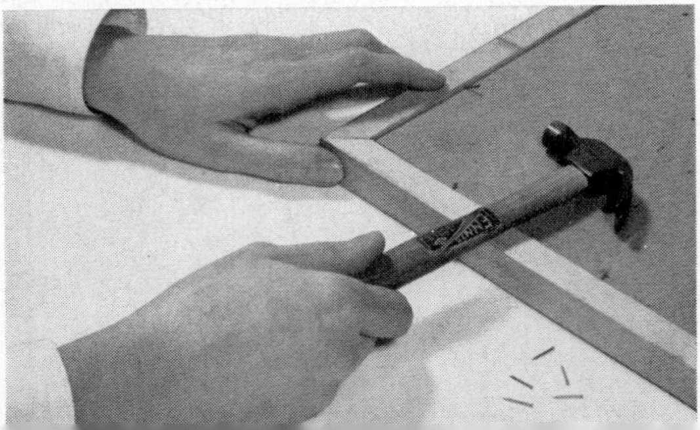

Step 5. To keep out dirt and dust and to make a neat job of it, the next (and optional) step is to cut a sheet of brown paper the size of the frame and glue it onto the reverse side. Another optional step is as follows: Before the glue is dry, brush some water on the brown paper except on its glued edges. Stretch the paper out so it is smooth. When the glue and the paper are both dry, the paper will be taut and make a neat appearance.

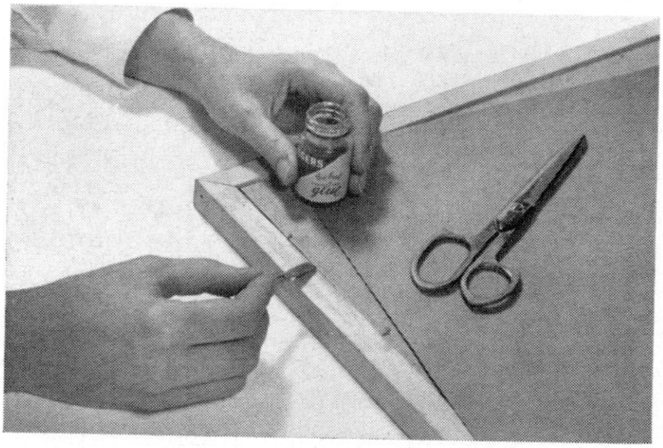

Step 6. Screw in one small-size screw eye on each side of the frame and about one-third of the distance from the top of the picture. Then stretch the picture wire between the eyes and twist it securely in place.

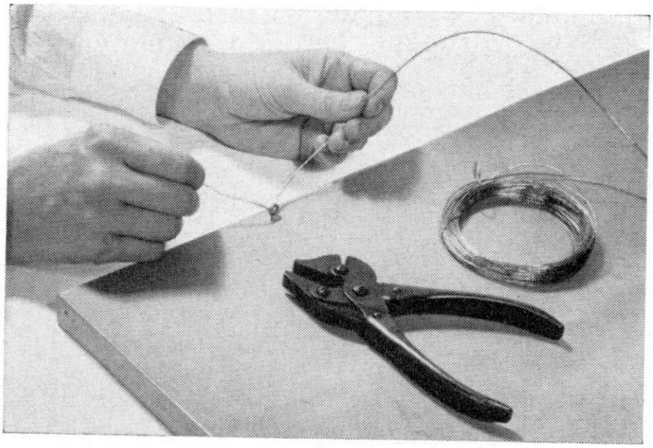

FINISHING THE FRAME

Finishing frames is much like finishing furniture except that it's easier because there isn't so much to do. The time to start finishing frames is while they are still in individual stick form, after the pieces of molding have been cut to size.

The first step, regardless of the finish planned, is to rub them to a shine with #0 or #00 steel wool. Wipe off the dust with a rag and then assemble the pieces. Fill up small nail holes or badly joined corners with any of the plastic-wood-type fillers or putty available from paint stores. Lacking this, beeswax will do. The actual finish is then up to you. The wood can be painted, stained, gilded, bronzed, antiqued, silvered, lacquered, pickled, bleached, or left in its natural state and only waxed.

For metallic finishes, as a general rule the frame is first given a coating of shellac. After the shellac is dry, a protective glaze or clear-lacquer coat is applied, followed by the metallic coat.

It is often desirable for the frame to repeat or "echo" some color in the picture. With toned prints or color photographs, more color can be used successfully in the frame than with black-and-white photographs. Photographs are usually enhanced by frames of natural or dark-wood finishes or by "off-neutral" frame colors. A suggested frame finish for black-and-white photographs is produced as follows:

Naturally, the subject, the tone of the print, and its surroundings are going to influence the method and colors chosen for finishing the frame. Frames should not call undue attention to themselves, since their purpose is to complement or enhance the picture, not to steal the show from it. But, within reason, frames can be tinted subtly to match their surroundings. Perhaps a light bluish gray would make a pleasing frame color for a high-key photograph. An antiqued metal leaf with a warm-gray overtone might go well with a middle-key portrait. Perhaps, in a striking modern setting, a bright silver mat would be a neat decorator's trick—or perhaps not. Just remember that the picture's primary aim is to achieve balance and harmony in a room. The right frame can add greatly to a picture; the wrong one can spoil it.

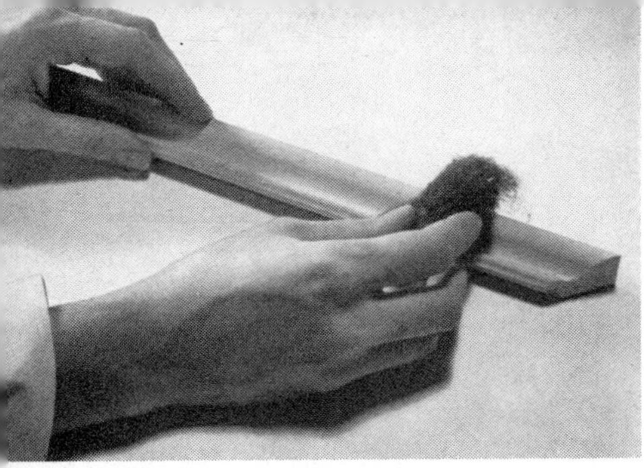

Step 1. Rub with steel wool.

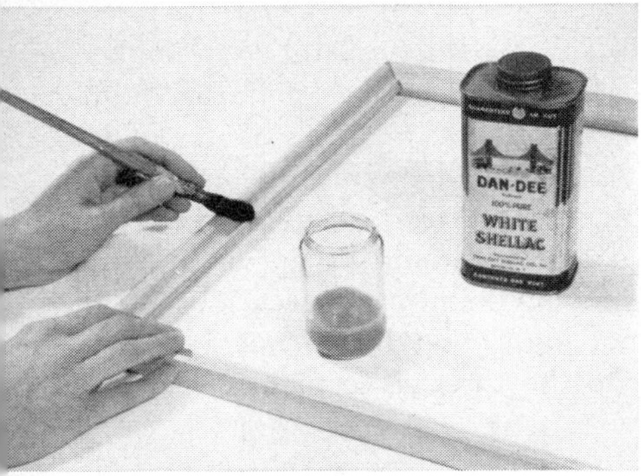

Step 2. Apply clear shellac.

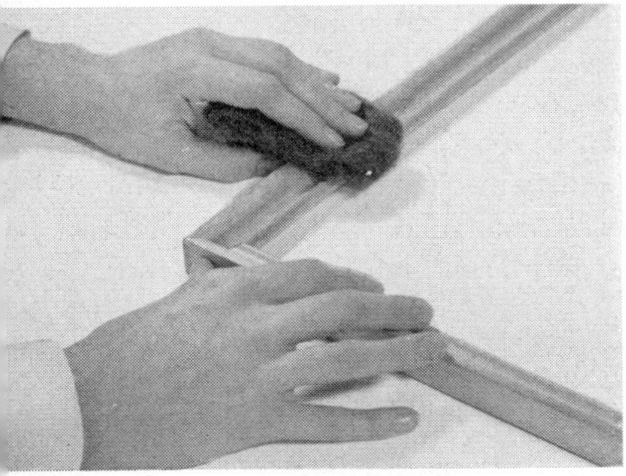

Step 3. Rub with steel wool.

Step 4. Apply black paint on only raised portions of the molding.

Step 5. Rub very lightly with steel wool to blend the black into the light areas.

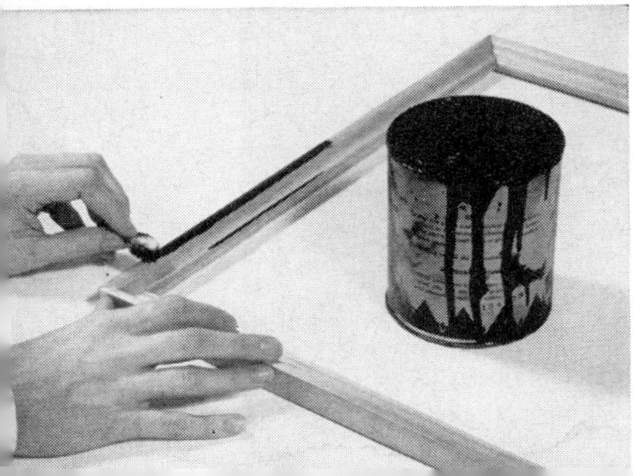

HANGING PICTURES

Too much importance cannot be given to the proper hanging of a single picture or to the grouping of several pictures. Rules can serve as very helpful guides, however, only if they are interpreted with artistic judgement. Here, then, are some rules for correct picture hanging:

Hang them at about eye level. Pictures are meant to be looked at conveniently, so don't place them too high—a common fault. An even more specific guide is to put the picture's center of interest at eye level. An exception would be when the picture is over a mantel or piece of furniture which in itself dictates the approximate hanging height. The picture should be flat against the wall. If it leans forward, producing an unnatural, precarious effect, the screw eyes are probably not high enough. Do not, however, place the screw eyes so close to the top of the picture that the picture hook or wire will show.

If there is only one picture to be hung, it probably should occupy a place of importance, such as over the mantel.

Do not hang a single picture where it will be partially obscured by a piece of furniture or between two windows where it will be difficult to see. Place tall pictures on vertical wall spaces, and hang wide pictures on horizontal wall spaces: this will help to insure harmony of related areas. Also, small, individual pictures should be used in small rooms, and large pictures in large rooms.

If there are several pictures to be grouped, be sure that the subjects harmonize with each other. Two fine character studies of elderly people do not, of course, belong in a grouping with modernistic still-life pictures.

Several small pictures can be used in place of one large picture in a large room, provided the pictures are framed as uniformly as possible and are grouped artistically. Before pounding any picture hooks into the wall, determine if the group is better in a dynamic or unusual arrangement than in a static form consisting of balanced sizes and groupings. If there are several odd-shaped pictures to be grouped together, place them on the floor and try various arrangements. This will help you to fit them together and hang them in a casual group so that together they will create a balanced, over-all design.

A natural way to arrange a group of similarly framed small-to-medium-size pictures is to march them up the stairway. Make sure that the centers of all such stairway pictures form a line parallel to the baseboard or dado. Larger pictures in groups, such as a collection of salon prints, can often be arranged in a close, geometric order over a davenport or some other piece of furniture, or in a hall so that each group is a neat, attractive unit. After all, it is a good idea to let pictures associate themselves with the furniture rather than the ceiling.

Another suggestion is to use a grooved molding to hold mounted but unframed prints that are covered with glass. It is a matter of moments to change prints hung in this manner when a new addition to the collection takes the place of a less desirable one. Grooved moldings are available in wood which can be painted in any color, or in chromium; since these moldings are fastened to the wall, they never permit the prints to hang crooked.

P.S. *Remember, pictures are made to be looked at and enjoyed. Just making an enlargement is only part of the story. After the print is made, let's be sure that it is well framed and correctly hung so it may be fully appreciated by all who see it.*

Chapter 16

Using the Enlarger to Make Slides

THERE MAY come a time in an amateur photographer's life when his interest in photography—or more specifically, in print making—begins to lag. Perhaps he has become the star of his camera club, or possibly his salon record is so excellent that making beautiful exhibition prints is no longer a challenge. But wait, friend: Before you lay aside your camera to take up the tuba or start to raise tropical fish, have you thought about making slides of your negatives to rekindle that lagging photographic interest?

SLIDES VERSUS PAPER PRINTS

"Why slides?" you might ask. Alright, here are a few answers—and see if you don't find yourself interested!

In the first place, you want only high-quality results—or you wouldn't have purchased this book. A photographic print is a poor running mate to a properly projected slide of the same subject, when it comes to creating a lifelike reproduction. Let's consider the reason for this statement: An average sunlit scene has a brightness range of about 1 to 170. Film retains most of this range (certainly the important middle portion of it) satisfactorily. But a matte print viewed by reflected light has only a range of about 1 to 30. Something was lost somewhere! Usually it is the details in the deepest shadows and, to a lesser extent, in the lightest highlights.

But a slide is different. Being itself a film (or plate) transparency, it retains nearly all of the density scale of the original negative. Then, when the slide is projected properly—say, with an efficient projector, in a dark room and on a beaded screen, the avail-

You can't beat slides for photographic quality, realism, and as entertainment for a group of friends.

able density range is about from 1 to 120, or *about four times the range of the matte print!* Thus, in looking at a projected transparency, one experiences a high degree of realism. In other words, it's much easier with a slide than with a print to imagine that you are looking directly at the original scene through a window in your living room.

USING SLIDES

Many enthusiastic amateur photographers have files of unprinted negatives. Perhaps these have resulted from a vacation trip or a camera-club outing. After the many exposed films are developed, only a comparatively few ever see the light of day in print form. Those are the negatives which "look interesting" from a pictorial standpoint. But consider this same group of vacation negatives from a slide standpoint. Even the less pictorial ones probably have interesting story-telling potentialities and, together, the entire group would make a good travelogue-type of slide presentation for viewing at the camera club or even for entertaining non-bridge-playing friends and neighbors. It is difficult to entertain a large audience, for example, a service club, with a selection of ordinary paper enlargements. But with slides projected on a screen, it's easy.

The important thing is, however, that slides are prints—prints which are probably made best with an enlarger—and all the customary techniques of enlarging can be used to make technically excellent and pictorially beautiful results. For example, only the best portion of a negative need be used for projection onto the lantern slide plate. And, during projection, the image can be dodged or printed in where necessary. The processed slide can be reduced, toned, tinted, spotted, and bound with whatever shape of slide mask best suits the need of the particular subject.

Slides are not only projection prints but they are, in a sense, miniature prints. Consequently, they require a commensurate amount of skill to produce really artistic results. Anyone can dodge a 16 by 20-inch paper print without difficulty—but now try your hand at dodging the same respective areas for a 3 by 4-inch or even a 2 by 2-inch slide, if you think print making has lost its challenge! However, it's not so difficult: miniature dodging implements and a bit more patience are the prime requisites.

MAKING GLASS LANTERN SLIDES

There are a few points about lantern-slide materials and the technique of making slides with them which, if kept in mind, will make the job much easier.

Equipment and materials. If you own an enlarger, or have the use of one, you're practically in the fun of slide making already. Most enlargers can project an image with a minimum magnification ratio of about 1 to 1 (1 inch on the negative would be equal to 1 inch on the projected image), particularly if the easel is raised or propped up somewhat above its usual position on the enlarger baseboard. Undoubtedly, to make the slide, you will want to use only that area of each negative which will present the subject at its "compositional best." This means, of course, that, for the most part, it will not be necessary to make reductions past the capacity of your equipment.

Although slides can be made on film as the printing material, probably the most convenient product for this purpose is Kodak Lantern Slide Plates. These are available in two grades of contrast capacity and in the popular 2 by 2-inch size, as well as in the "old-fashioned" size of $3\frac{1}{4}$ by 4 inches. It's somewhat more difficult to dodge and spot the smaller slides, but they have the advantage of being fairly inexpensive and capable of being projected in the readily available miniature slide-film projectors.

Preparation. Immediately prior to printing the negatives you have selected, clean them thoroughly of finger marks, dirt, etc., with a film cleaner, such as Kodak Film Cleaner or carbon tetrachloride. Give each negative a final dusting with a soft brush to remove any dust particles which may have been attracted by the static electrical charge usually built up in the cleaning operation.

In slide making, an ordinary paper masking easel obviously isn't needed to hold the glass plate flat or to provide margins. However, some system is necessary to locate the lantern slide plate so that the desired area of the projected image can be positioned at the center of the sensitive plate. Here's a method which works very well:

First take a slide mask and trace its complete outline on a sheet of white paper and again on a sheet of black paper. With the white paper on the enlarger easel, you can use the outline of the mask opening as a guide for composing and focusing the projected negative image. When this is done, substitute the black paper for the white paper, being sure that the outlines of the mask opening are located exactly where you wish them to be with respect to the projected image. Tape down the black paper if you want to insure against moving it accidentally.

Then turn off the enlarger and the white room lights. The pencil lines on the black paper can be seen readily if you glance across them obliquely. Place the lantern slide plate, emulsion side up (red side down), on the guidelines, and you are now ready to make the exposure.

Exposure. Kodak Lantern Slide Plates, Medium, are quite high in speed as compared with conventional paper printing materials. Even with the enlarger lens stopped down to about *f*/16, a 1 to 1 projection of a normal negative may require a rather short exposure—say, in the neighborhood of about 3 seconds.

Exposures as short as this are quite susceptible to seemingly narrow margins of error, for example, an extra, accidental, second means an exposure error of 33 percent. Then, too, this short total exposure time leaves precious little opportunity for dodging or printing in. The best way to solve this problem is with a neutral density filter placed in front of the enlarger lens. These filters are available in several standard densities in inexpensive gelatin-film form. The Kodak Wratten Neutral Density Filter, No. 96, with a density of .70 transmits 20 percent of the light and is a good average density to use for most slide exposures. If, for example, a normal exposure were 3 seconds, with the filter in place over the enlarger lens the exposure would be a more handy and easily reproducible 15 seconds.

If you do not use a neutral density filter, the best alternate procedure is to stop the enlarger lens down as far as possible and to time the exposure with an electric push-button type of darkroom timer. A yellowish filter will decrease the exposure because lantern slide plates are blue-sensitive, and the yellow filter will absorb a lot of the actinic blue light. However, a yellow filter will probably give increased slide contrast and upset your expectations in this connection.

Development. Practically any normal paper developer can be used with approximately the same development range as is used for prints. However, unlike paper prints, the contrast of the slide print can be varied through quite a wide range, depending on the length of the development time. As would be expected, a short exposure time, together with a comparatively long development time (up to 6 minutes), yields a high degree of contrast, whereas a long exposure plus, say, a 1-minute development, results in fairly low contrast. If you know that a particular negative results in a print of normal contrast when projected on Kodabromide Paper No. 2, then a slide of normal contrast on a Kodak Lantern Slide Plate, Medium, would require about 2 minutes' development in Kodak Dektol Developer or Kodak Developer D-72 diluted 1 to 2. From this point, the contrast can be adjusted either way. The printing contrast of a condenser enlarger can be reduced by inserting a sheet of matte acetate or ground glass between the light source and the top condenser lens. This will also help to slow down the enlarger's printing speed.

When you make your first slides, don't be misled by the abnormally dark appearance of the slide as it is nearing the end of development. Don't take it out of the developer prematurely: let it continue for the allotted time. Then, agitate it in Kodak Indicator Stop Bath or Kodak Stop Bath SB-5 for about 30 seconds and place it in the fixing bath.

Fixing. Although any normal fixer, such as Kodak Acid Fixer or Kodak Fixing Bath F-5, can be used, far more rapid clearing can be obtained by using Kodak Rapid Liquid Fixer with Hardener. Remember that you are working with glass plates, not paper. Any solution takes longer to penetrate an emulsion coated on a plate because it can be absorbed from only one side of the material. Thus it is a good idea not to hurry the plate through to the stop bath and the fixing bath. Kodafix Solution or Kodak Rapid Liquid Fixer with Hardener will, however, clear the plate rapidly enough to satisfy even the most impatient photographer who has difficulty in waiting that long minute or two before it is advisable to turn on the white light to examine his masterpiece.

Washing and drying. Wash the plate for at least 30 minutes in running water and, to minimize drying marks, dip it briefly in a bath containing Kodak Photo-Flo Solution before drying. Probably the most convenient method of drying slides in plate form is to use a simple wooden rack made of an inclined board which has been scored with a saw at ¾-inch intervals so that it will hold the plates in an upright position.

Toning. For a "rotogravure-brown" tone use Kodak Sepia Toner or Kodak Sulfide Toner T-10. Although both of these toners will swell and soften the emulsion, no difficulty should be encountered with scratching, abrasions, etc., if: (a) the plate is treated carefully and nothing is allowed to come in contact with the emulsion, and (b) the toner is not used at temperatures higher than about the usual 68 F.

It is quite well known that these toners of the polysulfide type cause a lowering of average print density as a result of their toning action. This is as true with lantern slide plates as it is with paper prints. Accordingly, it is very desirable to increase the exposure of a plate about 25 percent over that required for a normal, untoned slide. The actual increase will depend on the development time. If the original slide has received full development, somewhat less exposure increase will be required. If you add a pinch of hypo to the sulfide redevelopment bath (say, 65 grains of hypo per 32 ounces of the redeveloping bath), as recommended for increased transparency of the toned image, it is advisable to make slightly darker originals than a 25 percent overexposure will provide. Another way to utilize this lightening effect of the toner is to sepia-tone dark slides and thus reduce them to more normal density.

Kodak Brown Toner and Kodak Rapid Selenium Toner have no appreciable toning effect with lantern slide emulsions, so save yourself the trouble of experimenting with them.

For blue tones, use Kodak Iron Toner T-11; or for blue shadows with dyed middle tones, use Kodak Single Solution Dye Toner T-20 with Kodak Toner T-18. Complete directions are given in the Kodak Data Book on Processing and Formulas.

Spotting. Small, seemingly inevitable, dust spots most evident in areas of uniform density, such as the sky, have to be spotted in with a finely pointed brush. Dyes, such as Spotone or Kodak Flexichrome Colors, are recommended in preference to the pigment type of spotting colors because they make it somewhat easier to achieve a good "blend" between the objectionable light spot and the darker surrounding area.

By all means use a magnifier as a guide in spotting. Also, in order to work under optimum spotting conditions, be sure to mask off with opaque paper the slide area from the rest of the illuminator. Use a fairly "dry" brush and attempt to build up gradually the area to be darkened. Spotting slides, particularly the 2 by 2-inch size, is admittedly more difficult than working on a large paper print. But by working slowly and patiently *and with the aid of a strong magnifier,* the spotting should be imperceptible in the projected image.

For "dirty" negatives which do not clean up very well with carbon tetrachloride and may eventually present you with a tedious spotting problem, here's a partial answer: Provided that the subject sky area is without clouds, try flashing this sky area as described on page 121. The flashing exposure darkens highlights more than it does shadows, so the tiny white spots will be darkened enough so that they will be much less apparent and therefore will need far less spotting than if the entire slide had been printed "straight."

Projection. Since you are interested in results of the highest quality, project your slides if possible, in a darkened room, on a beaded screen, with an efficient projector, and with the audience sitting fairly close to the projector's axis. Ideally, without a slide, the projector should throw about 5 foot-candles of illumination on a beaded screen (if necessary, this may be effected by changing lamps or moving the projector). Incidentally, some exposure meters, such as the *General Electric,* are calibrated directly in foot-candles. If you are using a matte screen, adjust the illumination from the projector to produce about 8 to 10 foot-candles at the screen. The difference between the two screen types *to the observer seated near the projector axis is appreciable.* The difference in brightness is enough so that slide density should be planned in the darkroom to fit your particular screen-projector combination. Accordingly, at the outset, it is advisable to make a few sample slides, perhaps of varying density and contrast, from the same negative. Then decide, after projecting them, which one will serve as your master guide for the exposure and development of the remaining slides to be made.

Chapter 17

Pictures with a Purpose

Have you ever watched a group of boys build a hut in a vacant lot? They have a great time of it, don't they—until the hut is completed. Then, unless they use the hut for some further purpose, their interest is soon lost.

Much the same situation is found among collectors: the real fun of collecting nearly anything—from stamps to stuffed owls—is not in *being* a collector, but in *doing* the collecting.

You might generalize the moral by saying that fun is doing, not being. It's really that simple.

The same sort of thing affects photographers, too. Sure, it's fun to take pictures and make enlargements. But then what? Fortunately, with photography, there's no reason to let interest lag since all the steps in making an enlargement are only half the story, and so far the print hasn't even started to speak for itself! A print *can* speak, for photography is a sort of language—a means of communicating facts, ideas, or emotions.

But, before a picture can speak, it must be seen. Obviously, a picture can be presented in many different ways other than being adorned by a cardboard portrait folder and placed in that most classic spot, on the top of the parlor piano. Surely the piano top, and the mantel, too, has long ago reached a saturation point insofar as pictures are concerned! And that is where this chapter can perhaps make some helpful suggestions.

How are some of the ways that you can have fun with photographic prints? Let's list a few print uses, keeping in mind that an enlarger can make a print of nearly any size, from one as small as a postage stamp to one which serves as wallpaper.

- Calendar Covers
- Postal Cards
- Picture Albums
- Bookplates
- Bookmarks
- Book Covers
- Lantern Slides
- Photomurals
- Salon Exhibition
- Match-Book Covers
- Lamp Shades
- Jigsaw Puzzles
- Cutout Statuettes
- Basis for Oil Paintings
- Sale to Customers
- Montage
- Photo Miniatures
- Jewelry Inserts
- Framed Gifts
- Greeting Cards
- Thank-You Cards
- Calling Cards
- Invitation Cards
- Announcement Cards
- Posters
- Table Place Mats
- Coffee-Table Tops
- Glass-Covered Trays
- Screens
- Room Decoration
- Publication
- Instruction and Demonstration
- Photo Drawing and Etching

You, yourself, can doubtless add numerous other clever or specialized print applications to this list.

Would you like additional information on one of the topics in the above list? Since interests are so varied, the most sensible way to treat this matter is by giving a bibliography of helpful references; then you can look up several articles dealing comprehensively with the subject of your choice.

Sources of picture uses

Calendars

How to Make Photo Calendars
  ELMA WALTNER. *Pop. Phot.*, **21**: 60-61, No. 6, Dec. (1947)
How to Make Personalized Calendars
  I. G. EDMONDS. *Minicam Phot.*, **11**: 80-81, 110-11, No. 5, Jan. (1948)
Photo Calendars Make Novel Gifts
  W. R. OSBORNE. *Pop. Phot.*, **9**: 32, 117-18, Dec. (1948)

Bookplates and bookmarks

Making Photographic Book Plates
  WILLIAM E. BOOTH. *Amer. Phot.*, **31**: 44-46, Jan. (1937)
What to Do With Your Pictures
  H. BEZOLD. *Mechanix Illust.*, **40**: 128-29, No. 5, Mar. (1948)

Photographic Book Plates
C. W. GIBBS. *Better Phot.*, **2**: 24-26, May (1939)
Photographic Bookplates
IRA CURRENT. *Amer. Ann. Phot.*, **53**: 247-49 (1939)
How to Make Photographic Designs for Invitations and Greeting Cards, Bookmarks, and Other Purposes
HAROLD G. GRANGER. Practical Photography and Amateur Cinematography, E. Molloy, Editor. Newnes, London, 1934, Vol. III, pp. 830-36.

Lamp shades

Picture Lamp Shade
H. LEEPER. *Mechanix Illust.*, **41**: 132-33, No. 1, May (1949)
Lampshades
JACOB DESCHIN, in "New Ways in Photography," McGraw-Hill Book Co.
Photographic Lamp Shades Using Transparencies
F. R. FRAPRIE and F. C. O'CONNOR, in "Photographic Amusements," American Photographic Publishing Co., Boston, 1937, p. 40

Match-book covers

Book Matches Made Easy
RALPH ENDSLEY. *Pop. Phot.*, **24**: 68-69, 128, No. 4, Apr. (1949)

Postal cards

How to Make Your Own Post Cards
RUSS WHITAKER. *Pop. Phot.*, **24**: 52, 106-8, No. 5, May (1949)

Photo novelties

Photo Novelties You Can Make

K. MURRY. *Pop. Phot.*, **27**: No. 5, Nov. (1950)

Place mats

Photographic Place Mats

TIMOTHY STRATTON. *Pop. Phot.*, **24**: 42-43, No. 3, Mar. (1949)

Miscellaneous cards

Photographic Calling Cards

ANON., in "Popular Mechanics Photo Guide," Popular Mechanics Co., Chicago, 1942, p. 175

Making Photo Greetings With Standard Kits

ANON. *Camera (Balt.)*, **65**: 46-51, Oct. (1943)

Personalized Photo Birthday Cards

BOB KREIDER. *Pop. Phot.*, **17**: 72, No. 4, Oct. (1945)

How to Make Simpler and Better Greeting Cards

JACK WRIGHT. *PSA J.*, **16**: 588-90, No. 10, Oct. (1950)

Albums

Albums, Still and Cine

ROBERT BROWN. *Complete Photo.*, **1**: 153-57, Issue 3, (1941)

Lantern slides (black-and-white)

Making 35mm Slides

A. K. ASTER. *Amer. Phot.*, **37**: 39, Apr. (1943)

Making Miniature Slides

CORTNEY BRYSON. *Amat. Photog.*, **94**: 711, Oct. 18, (1944)

How to Prepare and Deliver a Lantern Lecture

R. GARBOLD. *Phot. J.*, **84**: 299-301, Oct. (1944)

Show Your Pictures By Projection

EVERETT I. MILLER. *Amer. Phot.*, **41**: 30-32, Apr. (1947)

The Advantages of Lantern Slides

HAROLD K. PLUMMER. *Amer. Phot.*, **42**: 105, No. 2, Feb. (1948)

How to Project Your Slides (Camerette No. 85)

RAY BULGER. *Camera Mag.*, **73**: 91-114, No. 1, Jan. (1950)

Lantern Slides

JULIAN M. BLAIR, in "Practical and Theoretical Photography," Pitman Publishing Corp., New York and Chicago, 1938, Chapt. XII, pp. 112-120

Salons and exhibitions

What's In A Name?

HADEN HANKINS. *Camera (Balt.)*, **57**: 84-87, Aug. (1938)

Titling Salon Prints

BARBARA GREEN. *Camera (Balt.)*, **57**: 244-46, 250-52, Oct. (1938)

Give Your Picture a Title That Tells (And Sells It)

WILLIAM TIGER. *Minicam Phot.*, **5**: 26, 88-89, Nov. (1941)

What Makes A Salon Print?

FRANKLIN I. JORDAN. *Amer. Phot.*, **37**: 8-11, June (1943)

Exhibition Photography
John S. Rowan. *Camera (Balt.)*, **66**: 42-52, Aug. (1944)
The Key to Salon Success (Camerette No. 66)
C. Stanton Lober. *Camera (Balt.)*, **70**: 82-104, No. 10, Oct. (1948)
Preparing The Exhibition Print
R. W. Fanstone. *Amat. Photog.*, **99**: 509, July 20, (1949)

Christmas cards

Send Your Own Photo Drawings For Christmas
Grace Hooper. *Camera (Balt.)*, **68**: 30-35, Nov. (1946)
Ideas For Christmas Cards (Camerette No. 67)
Roland Wolfe. *Camera (Balt.)*, **70**: 90-103, No. 11, Nov. (1948)
Expediting Christmas Cards
Franklin I. Jordan. *Amer. Phot.*, **43**: 682-84, No. 11, Nov. (1949)
Christmas Greetings—How to Make Them
Peter Gowland. *Pop. Phot.*, **25**: 62-65, 164-67, No. 6, Dec. (1949)
Christmas Cards With Your Camera
Robert Brightman. *Mechanix Illust.*, **42**: 124-25, No. 2, Dec. (1949)
Try Card Tricks This Christmas
Rita Connelly. *Camera Mag.*, **73**: 62-66, No. 11, Nov. (1950)

Photomurals

Photo-Mural Process of Decoration
W. G. Raffee. *Brit. J. Phot.*, **83**: 308-9, May 15 (1936)
How to Make Photo Murals and Decorations
Anon. *Minicam*, **1**: 76-82, 88-93, 95-97, No. 2, Oct. (1937)
How Photo Murals Are Made
Arthur E. Clason. *Pop. Phot.*, **4**: 20-21, 97-101, Feb. (1939)
Modernistic Murals for Your Home
Dan N. Steffanoff. *Pop. Phot.*, **5**: 25, 99-101, Sept. (1939)
Blowing 'Em Up Big
Hamlin Wellig. *Minicam*, **3**: 70-73, Feb. (1940)
Photo Murals
Ansel Adams. *U. S. Camera*, **3**: 52-53, 61-62, 71-72, Nov. (1940)
Photo Mural Technique
Marvin Black. *Photo Technique*, **3**: 36-39, Jan. (1941)
Murals are Easy with this Tray-Easel
Frank McCarty. *Pop. Phot.*, **8**: 32, 94, June (1941)
Photo Murals
Robert J. Rogers. *Complete Photog.*, **8**: 2866-75, No. 44 (1942)
Photomurals
Tom Gerson. *Minicam Phot.*, **8**: 31-33, November-December (1944)
Photographs in the Home
Jacqueline Judge. *Pop. Phot.*, **19**: 54-55, 136, 138, 140, 142, 144, 146, No. 4, Oct. (1946)

Making a Photomural
ALDEN STAHR. *Amer. Phot.*, **44**: 19-22, Jan. (1950)

Photomontage

Making Photomontages in the Enlarger
FRED G. KORTH. *Amer. Phot.*, **31**: 22-26, Jan. (1937)

Let's Make a Montage
JACOB DESCHIN. *Minicam*, **1**: 8-11, Jan. (1938)

Montage Magic
IRVING BROWNING. *Good Phot.*, **1**: 32-35, 133, 148, No. 3 (1939)

Photo-Montage
WILL CONNELL. *U. S. Camera Mag.*, **1**: 50, 65, Oct. (1939)

Photomontage Tells the Story
HARRY K. SHIGETA. *Pop. Phot.*, **5**: 20-21, 113-16, Oct. (1939)

Photomontage
JACOB DESCHIN, in "New Ways in Photography," McGraw-Hill Book Co., Inc., 1936, Chapt. XIII, "Photographic Multiplication," pp. 181-97

Photomontage
BARBARA MORGAN, in "Miniature Camera Work," edited by Willard D. Morgan and H. M. Lester. Morgan & Lester, New York, 1938, pp. 145-66

Photograms

A New Technique In Photograms
VICTOR KILLING. *Amer. Phot.*, **46**: 13-16, Jan. (1952)

Photoetching and photo drawing

The Missone Process
L. Missone. *Amer. Phot.*, **18**: 338-44, June (1924)
Some Suggestions on Photo-Sketching
E. A. Yunker. *Amer. Phot.*, **29**: 746-60, Dec. (1935)
Photo-Etching
C. A. Norgren. *Amer. Phot.*, **32**: 640-42, Sept. (1938)
Etchcraft for the Beginner
E. W. Donaldson. *Amer. Phot.*, **32**: 642-44, Sept. (1938)
Making Photographic Etchings
C. H. Fitzpatrick. *Photo Art Monthly*, **8**: 283-92, June (1940)
How to Make Photographic Drawings
Charles S. Martz. *Camera (Balt.)*, **69**: 44-51, 94-95, Mar. (1947)
Anyone Can Photosketch
Charles E. Emery. *Camera (Balt.)*, **70**: 108-9, No. 6, June (1948)
Sketching with Your Camera
Hillar P. Maskar. *Pop. Phot.*, **24**: 47-49, 118, No. 5, May (1949)
Photo Etching Made Easy
Raymond F. Barbera. *Pop. Phot.*, **27**: 76-79, No. 4, Oct. (1950)
Photo Sketching
E. E. Yunker, in "Photographic Amusements," by F. R. Fraprie and F. C. O'Connor. American Photographic Publishing Co., Boston, 11 Ed.
Photo Drawing
Leonard Missone, in "Photographic Amusements," by F. R. Fraprie and F. C. O'Connor. American Photographic Publishing Co., Boston, 11 Ed., 1937, pp. 148-49

Miscellaneous masking techniques

Bas Relief Photography
Anon. *Complete Photog.*, **2**: 395-96, Issue 7, (1941)
The Persson Process In Commercial Photography
Boris Dobro. *Photo Technique*, **3**: 10-13, Dec. (1941)
Posterizing Photographs, By a Very Useful
and Interesting Variation of the Persson Process
Roger W. Wade. *Amer. Phot.*, **36**: 8-10, Nov. (1942)
Bas Relief Is Easy
Leon Cantrell. *Pop. Phot.*, **13**: 23-24, 84, Sept. (1943)
Tone-Separation Prints (through the Persson Process)
Julio Zadik. *Camera (Balt.)*, **69**: 52-59, 137, No. 9, Sept. (1947)
A Combination Negative Produces This From This
(A method of emphasizing highlights with a high-contrast negative mask.)
Lee Ellis. *Camera Mag.*, **75**: 56-61, 135-36, May (1950)
Photo Posters
Gertrude Fehr. *Pop. Phot.*, **27**: 50-53, 182, 184-85, No. 6, Dec. (1950)

THE WINNER!

Chapter 18

All's Well That Ends Well

THE TWO of us, my photographer friend and I, sat in front of the fireplace and watched the flames consume the remainder of a solitary pine log. We had spent all the day and a good portion of the evening reading the galley proofs for this book. They were completed at last, and tomorrow they would be on their way to the printer.

My friend broke the long silence. "There's one person I wish could have read your book."

I smiled faintly. "Only one?"

"One person in particular," he continued, "the late George Bernard Shaw. You know, Shaw once said, 'The photographer is like a codfish. It lays a million eggs in order to hatch one.' I think he might have changed his mind a little. The way you've explained it, artistic photography is just *not* a hit-or-miss proposition. I think that anyone who practices 'shotgun' photography will change his methods after reading what you have to say."

"Well," I replied, "I hope so, and I hope it's clear. Even if it does take practice and experiment to become a skilled photographer, it doesn't take a thousand negatives and sheets of photographic paper to make one good print."

My friend nodded, "True! A lot of paper and supplies may be *used*—but they won't be *wasted*. After all, by learning the art of

print making, anyone can do a better job of expressing himself through photography. Prints are not an end in themselves; they are a way of talking to our fellow men. A photograph of a beautiful group of trees on a misty morning should tell what the photographer thought and felt—his opinions and emotions—about those trees at the moment of exposure. But it isn't until a *print* is made that this interpretation can exist, for art consists in bringing something into existence. Furthermore, the print maker's feelings can be understood fully by others who see his print only if the techniques and suggestions of the preceding chapters are understood and applied. To make others see and feel as you do: that's the challenge of photography!

"An old professor of mine once said the same thing but with a little different twist: 'Photography is mechanical, art spiritual; one a word, the other a thought. But photography can be elevated to a true art by breathing into it the spirit which it lacks.' "

A handful of glowing embers in the hearth was all that remained of the fire. "I wonder if our silhouettes before the fireplace would have made a good picture," I idly mused.

"I think," came the reply, "that *now* I would know just how to print that negative."

ALPHABETICAL SUBJECT INDEX